FROM SPINSTER TO CAREER WOMAN

From Spinster to Career Woman

Middle-Class Women and Work in Victorian England

ARLENE YOUNG

McGill-Queen's University Press
Montreal & Kingston • London • Chicago

ISBN 978-0-7735-5706-2 (cloth)
ISBN 978-0-7735-5707-9 (paper)
ISBN 978-0-7735-5848-9 (ePDF)
ISBN 978-0-7735-5849-6 (ePUB)

Legal deposit second quarter 2019
Bibliothèque nationale du Québec

Printed in Canada on acid-free paper that is 100% ancient forest free
(100% post-consumer recycled), processed chlorine free

This book has been published with the help of a grant from the Canadian Federation
for the Humanities and Social Sciences, through the Awards to Scholarly Publications
Program, using funds provided by the Social Sciences and Humanities Research
Council of Canada.

Funded by the   Financé par le
Government   gouvernement
of Canada   du Canada

Canada Council   Conseil des arts
for the Arts   du Canada

We acknowledge the support of the Canada Council for the Arts, which last year
invested $153 million to bring the arts to Canadians throughout the country.

Nous remercions le Conseil des arts du Canada de son soutien. L'an dernier, le Conseil
a investi 153 millions de dollars pour mettre de l'art dans la vie des Canadiennes et des
Canadiens de tout le pays.

Library and Archives Canada Cataloguing in Publication

Title: From spinster to career woman : middle-class women and work
in Victorian England / Arlene Young.
Names: Young, Arlene, author.
Description: Includes bibliographical references and index.
Identifiers: Canadiana (print) 20190069023 | Canadiana (ebook) 20190069112
  | ISBN 9780773557079 (softcover) | ISBN 9780773557062 (hardcover) | ISBN
  9780773558489 (ePDF) | ISBN 9780773558496 (ePUB)
Subjects: LCSH: Middle class women—Employment—England—History—
  19th century. | LCSH: Nursing—England—History—19th century. | LCSH:
  Typewriting—England—History—19th century. | LCSH: English fiction—
  19th century—History and criticism. | LCSH: Women employees in literature.
Classification: LCC HD6136 .Y58 2019 | DDC 331.40942—dc23

This book was typeset in 10.5/13 Sabon.

To my daughters, Laurel and Jenny,
and my granddaughter, Charlie – the career women
of the present and future

And in memory of my mother, Diena,
who knew that doing any job with pride and dignity was
the essence of a career

Contents

Figures

Acknowledgments

I wish to thank the institutions and people who have made the research, preparation, and publication of this study possible. My thanks to the Social Sciences and Research Council of Canada and the University of Manitoba for funding to do research in London, England. My thanks also to the institutions in London and their helpful staff for access and assistance – the British Library, the Women's Library, and the Wellcome Institute. I have benefitted at several stages of writing from colleagues, friends, and relatives – from Vanessa Warne, Glenn Clark, and Aaron Heisler, as well as from the many participants at conferences where I presented early versions of chapters as works in progress. I also want to express my sincere appreciation for the helpful commentary from the anonymous readers of my manuscript and for the advice and assistance I received from the editorial and production staff at McGill-Queen's University Press – Richard Ratzlaff, Jeremy John Parker, Elena Goranescu, Kathleen Fraser, Casey Gazzellone, and Colleen Gray. Last, but never least, I thank my ever-supportive husband, Robert O'Kell, for his sage advice and his enduring patience.

Portions of chapter 2 were published in the *Journal of Victorian Culture* 13, no. 1 (Spring 2008) as "'Entirely a Woman's Question'? Class, Gender, and the Victorian Nurse" (18–41) and are reproduced here with the permission of Oxford University Press.

Portions of chapter 1, chapter 4, and the conclusion were published in *Victorian Periodicals Review* 40, no. 3 (Fall 2007) as "Ladies and Professionalism: The Evolution of the Idea of Work in the *Queen*, 1861–1900" (189–215) and are reproduced here with the permission of the review.

The images and cartoons are reproduced with the permission of the British Library.

FROM SPINSTER TO CAREER WOMAN

Victorian Spinster to New Career Woman

The theory of civilised life in this and all other countries ... is that women of the upper and middle classes are supported by their male relatives: daughters by their fathers, wives by their husbands. If a lady has to work for her livelihood, it is universally considered to be a misfortune, an exception to the ordinary rule.

Bessie Rayner Parkes, "The Market for Educated Female Labor," *English Woman's Journal* 4, no. 21 (1859): 145–6.

At the beginning of the Victorian period, to be a middle-class woman was to be a dependent – a daughter, a sister, a wife, a mother. A middle-class woman who had no father, brother, or husband to provide her a home was an unfortunate, a castaway doomed to eke out a subsistence working in the household of strangers as a governess or companion. By the end of the century, middle-class women had options not readily available to their grandmothers. They could *choose* not to be dependent, not to be limited to a domestic life. For middle-class women, this change was little short of revolutionary. It may not have produced a major upheaval in British society as a whole, but it did expand the horizons for young women beyond anything their grandmothers could have imagined. Why and how this change came about is the subject of this study.

There are, in my analysis, two fundamental drivers of change. The need for work and the eventual opening up of employment opportunities for middle-class women was motivated initially by the growing demographic imbalance between men and women in Britain in the nineteenth century and subsequently by the manipulation of cultural perceptions of respectability, femininity, and class in the print media and in fiction. Work had to be recognized as both necessary for a middle-class woman and seemly. In essence, women and women's work had to be professionalized, requiring a radical change in what nineteenth-century surgeon and philosopher James Hinton called the "habit of thinking" of an entire culture.[1]

In the words of an anonymous contributor to the *Woman's Herald* in 1892, "ideals of womanhood are largely originated by heroines in real life, and by heroines in fiction, as well as by the unconscious but powerful interaction of these two factors."[2] In the chapters that follow, the assessment of the protracted campaign to provide middle-class women with suitable employment engages with this "powerful interaction" by analyzing the treatment of two culturally and historically complex figures, the hospital nurse and the typewriter,[3] in the media and in fiction – in other words, the "real life" and the fictional versions of those figures. This "unconscious but powerful interaction" of life and fiction enabled women to gain a level of social and cultural empowerment. Their determined efforts to use new or renewed areas of work to redefine their place in culture align with cultural theorist Raymond Williams's concept of "real and persistent elements of practice" – in this case in the form of challenge or resistance – that create the process of "a lived hegemony."[4] My analysis also aligns with Mary Poovey's concept of "ideological work," which she presents with dual emphases. In the first, which she terms "the work of ideology," Poovey interprets representations of gender as "part of the system of interdependent images in which various ideologies became accessible to individual men and women." Poovey's second emphasis is on certain representations of gender as "contested images, the sites at which struggles for authority occurred."[5] Rather than analyzing the "ideological work of gender," however, this study explores the ideological work of work. The focus here is not only on work as part of a system of interdependent, often gendered, assumptions and ideologies; it is also on representations of certain kinds of work and workers as contested sites "at which struggles for authority occurred." Work, in this formulation, functions less as a Marxian process that defines identity than as potentially gendered forms of activity that are manipulated to alter identity. Over the course of the Victorian period, ideals of middle-class womanhood, of what the Victorians would call ladies, changed – a change brought about by the manipulation of perceptions of femininity and respectability in media and in fictional treatments of women and work, and of women as workers. Arguably the most prominent of these workers were the hospital nurse and the typewriter (the term used for typist in the nineteenth century). Both figures and both areas of employment were discussed in the mainstream media (newspapers such as the *Times*, periodicals such as *Blackwood's* and the *Nineteenth Century*), the popular press (e.g. provincial weeklies, the *Idler*, *Cassell's Family Magazine*), and the women's press. The range in the last of these is remarkable, as it includes, among many others, such patrician publications as the *Queen, the Lady's Newspaper and Court Chronicle* (hereafter referred to as the *Queen*), the functionalist *Work and Leisure*, and the often pedestrian *Girl's Own Paper*, an organ of the Religious Tract Society. The scope of fictional treatments is equally extensive and diverse, encompassing novels from Elizabeth Gaskell's culturally groundbreaking and poignant *Ruth* (whose eponymous protagonist works as a hospital nurse in the latter part of the novel) to Grant Allen's zany and exuberant *The Type-Writer Girl*.

Hospital nursing and typewriting were by no means the only occupations adopted by middle-class women in the nineteenth century, as evidenced in a series of interviews with professional women conducted by the women's employment editor of the *Queen*, Margaret Bateson, and published in that newspaper in 1893.[6] Bateson subsequently published an expanded version of the interviews in a volume, *Professional Women upon Their Professions*, that indicates the range of employments undertaken by middle-class women by the last decade of the nineteenth century: art, music, accounting, stockbroking, medicine, dentistry, various kinds of administrative work (e.g., Poor Law Guardian, School Board representative), office work (which generally entailed typewriting), various areas of education and nursing, and the author's own area of special expertise, journalism.[7] Although not an exhaustive list of the areas of work open to women (the law and architecture, for example, are not mentioned),[8] the occupations represented by Bateson's interviewees give a sense of the expansion of professional opportunities, along with the requisite education, open to women by the close of the Victorian era. Bateson's idea of professionalism adhered to the most general of interpretations of the term. In the introduction to her collection of interviews, she encompassed under the term profession "any form of work which a woman is paid by the public, or entrusted by the public to do, and which she performs under that full sense of responsibility which we term the professional, in contradistinction to the amateurish spirit" (viii).

While this general and rather amorphous perception of professionalism did obtain in the Victorian period, the development of new areas of knowledge and expertise had also generated more restrictive, if not necessarily clear-cut, ideas about what a profession, and consequently what professionalism, meant. As W.J. Reader points out, the definition of profession is not precise, but "emerge[s] rather hazily" from "particular cases."[9] Over the course of the nineteenth century, the traditional definition of a profession, which in the eighteenth century had been limited to the clergy, the law, and medicine,[10] expanded to include other occupations in art, music, writing and editing, teaching, architecture, engineering, accounting, and business. The traditional professions had been confined to occupations undertaken by men with social status and education, men who were culturally defined as gentlemen. The expansion of professions prompted intensive debate over what constituted professionalism, as the social status of some members of these new professions was in question. The ideal of professionalism as it evolved in the nineteenth century reconceived traditional gentlemanly values such as education and social standing. Training and expertise replaced liberal education; altruism superseded *noblesse oblige*; and hard work and accomplishments replaced birth as the source of social standing.[11] What Harold Perkin terms the "higher professions" (in essence, those that enabled their members to earn significant wealth, such as law, medicine, architecture, and engineering) maintained their status and exclusivity through the establishment of professional associations that oversaw self-regulation, certification, and the publication of specialized journals.[12] Professions were recognized in the decennial census records, and eventually (after 1861) listed men and women separately, acknowledging women's entrance into the professional ranks. Nursing was not listed as a profession until 1891.[13]

Education for middle-class women was central both to the development of the professional ideal and to the availability of work, as the contemporary debates over suitable instruction for girls discussed in chapter 1 indicate. Until midcentury, most middle-class girls were educated at home or at small privately run schools that emphasized deportment and genteel accomplishments. Between 1848 and 1850, three schools aimed at providing improved academic education for young women opened in London – Queen's College, Harley Street (1848), Bedford College (1849), and the North London Collegiate (1850) – followed by the establishment of Cheltenham Ladies' College in 1854.[14] Between 1869 and 1873, funds from the fixed-term Endowed Schools Commission (established by the Endowed Schools Act) enabled the opening of academically oriented schools for girls in other areas of the country. While the curricula of many of these schools were directed to teachers' training, the academic programs available to girls allowed them to pursue other areas of interest and further training or study, whether that be an occupation, paid or unpaid, or university education. Since their establishment in the Middle Ages, British universities had been the sole domain of men, as both students and professors, and there was strong resistance to admitting women, especially at the oldest institutions, Oxford and Cambridge. In the 1870s, however, several university colleges for women were founded: Newnham College (1871) and Girton College (1873) in Cambridge, and Somerville College (1879) in Oxford. Although women were permitted to sit the general examinations, they were not granted full status at these universities and were not granted degrees until the twentieth century. As Carol Dyhouse observes, "their status was anomalous – they were there on sufferance."[15] The University of London was more progressive, admitting women to its degree programs in 1878 and conferring BA degrees to four women in 1880.[16] The number of women attending university colleges at the time, however, was small; still fewer obtained degrees.[17] Accordingly, even fewer women entered male-dominated professions such as the law or medicine.

While the protracted struggle to enter the medical profession in England is arguably the most celebrated of all women's successful inroads into an uncompromising male preserve in the nineteenth century, the women involved were a privileged few;[18] they represent the entrance of women from the middle and upper classes into established and male-dominated professions, rather than the professionalization of women's work. By contrast, although nursing had no established professional status at midcentury and typewriting had yet to appear as an employment option, by the end of the century nursing and typewriting were to become employments that women by the tens of thousands would undertake. Moreover – and perhaps because of the numbers of women involved – vexed social attitudes tended to cluster around these areas of work. As a result, contemporary discursive treatments of hospital nursing and typewriting provide particularly productive insights into the mechanisms used by advocates of women's work to change cultural attitudes, transforming nursing from a menial job into a respected profession and appropriating typewriting as an as-yet ungendered occupation that initially offered the cachet of technological advance to women's work. These two occupations, accordingly, represent two ends of the spectrum of newly professionalized women's work – the old and traditional (nursing) made new again and the modern and innovative (typewriting) made gender-specific. The promise that these two areas of employment presented to Victorian women was immense.

Teaching, another traditional area of women's employment, is less suitable for my analysis for several reasons. First, teaching was and is less gender-specific. Second, teaching (whether as a governess or as a schoolmistress) had always been the area of employment favoured by and for nineteenth-century middle-class women; it was not perceived as new or exciting in the nineteenth century, and indeed in the literature of the time seems to carry the stigma of the conventional last resort for the unwanted and unprotected woman of otherwise good social standing. Third, the class status of teaching was seen by some commentators of the period as in danger of being eroded by the influx into the profession of graduates of the Board Schools established after the passing of the 1870 Education Act. The result, according to Frances Low, was that "a large and entirely different class of women" – the "semi-educated" graduates of Board Schools – were competing with women "of birth and culture for educational functions which were formerly in the hands of the latter only." Another result of the Education Act, according to Low's analysis, was to reduce the aggregate number of teaching positions by replacing private governesses with the schoolmistress who teaches children "in herds."[19]

While thus not one of the major foci of my study, teaching will nonetheless function as a point of departure, as it did for many of the working women in literature in the 1890s. Juliet Appleton in Grant Allen's *The Type-Writer Girl*, and Rhoda Nunn and Eve Madeley in Gissing's *The Odd Women* and *Eve's Ransom*, for example, all reject teaching in favour of what they perceive to be the more progressive field of typewriting and clerical work. And progressive it was. During this period, the rapid growth in the number of female clerical workers coincided with the introduction of new business technologies, most notably typewriters and telephones. In the 1880s and 1890s, female clerical workers appeared with some regularity in British fiction, often in portrayals that emphasize their technological skills. Women's newspapers, from the *Queen* to the *Women's Penny Paper*, likewise endorsed typewriting as a desirable area of employment for middle-class women, with its advocates taking pains to construct it as a vocation requiring education and refinement in addition to technical skill. The professionalized hospital nurse similarly featured prominently in discussions of desirable but demanding careers for middle-class women. While nursing lacked the cachet of technological progressiveness, it was nevertheless perceived to be a vocation in the throes of a renaissance, which indeed it was. It was during this period that the British Nurses' Association was founded and received its Royal Charter.

This study follows in the wake of numerous fine analyses of middle-class women and work in nineteenth-century Britain, beginning with Lee Holcombe's pioneering historical account, *Victorian Ladies at Work: Middle-Class Working Women in England and Wales, 1850–1914*. Holcombe provides an invaluable survey of employment options, including teaching, nursing, and clerical work; she also discusses shop assistants, a position that would have been considered *déclassé* by most Victorian ladies. Ellen Jordan likewise discusses middle-class women in the British workforce in the nineteenth century in *The Women's Movement and Women's Employment in Nineteenth Century Britain*, which, as the title suggests, focuses on the role of members of the Women's Movement in expanding employment opportunities. A more recent study that also comprehends a wide range of occupations is Gillian Sutherland's *In Search of the New Woman: Middle-Class Women and Work in Britain 1870–1914*. Rather than being a survey, however, Sutherland's account focuses on the experiences of specific individuals and on the concept of the New Woman. Other interpretations of middle-class women and work in the Victorian period tend to examine specific areas of employment, especially nursing and clerical work, the subjects of this study. Accounts of Victorian nursing range from biographies of major figures, such as Florence Nightingale or Dorothy Pattison,[20] to histories and analyses of nursing in individual hospitals and sisterhoods,[21] to overviews of the development of nursing practice over the course of the century.[22] As Sue Hawkins observes in her able overview of trends in nursing history in the last fifty years, until the late twentieth century the literature was dominated by "accounts of nursing's relentless progress," while more recent studies have provided more nuanced accounts that place nursing history "in a wider context" that allows the "politics of nursing" to take "centre stage."[23] It is not only the politics of nursing, however, that emerges in more nuanced studies, but also the politics of hospital organization. The influx of middle-class women into hospital nursing – women who defined nursing as a career rather than as employment, women who had the confidence and social cachet to challenge some of the entrenched practices of the male medical staff – had a profound effect on the organization and provision of nursing services, especially in the major training hospitals throughout Britain.

While discussions of Victorian hospital nursing are generally based on historical records,[24] treatments of clerical workers range from economic histories to cultural-cum-literary studies. In the latter category, Christopher Keep's ground-breaking study of the typewriter girl addresses the imperative of securing "in the public mind the propriety of middle-class women working in the public space of the commercial office."[25] Much of Keep's analysis, however, focuses on the closing years of the nineteenth century and on the early years of the twentieth century, when typewriting was already losing its cultural prestige. Moreover, the eroticized image of the typewriter girl that Keep sees as emerging by the early twentieth century is not one that accords with the status and respectability that late-Victorian middle-class women were seeking. More recently, Katherine Mullin has also interpreted the Victorian typewriter as an erotic figure. While acknowledging the promotion of typewriting in the 1880s as an occupation suited to educated and refined women, Mullin quickly shifts her focus to typists "as powerful sexual agents."[26] Both Keep and Mullin accordingly emphasize external perceptions of typewriters and issues of general cultural anxiety rather than middle-class women themselves and their efforts to define certain venues of employment as respectable.

Like Keep's and Mullin's cultural analyses, most economic histories consider the circumstances that obtained in the 1870s or 1880s, when clerical work in government offices was first available to women, but then shift their focus to later developments in white-collar work for women.[27] Histories that examine the increased number of women in clerical jobs emphasize the growth of capitalist economies and the expansion of the service sector, growth that provided opportunities for women to enter this segment of the workforce. Graham Lowe, for example, sees the administrative revolution – "the reorganization of offices into multi-departmental bureaucracies, the rationalization of clerical work by managers vigilant of inefficiencies and rising costs" – as the force that "ushered out the traditional male bookkeeper with his pen and ledger book and marched in battalions of routine female functionaries."[28] The title of Susanne Dohrn's 1988 essay on women office workers in the late Victorian period, "Pioneers in a Dead-End Profession," encapsulates the kind of pessimistic vision that colours most historical analyses of women entering the clerical branch of the service economy.[29]

As Ellen Jordan has observed, the standard historical interpretation of the opening up of most areas of work to middle-class women in the nineteenth century has been that demographic determinates (the imbalance of the ratio of women to men) were negligible and economic ones (the expansion of industry and commerce) were decisive.[30] Jordan, however, downplays the impact of industrial and economic changes on the dearth of employment opportunities for young women at midcentury, the shortage being "contingent" but "not an inevitable outcome of these changes." The more significant causes, she posits, were cultural and linguistic: culturally accepted gender differences were "embedded in the practices of the preindustrial workplace and in the new discourses that were emerging" in order to comprehend "the changes taking place." Jordan argues persuasively for the influence of "intellectuals of the Women's Movement" and their "attack on the sexual division of labour" as the prime movers in changing attitudes among employers about the place of middle-class women in the workforce.[31] I argue for a not dissimilar but more extensive challenge to existing assumptions about women and work, a challenge that comprehends a broader range of cultural voices – the voices of activists, to be sure, but also those of ordinary women and men writing letters to newspapers for advice or comment, women workers recounting their experiences, and novelists imagining the challenges and adventures encountered by working girls and women. My analysis also crucially includes the voices of influential men since, in Victorian patriarchal society, the endorsement of powerful men was essential to ensuring the credibility of perspectives presented by women themselves. Moreover, I eschew the argument that demographic determinates were insignificant. The census statistics that revealed the higher proportion of females to males in Britain throughout the nineteenth century are real and the so-called problem of redundant women generated extended debate over possible solutions at the time. While the scope of the problem may have been exaggerated by some observers, the situation was nevertheless widely perceived as alarming, for in the lived experience of Victorians there was acute cultural anxiety over the future prospects of middle-class women.

In overlooking the plethora of voices engaged in the debates over middle-class women and work, the approaches cited above, though based on historical, social, and political realities, miss the intense human elements of middle-class women's entry into the workforce: the at times desperate need for work, the hope afforded by new opportunities, the excitement of independence, the satisfaction of professional achievement. Rather than read these moments through the lens of a later historical reality of multidepartmental bureaucracies or dead-end jobs, this study attempts to capture the frustrations and excitement experienced at the historical moment, and so provide new insights into the past and into women's lives. We can then understand more fully that the steadily growing numbers of unattached and educated middle-class women were not simply there, waiting for the administrative revolution to provide opportunities for them; these women in a very real sense enabled the administrative revolution by providing able and plentiful workers who could be paid less than their male counterparts. If there had been no demographic imbalance, along with the anxiety produced by that imbalance, if, to paraphrase one late nineteenth-century commentator, there had been "enough husbands to go round,"[32] bureaucracies and the service industry would have had a more limited workforce to draw on and of necessity would have grown more slowly, would have been more costly to maintain, and would likely have been smaller. The advances in science over the course of the nineteenth century likewise could not have been translated effectively into superior medical treatments if educated women had not been available to provide professional nursing care. That middle-class women in need of work and their supporters over the course of the century advocated for greater opportunities for women with such pertinacity and that they redefined certain areas of work as suitable and acceptable for middle-class women to undertake in fact established the workforce that enabled the growth of the service sector and advances in patient care in British hospitals.

The lively dialogue that addressed issues of women and work over the course of the nineteenth century inevitably intersected with or spawned related social or cultural fixations of the time: the Woman

Question, the Strong-Minded Woman, the Glorified Spinster, and the New Woman.[33] Chapter 1 accordingly opens with a consideration of the Woman Question and its relation to the demographic imbalance and women's employment and education. Using discussions of teaching and hospital nursing in the media, this opening chapter examines the various calls to professionalize middle-class women's work and closes with an analysis of the cultural constructions of the Strong-Minded Woman and the Glorified Spinster, both shaped by the newly assertive working woman. Chapter 2 follows the intense and sometimes acrimonious debates in the media over the entrance of middle-class women into hospital nursing, a move that was seen by its advocates as beneficial to patient care and progressive in terms of hospital organization. Detractors of the new style of nursing criticized it as disruptive to established practices and distressing for patients, as the new-style nurse, in the opinion of many, was a religious proselytizer, less interested in curing patients than in attempting to save their souls. The professionalized and respected Victorian nurse emerged from the crucible of this heated debate, but the male nurse faded from the public eye and, for the most part, from the hospital system. Chapter 3 examines fictional representations of the hospital nurse as part of the cultural response to the new-style nurse and to the new middle-class working woman in general. While almost universally positive about nursing, authors from the period struggled with the same perceived contradictions inherent in the concept of a working woman who was both professional and feminine, and most stories from the period fall back on the conventional marriage plot to establish the unimpeachable womanly credentials of the nurse protagonist. The record of public responses to the entrance of middle-class women into the civil service and other clerical jobs, the subject of chapter 4, reveals generalized skepticism about women's capabilities in these roles. Resistance to women office workers persisted, even in the face of universally positive reports on their exemplary performance. The advent of the typewriter solidified middle-class women's place in the Victorian office not, as other studies claim, because inventor Christopher Sholes and other men conceived of the new typewriting machine as a means to offer women employment opportunities, but because enterprising women recognized the potential of this new technology, set up typewriting services and training, and consistently demonstrated their superior skills in typewriting competitions in Europe and North

America. Chapter 5 then examines the cultural discomforts with the new woman office worker as revealed in fictional representations which, like those of the hospital nurse, were vexed by the conflict between ideals of femininity and competency in the workplace. Typewriting was ultimately a more problematic area of work for middle-class women than was nursing. The professionalized typewriter, a woman with education and status, quickly devolved into the underpaid and semiskilled typewriter girl. The promise of independence and the cachet of modernity, of being on the cutting edge of new workplace technology, insured that, despite its loss of status, the allure of the typewriter, both the machine and its operator, persisted to the end of the century. The typewriter was in many ways the quintessential New Woman, but she was specifically the New Woman as a modern worker. She becomes, along with the new-style nurse, a representative of what advocates for employment opportunities throughout the nineteenth century were striving to create – the New Career Woman.

The concluding chapter of this study analyzes responses in the media to the challenges faced by women and girls who were attempting to define their role in society at the dawn of the last decade of the nineteenth century. The women's press addressed the troubling realities of the labour market for middle-class women while the mainstream media engaged in a debate focused on how to prepare the girls of the period for the future. This protracted public exchange of concerns, hopes, and ideas – which continued sporadically from 1888 to 1895 and comprised the voices of prominent public figures as well as the general public – reveals the dramatic change in the "habit of thinking" about women and work that had taken place over the course of the century. However precarious the position of the New Career Woman remained by the end of the century, the culture at large nevertheless had, in the words of a correspondent to *Reynolds's Newspaper*, "come to a pretty unanimous conclusion that we must find 'work for our daughters to do.'"[34] The solution to the problem of "what to do with our daughters" was education – education of girls for a future in the workforce and education of the public to a new understanding of women's roles in the modern era.

I

The Woman Question and the One Thing Needful: Work

One of the most pressing social concerns of the Victorian era was what Victorians defined as the Woman Question. The Woman Question was an umbrella term – not a single question, but a series of questions encompassing numerous issues and problems related to the changing demands and expectations confronting women in the rapidly modernizing society of nineteenth-century Britain: How should women be educated? What is women's role in the public sphere? Should women have the vote? What work can women do? What is woman's true nature? What is her rightful place in society? Books and articles addressing aspects of the Woman Question often frame their titles as questions: *Can Women Regenerate Society?*; "What Shall We Do with Our Old Maids?"; "Why Are Women Redundant?"; "The Disputed Question." That these issues were so persistently presented as questions suggests the level of uncertainty that prevailed throughout the second half of the nineteenth century about how best to respond to such challenges. Aspects of the Woman Question remained a consistent component of public discussion over social policy and national values from midcentury on. For many Victorian women, the most urgent issue addressed in the ongoing public debates over their place in society was access to remunerative employment, a problem that, like the Woman Question itself, was multifaceted. Women, especially those in the middle classes, needed increased access to work; they needed work because of the redundant woman problem: there were more marriageable women than eligible men. In order to work, women required more education – or at least a different kind of education – from what was currently provided to them. For women in the middle and upper classes to engage in remunerative employment, however, was considered *déclassé* and unfeminine; in the parlance of the time, work in the public sphere would unsex women. For every argument in support of opening up job opportunities for middle-class women, there were counterarguments that raised fears of one or more dire outcomes threatening to change the status quo – women taking jobs away from men, masculinized women rejecting the natural roles of wife and mother, reformed education preparing girls for work but failing to prepare them for domestic duties, financially independent girls refusing to be guided by parents or established social mores.

The discourse in the press about women's work and related issues between the 1850s and the end of the century provides a record of changing conceptions of work, of evolving responses to the working woman, and of alterations in the position of middle-class women. The women's press was actively engaged in this discourse, with publications as divergent as the *English Woman's Journal* (directed at a middle-class readership) and the *Queen, the Lady's Newspaper and Court Chronicle* (which, as its title implies, was intended for an upper-middle-class to upper-class readership) weighing in. The number of women's newspapers and periodicals indeed grew between midcentury and 1900 to include more publications for more classes of women: *Englishwoman's Review of Social and Industrial Questions, Work and Leisure,* the *Girl's Own Paper,* the *Lady's Pictorial,* the *Lady,* the *Women's Penny Paper* (later the *Woman's Herald* and then the *Journal*), the *Gentlewoman, Shafts,* and the *Young Woman.* And all of these publications and more besides had something to say about women and work. The same issues were addressed in the mainstream press, in publications that included the most prominent and popular newspapers and periodicals of the time: the *Times, Nineteenth Century, Edinburgh Review, North British Review, National Review, Fortnightly Review, Westminster Review, Saturday Review, Blackwood's, Fraser's, Macmillan's,* and *Cassell's.* These publications were frequently in dialogue over these issues with each other and with the women's press.

That the question of women's work engaged public attention and inspired individual activism in the mid-Victorian period has been well documented. Historians, as well as commentators from the period, cite Harriet Martineau's 1859 article in the *Edinburgh Review,* "Female Industry," as the spur to interest and activism over women's access to work. According to Lee Holcombe, it "inspired Jessie

Boucherett to found the Society for Promoting the Employment of Women." A leader in a women's newspaper in 1883 similarly affirms that the society "owes its existence to an article in the *Edinburgh Review* for 1859, calling attention to the necessity for enlarging the sphere of employment for women."[1] Women's work was a topic under public discussion before Martineau's article appeared, however. The *English Woman's Journal*, founded as a forum to present and debate arguments about women and work, was first published a year before "Female Industry." Martineau's article is itself a review of ten reports and books on or related to the subject of female labour published between 1843 and 1858.[2] Comparable reviews, moreover, predate "Female Industry." One such piece in the *North British Review* in 1857 argues at least as forcibly as Martineau does for women's right to remunerative employment. The position adopted in this article is in fact more radical than Martineau's in that it argues for women's employment within the context of civil rights, a topic that the author, John William Kaye, had addressed two years earlier in response to Caroline Norton's infamous polemical pamphlet, *A Letter to the Queen on Lord Chancellor Cranworth's Marriage and Divorce Bill*.[3] In both arguments, Kaye deplores the "non-existence of women" before the law and the lamentable fact that women "are educated for the non-existence" that custom dictates for them.[4] Such a position, as the *English Woman's Journal* points out, was likely to be "sneeringly met with such terms as 'Emancipation,' 'Americanism,' 'Rights,' and the like," especially when presented by women.[5] With the lack of constraint afforded a man in his position in mid-Victorian culture, however – a man who had distinguished himself in public service, in the military, and in writing the history of recent military action – Kaye unabashedly enumerates the injustices of his society's treatment of women and emphatically asserts that society "must endeavour to open out new channels of female employment."[6]

THE DEMOGRAPHIC IMBALANCE

What ultimately made Martineau's argument more influential than Kaye's was that she forcibly drew public attention to the association between women's urgent need of employment and the demographic imbalance between men and women in England at the time, most notably in her analysis of *The Results of the Census in Great Britain in 1851.* Unlike previous discussions of work that noted the demographics, Martineau's provided abundant statistics from the census records, including ones previous to 1851, to demonstrate the evolving and increasing social dilemma that Britain was facing. And the demographic imbalance and its implications for women's economic security captured the public imagination more emphatically than perhaps any other in the conglomerate of issues that made up the Woman Question. As Kathrin Levitan observes, while single women "were not a new problem," the 1851 census "confirmed what politicians, economists, and novelists had been writing about for several decades" and, by providing "statistics to back up a formerly vague concern, ... sparked a massive increase in the volume of opinions on the problem as a whole." Discussions about surplus women, Levitan further points out, "often focused on the census itself, and nearly all of the writers on the subject used statistical figures to sharpen their arguments."[7]

As an observer at the close of the century notes, the growing numerical imbalance between the male and female population, tracked from 1810 onwards by the decennial British census, presented a challenge to the values and assumptions of the nation. "The old theory was," a contributor to the *Queen* comments in 1899, "that all women of the richer class should be wives, and work only on the domestic hearth; in a few cases unmarried women became governesses – though they were quite unfitted to teach. But this every-woman-a-wife theory received a rude shock when the figures of the census of 1861 were published, for they showed 2 ½ millions of unmarried women, and demonstrated emphatically that, so far as England was concerned, there were not enough husbands to go round."[8] The lack of husbands presented special difficulties for women of the middle classes, women who were not raised to work, who had neither the education nor training for work, and whose family fortunes were not extensive enough to provide lifelong support for unemployed spinsters. Moreover, as Kaye observes in his 1857 article, "in many respects their case is even harder than that of their more lowly sisters. There are fewer paths of occupation open to them."[9]

In 1858, the *English Woman's Journal* succinctly outlines the parameters of the mid-Victorian debate over women and work, noting that "it is still a disputed question whether women should work either with heads or hands, except in domestic life ... Social economists rather lament their employment otherwise than in the household as a temporary exigency, than admit it as a practical

axiom, while philanthropists are of the opinion that our superfluous numbers, to avoid starvation, must emigrate or become the
recipients of charity at home."[10] The opposing positions are clear,
even antagonistic, and are explicitly disputed in the print media.
J.D. Milne's argument for women's right to work and to compete
with men in the workforce in his *Industrial and Social Position of
Women in the Middle and Lower Ranks*, for example, is praised by
the *English Woman's Journal* as going "to the very root of the question" of middle-class women being "educated as responsible human
beings, trained to take their part in active life."[11] Milne's monograph
is assessed as illogical, however, by its reviewer in *Fraser's Magazine*,
who deems "female labour" a "hard necessity, which it would be
a social blessing rather to lessen than to increase." The reviewer's
own brand of logic is to adhere to the "time-honoured theory of
life" – "the world for men, and home for women" – which he finds
"beautiful" and "valuable."[12] In response to Bessie Rayner Parkes's
lecture for the Social Science Congress in 1859, in which she urges
middle-class parents to "teach every daughter some useful art," the
Saturday Review dismissively presents the remedy for the impoverished single woman as to "fall in love and get a husband." "Married
life is woman's profession," this respondent insists; "and to this life
her training – that of dependence – is modelled."[13]

MIXED MESSAGES

The stark contrast between the positions articulated in the *Saturday Review* and the *English Woman's Journal* might seem to suggest
that the main lines of opposition in this debate were drawn between
the mainstream media and women's publications. The battle lines
were not so clearly defined, however, either between the sexes or
between mainstream and alternative publications. The editors of the
Times, for example, were singularly supportive of the efforts of Emily Faithfull, Bessie Rayner Parkes, and the general mission of the
English Woman's Journal, the organ of the newly formed Society
for Promoting the Employment of Women.[14] The *Times* frequently
responded favourably to articles appearing in that journal and was
especially active in the public discourse about the plight of middle-
class women, publishing articles, leaders, and letters to the editor on
issues of women's employment, education, and emigration. While
the letters to the editor inevitably varied in their perspectives on

women's work, the leaders and articles in the *Times* not only were sympathetic to the cause of the reformers, but also enhanced the credibility of their position by presenting critiques of the status quo that would not have been well received if voiced by women themselves. The *Times*'s response to Parkes's address to the Social Science Congress is very different from that of the *Saturday Review*: the *Times* printed most of the lecture, along with a brief introduction stating that Parkes treats the issues related to female labour "sensibly and practically." Moreover, in editorials in the days following the reprinting of the lecture, the *Times* takes up the cause of female labour, backing Parkes's position that custom dictates female dependence and that there is "no room" in the "social framework for any other idea."[15] The *Times* sets the reality of women's position against the prevailing social assumptions about women's proper place in society, arguing that the current assumption that woman is destined to be dependent on man "is upset by facts."[16] Current social practice, one leader argues, "is found by experience to be impracticable ... The simple fact that women are constantly thrown upon the world to get their daily bread by their own exertions is a sufficient answer to those who think that dependence upon man is a woman's proper position." The editors are fully aware that this "simple fact" is one that many readers would probably prefer to minimize or even dismiss (as many other media commentators did), and that the ideas expressed in the leader "may in many quarters be distasteful." As if to counteract any reluctance to accept the reality of the situation, this leader is uncompromising in speaking to "the prejudices of society" and in affirming the unpalatable truth that "in this opulent and prosperous country" thousands of women are destitute.[17]

Given the *Times*'s endorsement of her perspective, it is perhaps not surprising that Bessie Rayner Parkes sees progress in public opinion "in regards to woman's work" as early as 1862. The continuing debate in the media, however, suggests that opinion in fact remained divided. W.R. Greg, one of the most noted of the proponents of female emigration, in "Why Are Women Redundant?" suggests promoting the emigration of working-class women, and compelling "every man among the middle and higher ranks ... to lead a life of stainless abstinence till he married" in order to provide eager husbands for the remaining redundant (middle-class) women. Greg argues that "to make women independent of men" or "to multiply and facilitate their employments" is to make "efforts in a wrong direction."[18]

Frances Power Cobbe directly challenges Greg's position in "What Shall We Do with Our Old Maids?" Although not opposed to the idea of encouraging working-class women to emigrate, Cobbe points out that, since most of the single women in search of work are in the middle classes, "emigration plans do not essentially bear on the main point." The kinds of "efforts in the wrong direction" that Greg warns against are exactly what Cobbe endorses, arguing forcibly that society should educate women so that they can work and be independent. Cobbe sets out the terms for the kinds of action that her society would have to undertake in response to the demographic realities that Martineau had laid out so starkly. "The old assumption that marriage was the sole destiny of woman … is brought up short by the statement that one woman in four is certain not to marry," Cobbe observes, "and that three millions of women earn their own living at this moment in England." To alleviate the problem posed by increasing numbers of destitute spinsters, especially in the middle and upper classes, Cobbe argues, "we must frankly accept this new state of things, and educate women and modify trade in accordance therewith."[19] Few Victorians were so sanguine about accepting the "new state of things" as a permanent state or about the idea of middle-class women being part of the workforce in perpetuity. Even Parkes demurs at the suggestion: "I never wished or contemplated the mass of women becoming breadwinners," Parkes avers; "the fact remains clear to my mind, that we are passing through a stage of civilization which is to be regretted, and that her house and not the factory is a woman's happy and healthy sphere."[20]

"DOUBLE ADDRESS" AND THE ARGUMENTS FOR EMPLOYMENT AND EDUCATION

As the arguments in support of employment cited above make clear, the expansion of opportunities for women is closely related to the improvement of the education provided to girls and young women. Women's education had been a topic of general interest since the early years of the century, and the issue of women's employment at mid-century developed in the context of debates over what kind of education was best suited to the girls and women of nineteenth-century Britain. Sydney Smith's 1810 discussion of "female education" in the *Edinburgh Review* established the dominant position of commentators on this subject for much of the century. The education of women and girls in England, he argues, is woefully deficient. If woman is to take her rightful place in society, she should be educated according to her abilities. While Smith's position is enlightened for its time, he, like many of his successors in the education debate, considers education for women as necessary for the full development of their characters and sees the educated woman as fulfilling her traditional role as wife and mother more effectively. Unlike men, Smith argues, "women have not their livelihood to gain by knowledge"; "the great use of ... [a woman's] knowledge will be, that it contributes to her private happiness."[21] While many observers after Smith would make similar arguments – most notably John Ruskin in *Sesame and Lilies* (1865) – the idea that "women have not their livelihood to gain by knowledge" is increasingly challenged as the century progresses. In 1858, the *English Woman's Journal* acknowledges Smith's essay as authoritative, but also cites the 1851 census results, arguing that the "whole social condition of woman, during these fifty years, has undergone a thorough revolution ... Now, more than ever, is there need of solid education for our girls, that our women may be fitted and trained to open other paths for themselves than the stereotyped and worn-out one of matrimony."[22] The education of women is also the cornerstone of John William Kaye's position in his review of arguments regarding "The Employment of Women." "We train our girls only to be useless," he asserts. "Instead of educating every girl as though she were born to be an independent, self-supporting member of society, we educate her to become a mere dependent, a hanger-on, or as the law delicately phrases it, a *chattel* ... We bring up our women to be dependent, and then leave them without any one to depend on."[23]

The combined call for better education and more employment opportunities for women dominates the discussion of the woman question for several decades, although some commentators turn out to be highly ambivalent about the real need for women to work. This ambivalence, or perhaps the perceived ambivalence of the reading public, results in discussions that are ostensibly about education becoming arguments for employment opportunities for women, and vice versa. In an article whose title defines its subject as "The Education of Women of the Middle and Upper Classes," Millicent Garrett Fawcett, for example, quickly and deftly switches the focus from education to employment. Garrett Fawcett begins by deploring the present state of women's education, almost immediately

modulating education into "mental training" largely denied to young
girls. She then calls not only for "equal educational advantages" for
women, but also for the opening of "all the professions to women;
and, if they prove worthy of them, to allow them to share with men
all those distinctions, intellectual, literary, and political, which are
such valuable incentives to mental and moral progress."[24] An argument for access to education has thus been parleyed, however subtly and indirectly, into an argument for access to full participation
in the intellectual and political life of the nation, without a word
about rights. A defence by "A Belgravian Young Lady" against Eliza
Lynn Linton's famous diatribe on the "girl of the period" – whose
legion failings include immodesty, vanity, frivolity, and extravagance
– becomes a call for employment opportunities. "Up to this time,"
the Belgravian Young Lady claims, "the only employment in which
a girl is not hindered is the pursuit of pleasure. We now ask for more
liberty of choice."[25] In response to this "cry" of "Nothing To Do,"
Reverend Daniel Fearon, by contrast, turns the tables the other way;
he begins by asserting that young ladies who want to work must
have a sound education, but ultimately argues that the provision of
more scope for women is unnecessary because "a better education
... [will] fit them to do their duty, in whatever state they may be
placed, with thoughtful intelligence."[26] In this case, in other words,
a response to the call for more opportunities becomes an argument
not for educating women for new roles in society but for educating
them to a becoming appreciation of the status quo.

An awareness of the sway of the status quo is what binds together
these contradictory interpretations of the relation between work
and education. It is at this point – in the complex interplay of concepts about work and concepts about education – that the evolving debates about women and work take on the characteristics of
"double address," defined by Johanna Smith as the stance a periodical adopts towards its readership when its implied audience com-
prises readers from more than one class or ideological position.[27]
As the exchanges in this debate ranged across a variety of media
and writers, they do not adhere to any single editorial policy, either
explicit or implied. The diverse arguments over women and work,
however, do demonstrate a similar awareness of incompatible ideological positions among potential readers that prompts writers to
engage in the journalistic bait and switch outlined above. But if ideas
about women's education and even about women's work might be

up for debate, entrenched assumptions about woman's nature were not. In a society as socially conservative as mid-Victorian England, no position that posited a radically new role for women would be seriously entertained by the majority of the reading public. And the most comprehensible way to reassure the general readership that English society and English womanhood are not at risk is to invoke the immutable laws of Nature (sometimes given even greater authority as the immutable laws of God), and that most natural of female roles, motherhood. Opponents of educational and employment opportunities for women routinely insist that such opportunities will undermine the health and well-being not only of young girls and women, but also of the nation. By contrast, the proponents of better education routinely argue that knowledge will help to develop and augment the skills required of good mothers. In his "The Non-Existence of Women," for example, Kaye supports the culturally accepted maxim that women's primary role, "ordained" by Nature, is to maintain "the well-being of the family." Not only will better education ensure that women perform their "primary duties" better, he argues, but training for active participation in the working world will also further improve their capacities within the domestic sphere. "There would be more good wives and good mothers," he asserts, "if women were better trained to take a part in the active business of life – if they were educated as though they might be neither wives nor mothers, but independent members of society, with work of their own to do seriously, earnestly, and with all their might."[28]

In her 1868 call for middle-class women's access to education and, by extension, to intellectual and political agency, Millicent Garrett Fawcett makes a similar point. She concludes her argument by invoking not rights and freedoms, but motherhood: the morally and intellectually developed woman will "be capable of affording ... [her children] that sympathy which an uncultivated mind can never feel."[29] Speaking in support of universal education in 1870, her husband, Liberal member of Parliament Henry Fawcett, contends that in "the interests of society ... not only with regard to those women who have to earn their own livelihood, but also with regard to those who are concerned in the rearing and training of children, it is of the utmost importance that they should be brought within the influence of the best available education."[30] While neither Kaye nor the Fawcetts take on the issue of the potential benefits of actual working experience, the "Belgravian Young Lady," cited above, does just

that by contrasting the accepted ideal of the idle young debutante
with the image of the serious young working woman: "Would an
apprenticeship in the arts of teaching, nursing, and managing be
more dangerous to the character of a future wife and mother than
an apprenticeship in dancing and flirtation?" ("Belgravian": 330).
The director of a nurses' training hospital, interviewed by the *Times*
in 1871, provides the answer to her question. To "console" himself
on the average loss of one trained nursing sister a year to marriage,
he tells the reporter, he thinks "what useful wives they will be to the
gentlemen who married them."[31]

Despite the by now long-standing emphasis on education, the lack
of suitable knowledge or training remained the greatest impediment
to middle-class women's employment. The *Englishwoman's Review*
notes the "ill-natured sneers" in the *Pall Mall Gazette* in response to
the efforts of the "Gentlewomen's Self-Help Institute," which was
attempting to provide an outlet for the sale of "ladies' handiwork,"
such as drawings, wax-work, lace, and "plain work of all sorts." While
deploring the tone of the *Pall Mall* article, the *Review* is nevertheless devastatingly forthright in its assessment of the situation of the
gentlewomen concerned, acknowledging that "these distressed gentlewomen ought not to exist; they ought to have been taught some
business in their youth, and to be self-supporting members of society."
The most pressing issue for the editor of the *Review*, however, is not
the current state of the distressed gentlewoman, as deplorable as that
might be, but the future of the next generation of women – "a fresh
generation of young girls" who must not be "brought up to be equally
useless." The way forward, the *Review* asserts, is "a good education"
and the removal of "every obstacle, whether social or legal, which
prevents women from engaging in remunerative employments" – and
therein, the editor is fully aware, lies the rub. "Here," she affirms, "we
meet with great difficulties" – the "strong ... prejudice against permitting women to enjoy these advantages."[32]

Until the 1870s, public debate remained grounded for the most
part in gender and ontology – the nature of woman, the nature of
woman's work, the appropriate education for girls. The reports in
the press cited above indicate that there was nevertheless a growing realization that it would be in the public interest actually to
induce middle-class women to work – at least in some sectors of
the economy. As a result, by the 1870s discussions in the media
about women and work changed. The conversation shifted from

philosophical or theoretical speculations about what could, or should, or would happen if middle-class women were to be admitted to the ranks of the educated, the trained, and the gainfully employed to more practical considerations of the kinds of work in which women were actually engaging. If some of this discussion was still speculative, it was nevertheless specific, providing concrete suggestions for new areas of employment. A letter in the *Times*, for example, presents a detailed argument for scientifically organized laundries, which would open "a field of work for women of many different classes and qualifications, from the refined and delicate to the rough and strong."[33] The growing demand for women workers in some areas – most notably nursing – produces commentaries and inducements that are both specific and pragmatic. The *Englishwoman's Review* reports that Florence Nightingale, in "a forcible appeal in *Good Words*" for women to enter nursing, "shows clearly that for a gentlewoman with strong health, nursing is a better paid and more interesting profession than teaching."[34] Several months later, the *Englishwoman's Review* cites entries in the *Daily Telegraph* and in the *Western Morning News* that note the high demand for trained nurses and the need to recruit capable women to enhance the image of nursing. The *Telegraph* argues that it is in "the interest of society ... to induce able women to make sick-nursing a steady and respectable profession."[35]

The movement to more practical treatments of middle-class women's employment began in the newspapers and in the women's press, and women's publications focusing on progressive issues related to their rights and their role in society were proliferating. The *English Woman's Journal*, published from 1858 until 1864, was succeeded in 1866 by the *Englishwoman's Review of Social and Industrial Questions*, which ran until 1910; the original title was the *Englishwoman's Review: A Journal of Woman's Work*. The *Woman's Gazette* (subtitled *News about Work*) appeared in 1876 and continued from 1880 until 1893 as *Work and Leisure*. The changes in titles are noteworthy, as they indicate that these publications were venturing into uncharted social territory, that their perspectives were evolving. Editors and contributors had to define their purpose and their content for themselves and for a new readership, indeed for a new category of woman: the middle-class spinster in search of stable employment – the New Career Woman. Such a term was never used at the time; even the appellation "New Woman" was not current until the 1880s and the 1890s. The concept, however, was already evolving by 1870, as the answer to the Woman Question increasingly became work and independence for middle-class women.

ENHANCING THE IMAGE: THE PROFESSIONALIZATION OF WOMEN'S WORK

The realization that society actually needed middle-class women for some areas of work and that middle-class women needed jobs was not enough on its own to transform the prejudices either of Victorian society or of the destitute ladies desperate for income. Redefining the Victorian woman as an individual with rights and potentially new social roles would, moreover, require the redefinition of the Victorian working woman and of the work she did. And the most urgent need, circa 1870, was to convince not only the general public but also middle-class women themselves that work was not degrading and that the working woman was respectable.

The process of enhancing the image of the middle-class working woman initially focused on two areas of work that were in the process of redefinition. The first was nursing, which, after Florence Nightingale's interventions during the Crimean War, was evolving from a low form of domestic service. The other was teaching, which, after the passing of the Education Act of 1870, was providing new opportunities. These two occupations also had the advantage, in terms of swaying public opinion in their favour, of representing work that conformed to Victorian ideals of femininity: caring for the sick and teaching children. Education still figured in the treatment of these areas of work, but the emphasis shifted to training and preparation for a particular occupation. This adjustment was part of a larger movement to transform the middle-class woman worker by elevating the status of her work, to make the jobs most available to her appealing. One means of elevating the status of women's work was to promote its professionalization. Professionalism accordingly becomes a defining issue as the media move more actively into the revision and reformulation of the idea of women workers and women's work. While the nineteenth-century media use the term "professional" loosely – "matronhood" is characterized as a profession in an 1879 article in the *Queen* – the concept of professionalism generally entailed a strong work ethic, an advanced level of general education, and specialized training.[36]

Because professionalism in the nineteenth century was in the masculine domain, professionalizing women's work entailed women's adoption of male work ethics, something that was actively promoted in venues as various as the *Times*, the *Englishwoman's Review*, and the main organ of the fashionable *beau monde*, the *Queen*. In this latter publication, the "first and truest of woman's work" is still identified as that of wife and mother. In the public sphere, the *Queen* cautions, women's performance is assessed by masculine standards: "good women's work, like good men's work, needs preparation."[37] Elsewhere, the *Queen* endorses a similar injunction emanating from the Society for Promoting the Employment of Women that admonishes women of all classes that "if they are to succeed as men do, they must give themselves to work, not as a temporary matter, to be thrown aside by-and-by, but as the business of life."[38] A correspondent to the *Englishwoman's Review* notes that women teachers "must obtain for themselves the same knowledge as a man would obtain."[39] The *Times* voices the persistent public misgivings about women's capacity to work effectively by attributing to women "much of the bad work which is done in the world," an "accusation" of which Emily Faithfull reluctantly admits the truth, but only because of women's "want of definite training."[40]

The focus in the media throughout the 1870s on the certification of teachers for the new Board Schools furthered efforts to professionalize women workers by equating women's professionalism with men's in a highly visible field comprising members of both sexes. In its editorial and correspondence columns, the *Times* engaged actively in the campaign to professionalize teaching by insisting on appropriate training and certification.[41] Women as elementary schoolmistresses elicited special concern over "the absolute necessity of a systematic training for young ladies" for such careers.[42] Commentaries in the *Times* merge discussions of higher education for women and of women's need for employment with considerations of the potential for women to be educators, to become certified schoolmistresses. One leader proposes teaching in elementary schools as an appropriate option for "the rising generation of young gentlemen and young ladies," although the leader concentrates on the options for young ladies, noting that Otter Memorial College at Chichester "shall be re-opened specially for the training of young women of a better class, in order to take [positions in] Elementary Schools."[43] Girton College is similarly presented as a resource for the training of schoolmistresses in a letter to the *Times* by the founder of the college, Emily Davies. "It has been one of the most important objects aimed at in the foundation of Girton College," Davies reminds the public, "to provide for girls and women a class of teachers answering to the tutors and schoolmasters provided by the Universities for boys and young men – a class of the same social standing, subjected to equally strict and systematic training, and having their qualifications similarly tested and attested."[44] The women's press also weighs in on the debate over the training of teachers, with the *Englishwoman's Review* insisting on "the value of a full college course of two years" over the pupil-teacher apprenticeship system of certification, and the *Queen* rather more aggressively calling for the "compulsory examination and registration of all teachers," including governesses.[45]

The *Queen*'s support for compulsory examination and certification of teachers reveals most starkly the class and gender cross-currents at work in the general movement to encourage middle-class women to join the labour market – the status implications of specific kinds of work and the unwillingness of "ladies" to espouse appropriate work ethics. Compulsory certification, the *Queen* affirms, has the potential to relieve two related social ills: on the one hand, the problem of the glut of unqualified governesses and the dearth of certified schoolmistresses, and, on the other, the problem of qualified governesses' unwillingness to become schoolmistresses "for fear of losing caste." While the *Queen* presents work as something that ladies will undertake only in response to misfortune, this leader nevertheless expresses no sympathy for social pretension or lack of pragmatism in the face of adversity, for those women who "will by no means be bound to punctuality, and will not learn or practise business habits." "There must not only be the stick held out to the drowning woman," the editor asserts, "but she must be willing to catch hold of it with a will." Those who do "catch hold" of opportunity with a will, according to the leader, reap financial benefits and personal fulfillment. "There have been instances," the editor claims, " – and they are honoured and honourable when they occur – of governesses receiving poor salaries, who have qualified themselves to become national-school mistresses, and are now leading happy, useful, and well-paid existences." There is a tacit recognition here that genteel poverty, or more to the point genteel destitution, has less social cachet than occupational success which, when it occurs, is "honoured and honourable."[46] While commentary in the *Times* frequently addresses the problem of perceived loss of status in becoming a schoolteacher, the aim is chiefly to reassure young women that this fear is only "a folly of the imagination" and that a "National Schoolmistress who was known to be a lady would be treated as a lady by those among whom she might be thrown."[47] One correspondent methodically catalogues the benefits of working in a national school, one such benefit being that "schoolmistresses almost always marry."[48] The *Queen*'s treatment of teaching, by contrast, forcibly makes the case that specialized training, conscientious effort, and fair remuneration – i.e., professionalism – make work "honoured and honourable"; in other words, make it respectable.[49]

THE TRANSFORMATION OF NURSING

Teaching circa 1870 accordingly had associations that allowed advocates for women's employment to claim it as both suitable for women, because it involved the care of children, and appropriate for ladies, because of its growing professional status. Nursing, by contrast, could claim to be "naturally" in women's realm, but establishing its professionalism and its respectability as a remunerative employment for middle-class women was a complex process. In the mid-Victorian period, nursing was a menial, quasi-domestic job carried out by women of the lower servant class, but nursing also had a vocational counterpart in genteel female philanthropy, in the ladies bountiful who visited the poor and the sick. Ladies from the middle and upper classes visited the sick in hospitals and workhouses as well as in their homes, and their work, as Susie Steinbach notes, "was seen as an extension of domesticity rather than as a transgression of its boundaries."[50] The more dedicated and determined, such as Louisa Twining, became involved in organizing such volunteer efforts by establishing philanthropic societies to coordinate the work, raise funds, and lobby for reforms.[51] Such philanthropy was typically associated with religious devotion, as it was for Elizabeth Fry, a devout and evangelical Quaker most famous for her work in prison reform, who founded the nonsectarian Society for the Sisters of Charity. More influential were the Anglican sisterhoods, modelled on Roman Catholic nursing sisterhoods. The most prominent of these was St John's House, founded in 1848 to train nurses to care for the sick poor in hospitals and in their homes. The sisterhoods typically had two classes of trainees – lady probationers, who paid

a fee and whose work was volunteer, and ordinary trainees, of a
lower social rank, who received board and wages. The sisterhoods
negotiated contracts with hospitals in order to have access both to
the objects of their philanthropy – the sick poor – and to a training
venue for their members.[52]

Because of the training that sisterhoods (and later the Nightingale
School of Nursing) provided, nursing acquired one of the distin-
guishing features of work considered appropriate for middle-class
women – specialized knowledge.[53] Training alone, however, did not
invest a role previously deemed degrading with the status required
by ladies seeking remunerative employment, but the sisterhoods also
linked nursing and philanthropy, a connection that enabled the move
from menial occupation to profession. The influence of Florence
Nightingale's interventions in the Crimea on the public perception
of nursing remain a given to this day, but the dedication of members
of nursing sisterhoods and of volunteer lady nurses during the 1866
cholera epidemic was equally crucial in cementing popular support
and respect for new-style nurses. Several letters and articles in the
Times in 1866 attest to the unstinting efforts of nurses in hospitals and infirmaries during the epidemic.[54] The *Times* also reprinted
a brief article from the *Globe* commemorating a nurse at Guy's
Hospital who had "attended to the [cholera] patients with unremit-
ting zeal, and has now … fallen a victim to her great exertions."[55]
In December of 1866, the bishop of London publicly acclaimed the
"great help which London received, during the late appalling sickness, from the self-denying efforts of Christian women [i.e. members
of Nursing Sisterhoods]."[56]

Nursing's respectability circa 1870 is accordingly guaranteed by
its vocational and charitable associations and by the public recognition and appreciation of nurses' dedicated and selfless service during
crises such as war and epidemics. The *Times*, the *Queen*, and the
Englishwoman's Review all reported regularly on the progress of
new and better training facilities for nurses, and on the exemplary
work that lady nurses undertake, but arguments in the media for
acknowledging nursing as a profession are based not on the concept of nursing as skilled work, but on nursing as charity. It was,
however, one thing to validate the vocational efforts of the lady
nurses in sisterhoods – affluent women who paid a large premium
to join these organizations – and it was another to enjoin women
from the middle classes to work in hospital wards in order to earn

a living. As "a means of livelihood," as remunerative employment, nursing's status remained uncertain and middle-class women were not flocking to training schools. The *Western Morning News* reports on a parliamentary subcommittee investigation that reveals "how very large is the demand – how very small the supply of trained nurses" in London in 1875.[57] Notices from training schools sent mixed messages about what kind of women they want to attract to their programs. The "respectable young women" that the Liverpool Nurse's Training School wants to "train and fit for superior head nurses" must be "of good character, and able to read and write."[58] The Committee of the Nightingale Fund aims higher, requiring more than basic literacy in their call for "a few well-educated intelligent young women."[59] Some of the confusion regarding qualifications for training arose from the intrusion of the class system into the practice of nursing, with trainees and staff divided into sisters, comprising "educated women only," and ordinary nurses, "drawn from the class of domestic servant."[60]

The level of physical exertion required of nurses could also be a deterrent for women accustomed to affluence and leisure. The *Englishwoman's Review* indeed attributes "the scarcity of nurses, especially the scarcity of lady nurses, to the very severe work required from them, which only exceptionally strong women are capable of sustaining without injury."[61] The *Woman's Gazette* warns aspiring probationers about elements of the work "which are far from agreeable, especially to refined and cultivated women."[62] As the *English Woman's Journal* had long since asserted, however, if women wanted to maintain a footing in the world, they "must work, and so work as they have not done yet."[63] The disagreeable elements of nursing included not only physical exertion, but an intimacy with human suffering and bodily functions foreign to most "refined and cultivated women," a kind of work they had not done yet, but which was increasingly being advanced as an option for them to consider, despite the warnings about the drudgery involved.

The contradictions inherent in the social and cultural perceptions of the relation among nursing, status, and employment are unmistakable in two treatments that appear in the mid-1870s. In its support of the establishment of training schools in all voluntary hospitals, *Fraser's Magazine* draws on the conventional link between philanthropy and lady nurses, but turns the charitable relation on its head, making nurses the objects of charity. "Is not this vast work then surely a work of charity?" the author asks – i.e., charity in the care of the sick and charity "to employ part of the surplus female population and to supply the deficiency of female occupations." "Here is surely a charitable work for the public," the author concludes, "for there is no class of the community that more often falls into needy circumstances as educated gentlewomen, or is so able to furnish intelligent and careful nurses."[64] A year later, an article in the *Queen*, recommending monthly nursing in the homes of the affluent as "a very hopeful and appropriate" employment for indigent gentlewomen, divagates from a consideration of the misfortunes of unprepared ladies "brought up in comfortable, if not luxurious, homes, without a thought of having to earn their own livelihood" to a series of rhetorical questions that maps out the qualities of a lady that would make her an ideal nurse: "Could not a lady, possessing an educated mind, be a great help and assistance to the doctor, and co-operate with him far more effectually than any ordinary nurse? Could she not, understanding so much better the laws which govern our health, look after the proper management and ventilation of the sick room?"[65] What begins as a suggestion to help ladies fallen on hard times becomes an argument for ladies – whom the author assumes to be educated and accordingly able to relate effectively to medical professionals and to understand the scientific management of the sick room – being the means of ensuring the prestige of nursing as a paid occupation. Whatever the assumptions of the article's author, however, the qualities of a lady are not sufficient to professionalize nursing, as the parenthetical intrusion by the editor at the end of the article indicates. "It is a good suggestion," she observes, "but does not a lady require special or hospital training for the post?"

To be perceived of as a profession, nursing must be an occupation that is suitable for ladies and that maintains standards of training and knowledge, and ladies who take up nursing must adhere to these standards. This crucial interconnection between status and specialized training is elaborated in a lecture delivered in May 1876 by Florence Lees, superintendent general of the Metropolitan and National Association for Providing Nurses for the Sick Poor. The *Queen* published a detailed and uncritical report on the lecture, silently endorsing Lees's argument for professional training schools and her singling out of "educated gentlewomen" as "the class best fitted" for nursing. Lees also suggests that one aim of training schools is to place nursing on an equal footing with medicine. "To make nursing equal, as a profession, to the medical," she comments, "a more comprehensive education and training was necessary than was required for the hospital nurse or sister [that is, women more or less apprenticed under the old system of training on the job]."[66] In alluding to potential equality between nursing and medicine as professions, Lees is also equating women's professionalism with men's.

The equation of nursing with medicine occurs frequently in arguments for the professionalization of nursing in the 1870s. In an article in *Cornhill Magazine*, surgeon and philosopher James Hinton compares nursing specifically with surgery, which like nursing had risen from an occupation of doubtful status in an earlier era, when, in public opinion, the "surgeon was a mechanic rather than a professional man." Surgery was then "supposed to be menial in its character," when it was in fact, as it eventually came to be recognized, "a profession of equal rank with that of the physician." Hinton sees his generation's idea of nursing as manifesting "a precisely similar mistake" and questions if "any occupation whatever [can] call more emphatically for the qualities characteristically termed professional." Hinton notes with regret that nursing is considered "an excellent and most respectable vocation" but "not one for a lady to follow as a means of livelihood, unless she is content to sink a little in the social scale. Charity, which dignifies all things, alone exonerates her from that penalty if she pursues it."[67] In an 1871 article in *Saint Paul's Magazine*, Charlotte Haddon similarly observes that ladies "nurse only for charity" because "nursing is considered menial." Like Hinton, Haddon draws parallels between nursing and surgery, noting that "surgery was counted menial a hundred and fifty years ago, and then the surgeons were servants to the physicians. But," Haddon continues, "it was made a profession by a few men who saw what it was capable of becoming, and brought scientific knowledge to bear upon their practice."[68]

Hinton interprets the problem as "a habit of thinking about nursing," rather than as a matter "founded in the nature of things" and advocates making nursing a profession by, among other things, making it a well-paid occupation. Haddon's remedy for what she sees as a false conception of nursing is for "a few qualified women to elevate nursing." Nursing, she contends, "is essentially a profession, and waits only for the right persons to practise it, in order to take its proper rank."[69] Leaders in professionalized nursing from this period apply the strategies prescribed by Hinton and Haddon – the elevation of the status of nursing by a few practitioners of the "right" sort and the recognition of its standing as an occupation by means of substantial salaries. Florence Lees, for example, one of the most influential nurses of the nineteenth century and author of the standard nursing manual of the day, worked without pay; by contrast Rachel Williams, a graduate of the Nightingale School of Nursing at St Thomas's Hospital and coauthor of another respected nursing manual, negotiated aggressively for increases in her salary as matron of St Mary's Hospital, insisting on a raise from her starting salary of £100 per annum in 1876 to £150 in 1878.[70]

Part of changing the "habit of thinking" about nursing, to use Hinton's phrase, involved changing the "habit of thinking" about the work required of nurses. For comparisons between nursing and medicine to sustain claims to professional status, nursing would have to be, in fact, in some way comparable to medicine, which was gaining prestige in the nineteenth century because of the advances in scientific and medical knowledge. The drudgery of the nurse's menial cleaning chores was accordingly recast as part of the "science of hygiene"[71] and commentaries posit that the conception and practice of nursing have developed as the result of the advances in medical science. "The development, if not the origin, of the art of nursing," declares Seymour Sharkey, a physician at St Thomas's Hospital, "is mainly a result of the progress of medical knowledge."[72]

CHANGING THE "HABIT OF THINKING"

Over the course of the Victorian period, there was as well a growing awareness among supporters of women's rights that, if their access to work was to be assured, they would need to enlist the support of public opinion to change the "habit of thinking" about women and remunerative work. That this change was in fact happening is reflected in the challenge in the media to certain categories of womanhood that were circulating at the time, challenges that invoked images of the working woman. As early as 1863, an article in *Fraser's Magazine* by George Whyte-Melville confronted the pejorative epithet of Strong-Minded Woman, commonly used to denigrate women who were assertive, energetic, and intelligent. Whyte-Melville derides men who develop "a general horror of any womanly trespass on their studies, their pursuits, or their prerogatives" and mocks a general public that imagines the most disagreeable representatives of their sex tied "together, so to speak, in one forbidding bunch" labelled "'Strong-minded Women.'" Invoking that most powerful icon of womanly caring and devotion to duty, Florence Nightingale, as the epitome of the Strong-Minded Woman, Whyte-Melville denounces the prejudices of his culture against women who exhibit "energy and judgment," arguing that "strength of mind, far from being a drawback to her other attractions, is a most desirable quality in a woman." "The real strong-minded woman," he asserts, "is patient, though right-thinking; forgiving, though clear-sighted; judicious in advice, entreaty, and even reproof."[73] The *Fraser's* article does not represent a wholesale revision in Victorian attitudes to women, but it does suggest some openness to the idea that women can and should be intelligent, informed, and earnest about their position in the world. The growing acceptance of this openness is further suggested by the fact that two of the most prominent publications for upper-middle-class ladies – the *Ladies' Own Paper* and the *Queen* – were adding articles on topical issues to their standard fare of fashion, recipes, and social gossip. The *Englishwoman's Review* remarks with apparent surprise on the alteration to the *Ladies' Own Paper*, welcoming these changes as indications of "the increased demand for serious literature, which has arisen amongst women."[74]

A generation after the publication of "The Strong-Minded Woman," Frances Martin recasts the spinster, a figure conventionally associated with loneliness, poverty, and disappointment. Martin's revision of the type becomes the Glorified Spinster, who is independent and vibrant and who, not coincidently, is employed among the ranks of "teachers, nurses, accountants, clerks, librarians, heads of certain business-departments." Unlike the Old Maid, who is "a woman *minus* something," the Glorified Spinster is "a woman *plus* something." The Glorified Spinster, as portrayed by Martin, is cultivated, self-reliant, and content. Having "tasted the sweets of liberty and independence ... she considers marriage as a last resort for those who lack sufficient strength of mind or body to maintain their footing in the world alone."[75]

These two revisions of female types differ in fundamental ways, although both are, as Judith Walkowitz says of the Glorified Spinster, "highly stylized cultural construction[s]" that represent the experience of a limited number of independent middle-class women.[76] These redefinitions nevertheless provide important insights into the evolving cultural response to middle-class women and work as they both rely, to a greater or lesser extent, on the concept of the working woman.

Whyte-Melville's idealized version of the Strong-Minded Woman is a woman who works, but her work is vocational – Florence Nightingale did not work because she needed money. This version of the Strong-Minded Woman also retains essential characteristics of the ideal Victorian woman: she is patient and forgiving; her archetype is the attentive and dutiful caregiver. The Glorified Spinster, by contrast, is iconoclastic. In delimiting her, Martin disdains concessions to conventional gender assumptions about femininity, domesticity, and motherhood. The Glorified Spinster is, in a sense, a career woman, except that she is defined less by work than by what work allows her do and to be. Work is what enables her glory, what allows her to "maintain ... [her] footing in the world." And, as the *English Woman's Journal* asserted thirty years before, if middle-class women are to "obtain a firmer footing on the earth's broad surface ... [they] must work, and so work as they have not done yet."[77] Work and cultural acceptance of the idea of the middle-class working woman were indeed fundamental not only to women's firmer footing in Victorian culture, but also to the changing attitudes toward womanhood that evolved over the course of the second half of the nineteenth century.

By the 1880s, supporters of working opportunities for women variously make appeals to public opinion, attempt to shape public opinion, and even imagine progress in the alteration of attitudes. Edith Simcox, writing in the *Fortnightly Review* in 1880, invokes the careers of cultural icons, in this case Mary Carpenter (who laboured tirelessly for educational reform for the underprivileged and penal reform for young offenders) and Sister Dora (second only to Florence Nightingale as the Victorian symbol of selfless nursing). Simcox casts them as the heroic ideals who, in altering public perceptions, removed some of the obstacles for a new generation of women who would follow their pattern. Moreover, "the same gradual change of social feeling which promises to allow women of heroic dimensions to use their powers undelayed," Simcox argues, "also promises to provide a modest field for the aspirations of the unheroic many."[78] In 1881, Margaret Harkness calls for a "frank discussion of ... [the] present position and future prospects [of women] as members of the working community," commending "the quiet and determined way in which women as a class have taken possession of every fresh field of labour thrown open to them."[79] In the opinion of some, as the comments of Reginald Brabazon in the *National Review* indicate, the bid for public awareness had already succeeded. "It is a satisfactory sign of the times, and of the progress of a sensible public opinion," Brabazon maintains, "that women are now-a-days not ashamed to confess that they support themselves by honest toil."[80] While Brabazon, writing in 1884, is undoubtedly overly optimistic about alterations in attitudes, and Harkness perhaps unmindful of the alarm that could result from the image of "quiet and determined" women taking "possession" of every area of work made available to them, the underlying awareness in these and other commentaries on women and work indicates an ongoing effort on the part of reformers to shape public perceptions and gain public acceptance for their cause.

That nursing had been particularly successful in shaping public opinion, in changing a "habit of thinking," is indicated by the respect nursing commands by the last decade of the century. In 1893, Gertrude Dix remarks in the *Westminster Review* that "the progress of medical and surgical science has been followed, step by step, by a corresponding advance in skilled nursing, and the character of a nurse's duties has completely changed ... From having been considered a work any woman was capable of performing – a something 'that came by nature,' nursing is now a recognised profession, requiring a system of theoretical and practical training extending over a definite period."[81] Two years earlier, another contributor to the *Westminster Review* observes that "we have to-day [1891], a 'Nursing profession,' such as had no real counterpart thirty years ago." This commentator also draws parallels between medical and nursing training, noting that "nurses, like medical students, learn their duties for the most part at the great medical charities [i.e., the large voluntary hospitals]" and that "the dignity of the calling" has been enhanced "by the increased confidence which is now reposed in nurses by medical men, both in the hospitals and in private practice."[82] The successful redefinition and consequent professionalization of nursing had demonstrated that not only could women work as they had not done yet, but women's work could command respect as it had not done yet, making nursing the vanguard of professionalized work for Victorian women.

The Strong-Minded Victorian Nurse: The Disputes over Nursing and Hospital Reform

When George Whyte-Melville invoked Florence Nightingale as the exemplar of the Strong-Minded Woman, his intention was to undermine the popular perception of intelligent and capable women as forbidding and objectionable. His version of the "real strong-minded woman" fits not only the public perception of Nightingale, but also the ideal of the late-Victorian nurse trained through the nursing sisterhoods or the Nightingale School: "patient, though right-thinking; forgiving, though clear-sighted; judicious in advice, entreaty, and even reproof."[1] By the end of the century, this was indeed the image of the nurse that prevailed, but the transition of the lady nurse from selfless volunteer to trained and efficient professional was anything but smooth. The reading public may have been open to the discursive reconstruction of the nurse from Sairey Gamp – the disreputable character in Charles Dickens's *Martin Chuzzlewit* whose name became the popular by-word for a coarse and incompetent nurse[2] – to ministering angel, but the reality of nursing practice required more than a change of image; it required nothing less than the reorganization of hospital management and patient care. The relations among hospital administrators, doctors, and nurses could be strained at best during the period of reorganization. At worst, these relations broke into what the *Queen* characterized as "civil war between governors and the medical staff."[3] Between 1873 and 1884 there were several crises precipitated by reforms in nursing practice in London hospitals, the most notable being at King's College Hospital, where nursing services were supplied by the sisterhood of St John's House, and at Guy's Hospital.[4] The media interest in these crises – especially the protracted one at Guy's Hospital – added yet another dimension to the complex public discourse over nurses and nursing.

The process of transforming nursing from menial to professional was complicated, as mentioned in the previous chapter, by issues of class and status related to old prejudices against the Gamps, the work involved, and the women that the new training schools were trying to attract. These were far from the only complications that nursing encountered, however. Before nursing achieved its status as the career *par excellence* for ladies, it was embroiled in acrimonious and well-publicized disputes over gender, class, religion, and even manslaughter. For a while, it was not even clear that nursing would remain a female vocational preserve. Initial public interest in nursing in the mid-nineteenth century in fact appeared not as part of the discourse over employment opportunities for women, but rather as part of the discourse over public health and sanitation. Attention to nursing in the *Times* first emerges in the context of reports on and public discussions of the administration of voluntary hospitals. An item in 1848 about the establishment of an institute "for the training of nurses for hospitals" reflects this context in the syntax of the announcement itself: this is not the training of women to be employable, but the training of a specialized workforce *for* hospitals – for the specific needs of hospitals.[5] With Britain's entry into the Crimean War in 1854, the context for discussions about nursing shifts dramatically to the provision of care for wounded soldiers and the urgent need for nurses in military hospitals. The highly publicized campaign to provide adequate medical care in the Crimea intensified public interest in nursing, especially as represented by Nightingale's work in Scutari.

VICTORIAN MALE NURSES

A surprising dimension of the evolution of nursing revealed in the discourse in the periodical press, both during and after the Crimean War, is the possibility that nursing in the Victorian period might not have developed into an exclusively female occupation. While Florence Nightingale's iconographic stature is generally presented in the most essentialist feminine terms,[6] the fact remains that her power and prominence in the movement for nursing reform resulted from the phenomenal public response to a military mission. It is therefore not illogical to consider the possibility that reformed nursing could have developed into a profession that included men from the outset. Orderlies and male nurses were caring for soldiers in the Crimea before Nightingale and her contingent of thirty-eight women arrived, and these men continued to work alongside the female nurses in the field hospitals. As Holly Furneaux attests, in the Crimean War hospitals "orderlies comprised the largest proportion of the hospital labour force," their duties being largely the same as those undertaken by female nurses: "preparing and administering medicine, food, and drink, dressing wounds, changing, washing, and combing patients' clothing, bedding, and hair, fetching water, and cleaning the ward."[7] Both in the field hospitals and on the field of battle, men in both medical and military capacities were providing services that would fall under the rubric of nursing. In the early days of the combat, a correspondent to the *Times* signing himself "A Medical Pupil" indeed offers nursing service to the war effort on behalf of his fellow students, noting that "the success of an operation depends as much upon the after-treatment as upon the operation itself" and that the "dressing and bandaging" that medical students could carry out would help to relieve the suffering of the wounded.[8] A poem appearing in the *Times* a few weeks later suggests that men are also eminently capable of ministering tenderly to the needs of the dead and dying; the speaker describes the sorrow and horror of finding a dead comrade, whom he buries on the battleground after he had "softly sealed ... [the] eyes" of the dead soldier "and set one kiss upon his brow."[9] Since the great impetus to public interest and support for nursing reform came from work in military field hospitals during a war, in a setting that demanded that men as well as women be involved in the care of the sick and wounded, what could be more natural than that reformed patient care in British hospitals continue to be provided by a similarly integrated workforce?

Census records indicate that there was a significant percentage of males in the ranks of hospital nurses in 1861.[10] By the time of the 1881 census, only a few hundred men list their occupation as some form of nursing, with categories varying from "domestic nurse" to "army nurse" to "hospital nurse." Even as the number of male nurses dwindled, however, the record in the mainstream press indicates that the public remained open to the idea of male nurses throughout the century. An 1874 article on reformed nursing in *Fraser's Magazine* indeed presents male nursing for male patients as the norm and the new hospital system as an anomaly: "In hospitals the first peculiarity to be noticed is, that women are employed to nurse both sexes; whereas in private families men nurses are frequently, if not generally, in attendance on men."[11] The following year, *Chambers's Journal* catalogues several London establishments that train and supply nurses, two of the five that are described in detail being listed as offering the services of male nurses and attendants.[12] An 1876 leader in the *Times* calling for the systematic training of nurses acknowledges that "some women, as well as a very few men, are naturally disposed to nursing."[13] Physician William Gull makes a similar point about the gender-neutral nature of nursing in an intervention during the Guy's Hospital crisis in 1880, stating that it is "a poetic fiction" to suppose that women have an "inherent fitness for nursing."[14]

The persistence of the idea that men could be nurses was concurrent with alterations in the treatment of disease, alterations that in many respects recast the nursing function in ways that were anything but exclusively feminine. Advances in medicine and science in the nineteenth century led to radical changes in medical education and hospital organization. Voluntary hospitals, with their populations of the sick poor, became the standard venue for clinical training, a necessary component of medical education even for men who had obtained degrees at universities. Medical students gained practical experience in patient care working as clinical clerks or dressers under the supervision of house physicians or surgeons. Students provided certain kinds of basic care that would fall under the purview of nurses in modern hospitals – for example, taking and recording temperatures, administering medications, and changing surgical dressings.[15] *Guy's Hospital Gazette*, a publication for the hospital's medical students, affirms that as a dresser on the surgical wards a medical student "learns in a great measure how to nurse" and that difficult surgical cases will "test his ingenuity and nursing skill."[16] As the organized and professionalized training of nurses also moved into hospital settings, what came to be called "higher nursing" became a contested area of responsibility between doctors and nurses, which is to say between men and women – a gender complication that would continue to influence relations between doctors and nurses and to shape the public debate over nursing for two decades.

The tactics used by advocates for professionalizing nursing – the comparison of nursing to the male-dominated field of surgery and even the emphasis on professionalism, conventionally associated with men's work in the nineteenth century – had masculine associations that subtly defeminize nursing. The role of male nurses in military and mental hospitals, the parallels between the development of nursing and the development of male-dominated surgery, and the overlap between the duties undertaken in "higher" nursing and in medical training (again, male-dominated) all suggest that a gender-specific occupation was not the inevitable result of these changes, even in a culture as tradition-bound as Victorian Britain. Moreover, there continued to be a public demand for male nurses, despite the growing female domination of the field. In 1881, the *Lancet*, the chief organ of the British medical profession, acknowledges that the "demand for nurses, male and female, gentle and simple, grows apace."[17] In 1885, when women had largely won the battle for control over the organization of hospital nursing, Jane Hamilton, an aging philanthropist, established and financed an association to promote the training of male nurses, "not to displace female nursing, but to supplement it by a branch for which there was urgent need." The association's first annual meeting was chaired by Sir T. Crawford, director-general of the Army Medical Department, who decorously noted that "in various surgical operations and other circumstances a male nurse is of the utmost service"; he also praised the skills of the male nurses of the Army Medical Staff Corps who were, he observed, "fully trained in the military hospitals." The association was supported by numerous prominent men, including several surgeons general and other military officers, a brace of archdeacons, several medical doctors, and "a number of the nobility and gentry."[18]

That prominent members of society supported Hamilton's initiatives no doubt in part reflects her social connections, but that they supported her publicly also indicates that they believed in the value and need of her association. That a relatively silent but committed interest in male nursing continued is, moreover, suggested by a flurry of renewed commentary on the merits of male nurses in 1897, at a time when the hottest debates in nursing were internal disputes in the newly minted nursing associations over what class of women should be recruited into nursing, how they should be educated, how they should be certified, and by whom. The *Westminster Review* published "Men as Nurses," a brief report on Hamilton's 1885 initiative, and followed that a month later with an article on the moral influence of nurses, the author asserting that "there are some men capable of filling the position, who can bring the necessary qualities to the work."[19] Eliza Priestley subsequently observes in the

Nineteenth Century that it is "strange ... that so little is done to encourage the training of male nurses," but she cites two examples of agencies that provide the services of male nurses. Priestley, who had a low opinion of the modern young female nurse, believes that male nurses would help the "profession ... take a more dignified place in public estimation."[20] The appearance of articles on male nurses in two such prominent periodicals within months of each other suggests that the idea of the male nurse generated more public interest than has hitherto been recognized.

PROFESSIONALIZING THE LADY NURSE

The process of establishing the identity of the nineteenth-century professional nurse as essentially female was heavily influenced by the growing need for work for middle-class women. The increasing influence of the sisterhoods and the establishment of the interconnectedness of class status and specialized training as the lynchpin of nursing's professionalism played a significant part in the cultural redefinition of nursing not only as progressive and scientific, but also as respectable and feminine. London hospitals contracted nursing services to nursing sisterhoods like St John's House, or established training schools for a new class of female nurse, such as the Nightingale School at St Thomas's Hospital. Both the sisterhoods and the schools used the wards as the training grounds for their probationary nurses and produced what was termed "new-style nurses" as opposed to the "old-style nurse" whose training had been less systematic and formal, and whose social background was generally working class. The medical establishment was initially in favour of some kind of nursing reform and expressed enthusiasm for lady nurses supplied by the sisterhoods. An 1866 article in the *Lancet*, reproduced in the *Times*, acknowledges that the "system of lady-nursing ... is attended with the greatest benefit, and with none of those evils which many at first feared from its introduction."[21] In an address to the National Association for the Promotion of Social Science in the same year, Elizabeth Garrett also notes that the *Lancet* "has recently given emphatic testimony" to the "immense improvement in the nursing" at hospitals where the new system of nursing had been introduced, and where the sisters were still working on a voluntary basis. The *Lancet*, Garrett observes, "prophesies that we cannot long refuse to adopt a system 'which embodies intelligence, the keenest sympathy, [and] refinement.'"[22]

That the work is voluntary is the key to the medical profession's initial public approval of nursing by ladies. The alteration in the status of the lady nurse from philanthropist to potential careerist, however, eventually produces equally public criticism of the new training programs and sympathetic revaluations of old-style nurses. By the dawn of the 1880s, medical men begin to complain about evils in the new system of nursing that had not alarmed them nearly as much when the ladies of the sisterhood had seen their mission as purely avocational. By enabling the movement of middle-class women into the workforce, as well as by generating alterations in hospital organization, professionalized nursing presented challenges to many strongly held Victorian values in the socially conservative ranks of medicine. On both counts, new-style nursing began to encounter resistance within the medical establishment that now saw not intelligence, sympathy, and refinement in nursing sisters, but ignorance, presumption and even downright cruelty.

THE SPECTRE OF RELIGIOSITY

Association with the sisterhoods afforded nursing the respectability vital to its acceptance as an occupation for ladies, but this advantage, it eventually emerges, came at a price. From their inception, nursing sisterhoods were subject to the general criticism that their medical mission was subordinate to their religious one, despite initial protestations from within the medical profession itself that this was not the case. The *Lancet*, for example, insists that there is "no interference with the religious convictions of the patients [on the part of nursing sisterhoods]. Nothing like proselytism is attempted."[23] A correspondent to the *Times* in 1869 who signed himself "M.D." confirms that "no difficulties of consequence have arisen" from religious sisterhoods undertaking hospital nursing; "M.D." asserts, moreover, "that the medical officers of every hospital in which lady superintendence has been introduced have become almost unanimously converted to this system of nursing."[24] As professionalized nursing gained a stronger foothold in hospitals in the 1870s and 1880s, however, it continued to be haunted by the spectre of religious fanaticism, by the fear that overly devout nurses would care more for the spiritual rather than the physical welfare of their patients. Medical men who had initially extolled the virtues of new-style nurses now engaged in often vitriolic public attacks. In 1879, surgeon George Barraclough, for example, sees sisterhoods as the source not of benevolence, but of inhumanity, and he finds their conduct so disturbing that he is moved to expound at length in *Fraser's Magazine* about the threat that lady nurses pose. While he warns that "narrowness and want of charity is, at times, encountered in all religious associations," Barraclough nevertheless fears that nurses outside the control of sisterhoods would be even more intemperate in their religious propagandizing and he fabricates alarmist scenarios in which uppity nurses warped by religious prejudice or steeped in apparently useless "medical Latin" cause unnecessary deaths.[25] Such fear of the possibility modulates into an assumption about the reality of the lady nurses' true mission and into a weapon in the arsenal of their most vituperative public critics, the medical doctors who resisted the change from old-style to new-style nursing. Whether or not nurses were attached to a sisterhood, they were plagued by charges of pernicious religiosity, of adding to the stress of illness by proselytizing or by annoying patients with prayers, and of neglecting nursing duties in order to attend rigidly scheduled prayer or religious services conducted by the nursing administration.

The issue of religion so clouded public perceptions that commentators in the newspapers and periodicals had to remind their lay readers that the highest position in nursing in London hospitals had always been termed "sister," a designation that did not indicate any affiliation with a religious sisterhood.[26] It is in fact true that nurses – especially those in training, who lived together in residences attached to hospitals – were expected to attend daily prayer services presided over by the matron. This practice was not limited to sisterhoods and such practices were hardly foreign to Victorian middle-class culture in general. It would have been unthinkable, for example, for regular prayers and church services to be omitted from the routine in public schools, and family prayers were common in many homes. Lady nurses were being denounced for a level of religious practice endorsed by Victorian society at large. Moreover, as one lady nurse points out in a letter to a women's newspaper, the demanding duties of a hospital nurse left her no time to indulge in proselytizing, even if she were inclined to do so.[27] The supposed religiosity of lady nurses was a red herring. The real threat that the lady nurse posed was to doctors, not to patients, and it was a function of her class status, not of her religious devotion.

Debates over professionalized nursing that appear in the periodical literature always confirm the subordinate position of the nurse to the doctor.[28] As noted in chapter 1, however, in making the argument for recasting nursing as elevated and honourable work rather than as menial, contributors frequently make the comparison between the rise in status achieved by surgeons a generation earlier and the rise in status aspired to by nurses. While the medical and surgical doctors are thus accorded their due authority in the workplace, surgeons are implicitly acknowledged as parvenus. They – and their profession – lack pedigree. And while nursing at the time also lacked pedigree, the ladies who were taking over the field most assuredly did not. The sisterhoods smacked of High Anglicanism at a time when the Tractarian Movement was still influential in upper-class circles. Many of the lady nurses, both inside and outside the sisterhoods, were the daughters of high-ranking members of the Anglican clergy.[29] The lady nurse's religiosity was what the doctors decried, but what they really feared was her class superiority. Many of the doctors in London hospitals had risen from humble origins. The lady nurses, by contrast, stooped to conquer.

OLD- AND NEW-STYLE NURSING AND THE DISPUTE OVER HOSPITAL REFORM

It is hardly surprising, then, that antagonisms developed between doctors and nurses, especially during the 1870s and 1880s when reforms in nursing were precipitating reforms in hospital management and when, as one commentator observes, "class distinctions were still hard and fast."[30] It was boards of directors, not the medical staff, that invited the nursing sisterhoods and training programs into the hospitals, and many doctors were dissatisfied with the resulting changes in the organization of wards and of patient care. Formerly, nurses had been trained on the wards by means of an informal apprenticeship, and while the results were anything but uniform, the best of these nurses were greatly valued by the medical men under whom they served. In some cases, nurses had worked on the same ward for a decade or more and knew the specific demands, techniques, and expectations of particular doctors. The new nursing system changed the role of the matron from the overseer of housekeeping, supplies, and food services to the administrator of nursing services and training, a role formerly shared by the sister and doctor in charge of each ward. The new system further demanded that nurses rotate from ward to ward every three months in order to gain experience and expertise in all types of nursing care, a system that doctors found disruptive. The lady nurses were doing more than introducing new-style nursing; they were imposing a new hospital culture, a culture in which many old-style doctors were ill at ease. It was, moreover, a culture that could not easily accommodate conflicting class and professional hierarchies.

The resulting conflicts between doctors and new-style nurses gave rise to highly publicized crises in the 1870s and 1880s in large London hospitals, making the "nursing question" a matter of public scrutiny. The nursing question was indeed raised so regularly and so repeatedly – most notably in articles, letters, and stories in the *Times* – that the public could not help but be acutely aware of the issues involved and of their importance not only to nurses and nursing, but also to the viability of major voluntary hospitals and, consequently, to public health and welfare. The most acrimonious and protracted crisis, and the one most damaging to the reputations of the hospital and the individuals involved, was the one at Guy's Hospital in 1880.[31] The principal adversaries in the dispute aired their grievances, both personal and professional, in the periodical press and the newspapers, leaving a record of events, attitudes, accusations, grievances, and wounded feelings that provides intriguing insights not only into day-to-day interactions within the walls of a Victorian hospital but also into the cultural battle, coloured by all the fraught gender and class sensibilities of the Victorian era, being waged there. Through their exchanges in the press, the self-possession of the genteel nurse and the insecurity of the doctors who resented the incursions of ladies into their territory – both physical and professional – are laid before the eyes of an appalled public and, incidentally, before a fascinated posterity. This exchange clearly reveals the workings of the class and gender politics that shaped the professional nurse and demonstrates how the warring parties used cultural stereotypes – like Sairey Gamp – and cultural biases – like the proselytizing lady nurse and the déclassé medical student – to sway public sympathies.[32]

CLASS, GENDER, AND THE CRISIS AT GUY'S HOSPITAL

The crisis at Guy's Hospital was precipitated by the hiring of Margaret Burt as matron, with the mandate to update the hospital's nursing services. The medical staff resisted, more on principle than on any practical grounds; they were incensed because they felt they had not been adequately consulted and their objections began before giving the new matron and her system any real opportunity to establish themselves. Miss Burt was appointed in November 1879 and took up her position in December; on 29 December, the medical staff collectively sent a letter to the hospital's treasurer, who functioned as the administrative CEO, condemning the new system and the new matron.[33] The strife at Guy's might have remained a largely internal matter if it were not for the notorious article by Margaret Lonsdale in the *Nineteenth Century* in April 1880. Lonsdale was virtually the sole representative of the lady nurses in the media firestorm that followed, her initial foray into the press being met with a barrage of criticism and attacks from some of the most prominent doctors at Guy's – Samuel Habershon, Walter Moxon, and William Gull. This cast of characters embodies the class dimensions of the nursing debate. Of the major respondents to Lonsdale, only Octavius Sturges, senior physician at the Westminster Hospital, was a gentleman in the true Victorian sense of the term, having been born into a prominent family and educated at Cambridge. Habershon, senior physician at Guy's, was the son of an ironfounder. Moxon's father was an inland revenue officer, and Moxon himself had worked as a commercial clerk while studying at the University of London to qualify for entry into Guy's training program.[34] Sir William Gull was arguably the most distinguished medical practitioner of his day. He was physician to the Queen and a consultant at Guy's at the time of the nursing crisis. But he, too, had risen from humble origins; his father was a wharfinger who had died when his son was ten.[35] Margaret Lonsdale by contrast was socially prominent, the daughter of a canon and the granddaughter of the bishop of Lichfield. She had been a lady nursing probationer at Guy's for about six weeks before writing the article for the *Nineteenth Century*. Previously, she had been a lady probationer at the small but well-respected Cottage Hospital in Walsall and had just published a highly popular biography of its revered charge nurse, Sister Dora. It was indeed Lonsdale's success as an author that had prompted such a prominent periodical to approach her to write an article on nursing.[36]

Lonsdale's exposé of the dispute at Guy's draws on numerous stereotypes, not just of nurses, but also of doctors and medical students. She argues that the old system of nursing at Guy's relied heavily on women akin to Sairey Gamp, women who were largely untrained and

ignorant and who drank on and off duty. She invokes the uncomplimentary popular image of medical students "as a class, universally
acknowledged to be uncouth."[37] Sisters, by contrast, come across in
Lonsdale's account as virtuous and knowledgeable models of efficiency. As with most stereotypes, there may have been some truth
in these characterizations. The governors of the hospital were not
likely to be bent on nursing reforms if there were no problems. Had
Lonsdale limited her comments to the putative deficiencies of the
old-style nurses, even with the offhand insult to the medical students,
she might not have drawn fire on such a grand scale.[38] These same
stereotypes had, after all, been used by the *Lancet* back in the 1860s,
when the medical community had supported new-style nursing. The
Lancet at that time made observations similar to Lonsdale's, assessing the nursing at Guy's as "but one degree removed from the Gamp
and Prig *régime* of thirty years ago" and the medical students as
deriving much needed "benefit from contact with ladies."[39] Lonsdale
goes on, however, to impugn the medical staff, implying that their
resistance to change is motivated by their desire to avoid objective
scrutiny of "practices and experiments indulged in by medical men
... which it is understood had better not be mentioned beyond the
walls of the hospital." Old-style nurses, Lonsdale alleges, are the perfect cover; if they talk, "their character is such that little credence
can be given their word."[40] It is hardly surprising, then, that while
she interprets the presence of "lady nurses" as a salutary "moral
restraint," many of the doctors term it espionage.

   That the social position of many of the new sisters was considerably higher than that of most doctors gave a particularly unpleasant resonance, as far as the doctors were concerned, to the putative
civilizing influence of the refined lady nurses on the medical staff.
Moreover, Lonsdale characterizes the relations between doctors and
nurses in "hospitals where the old system of nursing prevails" as
much the same as that of "head and under servants in a large household" between whom there is "a kind of tacit understanding" to
blind the master and mistress – i.e. the public – "on certain points."
This imputation further undermines the dignity and authority of the
medical profession by casting the doctor as merely a higher category of not overly scrupulous domestic servant.[41] "Is it any wonder," demanded the *Medical Times and Gazette* in response, "that
the Guy's men are wild?"[42] So wild, indeed, were the Guy's men
that they swelled the next issue of the *Nineteenth Century* with

thirty-seven pages of responses to Lonsdale's original eight-page article, and maintained a more or less continuous flow of indignant letters to the *Times* until the fall of 1880.

The whole affair was seen, and is generally still interpreted, as a crisis of authority, which undoubtedly it was. The medical staff initially stressed, and continued to complain about, the interference of the governors in matters of medical management and the high-handed behaviour of the hospital treasurer. The public debate, however, concentrated almost exclusively on the relations between doctors and nurses; the issue accordingly became one that in many ways pitted gender supremacy against class supremacy, at least within the walls of the hospital. In their series of responses to Lonsdale in the *Nineteenth Century*, the doctors are not content simply to point out that she was unfair in some of her criticisms of the former nursing staff at Guy's, which she perhaps was; rather, they attack Lonsdale herself, and lady nurses and sisterhoods in general, with a disconcerting lack of restraint, in one instance going so far as to characterize lady nurses as "agents of a system of espionage where truth is held lightly."[43] Nurses' attainments are elsewhere disparaged in the press as a "superficial polish of medical knowledge"[44] or they are personally dismissed as "a squad of half-instructed young women."[45] While some of the other doctors are willing to acknowledge that the new nursing system could be workable and even beneficial, none besides Octavius Sturges, whose family background and Cambridge education made him at least the social equal of any of the lady nurses, is prepared to grant that highly trained nurses have legitimate claims to specialized knowledge or expertise. "In this system of subordination on the part of the nurse," Sturges asserts, "there is no sufficient recognition ... of her trained skill and experience ... Nurses, being now recruited from a superior class, are entitled to take higher rank."[46]

In their attacks on lady nurses, the doctors never brand them as strong-minded, but the criticisms of Lonsdale and her counterparts nevertheless parallel the negative stereotypes of the Strong-Minded Woman. The doctors' most common complaint about the lady nurses is their lack of tact and humility. The doctors deplore what William Gull characterizes as the "alloy of self-assertion" that taints the "very advantageous stock" of feminine attributes that might otherwise make lady nurses admirable caregivers.[47] The self-assurance of women like Lonsdale irks medical men like Seymour Sharkey, who complains that "ladies who write and think in the tone which

pervades Miss Lonsdale's article are imbued with the most warped
and wrong-headed notions." Sharkey is scandalized that Lonsdale
"sneers at the idea" of nurses assiduously observing the special
demands of individual doctors and that she "seems to imagine [that]
nurses are placed in hospitals to correct the errors made by medical men."[48] Perhaps because of the positive connotations of "strong-
minded," especially as associated with Florence Nightingale, the
doctors prefer to concentrate on Londale's presumed ignorance
and callowness. In the spirit of age and experience prevailing over
youth and ability, particularly when the former is male and the latter female, doctors repeatedly attempt to undercut her credibility by
referring to her dismissively as a young woman lacking experience
and knowledge, or, in one case, as a "young girl."[49] Lonsdale was in
fact thirty-three, but her opponents were eager to disclaim her critique of Guy's as the rantings of jejune intemperance or as "the rav-
ings of a fashionable mania."[50] This last phrase is one that Lonsdale
had coined herself, in her initial discussion of nursing at Guy's in the
Nineteenth Century, to characterize the intensity of public interest:
"nursing," she observes, "is rapidly becoming a fashionable mania"
– "books about the subject are widely read."[51] Her detractors were
quick to seize on the phrase "fashionable mania" and use it out of
context, assigning the mania and the susceptibility to fashion to
Lonsdale and the lady nurses themselves. Media accounts go on to
disparage her representations of old-style nurses and the relations
between doctors and nurses under the old system as flights of a
mean-spirited and overwrought imagination, if not outright lies – "a
good story rather than a true one,"[52] "warped and wrong-headed"
and full of "exaggerated notions."[53]

Running through all the doctors' responses to Lonsdale and the
entire issue of lady nurses is the old theme of religious sisterhoods
and their supposedly pernicious influence. Although the new nursing
system at Guy's was not attached to a sisterhood, Margaret Burt had
trained at St John's House, and this was a sore point with many doctors at Guy's, not least Samuel Habershon, who pejoratively assesses
the changes there as "the development of a system of nursing, with
religious observances."[54] For Habershon, as for many of the doctors,
the putative High Church religiosity of lady nurses is all the more
disturbing for the taint of aristocracy. Moxon expresses their suspicions most unequivocally, maintaining that "this new system represents in short a determination ... to substitute for our old sisters

the closest approach possible to a religious sisterhood of an aristocratic turn." So strong is his mistrust of lady nurses and of Lonsdale
in particular that he imputes religious-cum-class motives rather than
professional ones to her criticisms of nursing at Guy's. "Only for
some such religious object could any lady write as Miss Lonsdale
writes," he insists. "Hence it is that social superiority is thrust forward at every turn as the character of the 'new system.'"[55]

THE STRONG-MINDED NURSE AND THE DISRUPTION OF HOSPITAL CULTURE

Underlying all the public protests by the Guy's doctors is the fear of
professional displacement, the "general horror" of "womanly trespass on their studies, their pursuits, or their prerogatives" that, according to Whyte-Melville, strong-minded women arouse.[56] Despite
the criticisms levelled at new-style nurses, the advances in medical
knowledge in the nineteenth century had in fact led to a greater understanding and valuation of basic nursing care. "One of the most
striking characteristics of modern medicine," one doctor observes,
"is the importance assigned to nursing in the treatment of the sick
... In the sick-room, the vast array of potions and unguents and the
odour of drugs has been replaced ... by a neat and skilful nurse and a
plentiful supply of fresh air."[57] But if nursing care is more significant
than prescribed drugs in the successful treatment of disease, what
then is the place of the doctor in relation to the patient? Medical
practitioners were alert to the potential disruption of doctor-patient
relations and were more than a little disturbed by it. "The true and
I believe the chief objection which medical men have felt against the
new order of nursing," William Gull contends, "is that it introduces
a new element between them and their patients."[58] Sturges is more
alarmist, if perhaps ironic: "The doctors having at length confessed
that drugs are nought, or almost nought, are distinctly informed that
the province of nursing, to which they would betake themselves, is
already occupied. They are as good as eliminated."[59] Moxon is more
direct: "We cannot at Guy's give the higher nursing up to the nurses.
It is essential to the existence of the medical school that the higher
nursing should be done by the [medical] students."[60] Implicit in this
injunction is a realization that more skilled nurses would mean a
generally diminished need for doctors, and an acknowledgment that
men could nurse.[61]

Underwriting these acrimonious responses to the Guy's crisis was a public apologia for a culture – the culture of the hospital that ensured the studies, pursuits, and prerogatives of the male doctors – that the medical establishment wished to defend and preserve.[62] Outside this culture, the granddaughter of a bishop would not take orders from the son of a wharfinger; inside the hospital, Margaret Lonsdale would certainly be expected to respond respectfully to the demands of William Gull. The persistent criticism of the insubordination of lady nurses indicates, however, that whatever the professional relations of the two groups, ingrained class attitudes continued to colour their interactions. The textual sparring between Lonsdale and the doctors at Guy's reveals the difficulty – perhaps the impossibility – of reconciling the imbalance between professional status and social class in the working relations of doctors and lady nurses. Despite Lonsdale's criticism of the old system of nursing and patient care at Guy's, she repeatedly affirms, both in her original article and in her subsequent responses to angry letters from doctors in the *Times*, that nurses must be subordinate to the medical staff. At the same time, her confidence, born of class and social position, allows her to be assertive and vocal when she sees what she deems to be poor practice, and subsequently to rebut her opponents by citing all the misinformation and factual errors in their arguments. The very fact that she had the temerity not just to voice her opinions in the press, but also to stand up for herself when faced with a barrage of abuse from the medical community, indicates that, however willing she was to be subordinate in a professional situation, in public debate outside the walls of the hospital she considered herself to be on at least an equal footing with her opponents. Margaret Lonsdale, in other words, was a strong-minded woman, but the confidence and aplomb such personal strength and integrity entailed prompted the doctors of the time to label Lonsdale and the other new nurses, especially those in positions of some administrative authority, as aggressive and wanting in tact. Lack of tact was one of the most common criticisms levelled against Margaret Burt by Guy's medical staff, and it became a virtual rallying cry against new-style nurses in public discourse for the next twenty years.

THE GUY'S CRISIS IN THE WOMEN'S PRESS

The public record of hospital relations of the period, dominated as it is by the conflicts between medical and nursing staff at Guy's, presents a prevailing image of doctor-nurse relations as uniformly confrontational. This is certainly the impression that emerges from the mainstream press. Women's periodicals and newspapers, as if to present a corrective to biased misrepresentations and popular misconceptions, suggest a very different situation. With the exception of Lonsdale, women had not been a part of the heated debate over nursing as it played out in the mainstream press, despite the fact that they had earlier produced assessments of the value of nursing as a career for ladies and continued to do so when the dust had settled after 1880. In 1880, however, their comments were either reserved for or restricted to the women's press, and their opinions varied. The *Queen, the Lady's Newspaper and Court Chronicle*, while siding with the doctors, also prints a letter from a correspondent who discreetly and logically points out that the major criticisms of lady nurses are unfounded. "We lady nurses," she notes, "are not anxious to be doctors or chaplains, and have neither time nor the inclination to force our religious opinions upon our patients."[63] A similar divergence of opinion appears in *Work and Leisure*, a women's periodical solidly middle-class in its vision and interests, which printed a letter from a reader giving credence to the doctors' numerous versions of Lonsdale's sins.[64] The editors in turn caution against hasty responses without consideration of evidence from all parties concerned.[65]

Not everything in the women's press was formulated to underplay confrontation, however. One of the great ironies of the controversy over nursing, and of the Guy's debate in particular, is that while so many of the doctors repeatedly betrayed intense class-based insecurities, at times bordering on paranoia, with regard to the motives and attitudes of high-born and strong-minded lady nurses, these same doctors – including those whose origins were humble – were receiving their staunchest public support from the *Queen*, the most aristocratic ladies' publication in the kingdom. The language in the *Queen* is as vituperative and the assessment of the lady nurses as prejudicial as those in the most heated responses to the crisis appearing in the mainstream press. The first leader on nursing in the *Queen*, published before Lonsdale's article was printed in the *Nineteenth Century*, asserts that "the 'sister' with views of her own is of all nurses the one most to be avoided."[66] A subsequent leader labels Lonsdale as "unscrupulous"; another refers to her critique of nursing at Guy's as "insolence."[67] Margaret Burt's efforts to update nursing services at the hospital become "the dictation of a woman ignorant of medical science."[68]

The *Queen*'s intervention in the Guy's debate culminates in the publishing of the names of the hospital's board of governors, a body that fares almost as badly as the nurses at the hands of the paper's editor. Not only is this the most dramatic intervention of the entire Guy's debate, it is also highly ironic. One of the major objections to lady nurses, in the *Queen* and elsewhere, was their lack of tact; they were deemed too assertive, too wanting in decorum – in short, too strong-minded. Here we have the lady editor of the *Lady's Newspaper* taking it upon herself to obtain, "at some considerable difficulty," she admits, the list of governors.[69] The list is marked "private," but, the leader asserts, "we recognise no private performance of public duties, and therefore print it in full, adding the addresses of the members." The leader goes on to make strong accusations of nepotism and despotism by an inner circle of governors, charging, among other things, that "when there is a vacancy [on the board], the small working body appoint an exalted individual, who is seldom likely to attend their meetings, and they are left to do as they please with the valuable property bequeathed by Thomas Guy."[70] In many ways the *Queen*'s championing of the doctors appears to be a case of gender trumping class: men (doctors), even without superior class status, are ceded authority over ladies (nurses) by the lady editor of the *Queen*. But the *Queen* then turns on the highly placed governors of the hospital, publicly impugning their motives and calling for the intervention of Parliament to regularize the hospital's administration. Their *bête noire*, Margaret Lonsdale, could not have been more strong-minded and imperious, nor could the situation within Guy's present a more complex and charged field of gender and class cross-currents.

The feature of the Guy's debate most deplored by all parties at the time was that it was so public and so charged – in many instances, so lacking in decorum on all sides. Commentators from both inside and outside the profession regret the "personal character of the controversy" and call for the termination of "a dispute which affects so damagingly the reputation of a noble institution."[71] And just when it seemed that the public dimension of the controversy would subside, the indictment and trial of one of the new nurses at Guy's for manslaughter in the death of a patient in the summer of 1880 rekindled the fires of outrage. Conflicting testimonies from Guy's doctors during the trial led not only to new attacks on Margaret Burt and her nurses but also to personal sniping among doctors, notably William Pavy, Walter Moxon, and William Gull, in letters to the editor of the *Times*. The anger and resentment of some of the major players in the crisis, expressed so persistently and so publicly, indeed led the governors of Guy's to demand – again publicly – the resignations of Samuel Habershon, senior physician, and John Cooper Foster, senior surgeon. The damage resulting from the public displays of indignation and professional distrust was considerable – the blighting of distinguished medical careers, the humiliation of nurses, and the dishonouring of a public institution. Late in 1880, the *Examiner* indeed considers "the resignation of the whole medical staff imminent," with the prospect that "no man in the profession with the least pretensions to self-respect could accept service in the establishment."[72] A generation later, feelings still ran so deep that when a young doctor asked his senior associates at Guy's about "the great 'Nursing Dispute,'" he was "met by a certain unwillingness to discuss it, sometimes even by an embarrassed silence."[73]

THE LASTING EFFECTS OF THE PUBLIC DEBATES

It was nevertheless the charged and very public nature of the debate that was its real value. The heated interchanges brought major issues of public interest to the public's attention, issues regarding the administration of hospitals and health care, the education of both doctors and nurses, and the development of professional opportunities for women. The vituperative character of the debate in the mainstream press, which seemed to disincline women from taking part, nevertheless inspired the women's press to open up its own avenue of engagement in the public discourse over nursing. And the disputes ultimately contributed to raising the status of nursing. The ladies who wanted the reforms also sought to elevate nursing to professional status; the doctors who wanted to maintain the old system argued that their nurses were not Sairey Gamps, but intelligent, respectable, and often refined women. The "nursing question," moreover, remained in the public consciousness for the remainder of the century. The Guy's dispute did not settle the controversies over nursing, but it did firmly establish the nursing debate as a pressing public issue. Subsequent discussions of disputes over nursing and hospital administration during the 1880s were more restrained and cautious, but they nevertheless kept the issues before the public with a fairly steady flow of letters to the *Times*. By the end of the 1880s,

reformed nursing had been embraced by the public at large and
hailed as the jewel in the crown of the Victorian social legacy. "The
future historian of the reign of Queen Victoria," a leader in the *Times*
presciently affirms in 1888, "will be likely to give a prominent place,
among other social improvements, to the institution and organization
of skilled nursing."[74]

The extent to which nursing had become a public issue is evident in the numerous brief notes and articles about the advisability
of registering nurses and about the activities of the British Nurses'
Association that abounded in both women's newspapers and
mainstream newspapers in the late 1880s and 1890s. While some
discussions revealed divisions in the public assessment of the professionalism of the new-style nurse, raising the old canard of the
fashionable mania and deploring the "too numerous vain, giddy,
and frivolous young persons who bring disgrace on the profession,"
discussions about nursing at the close of the century did not have
the sensational charge of publicly aired internal disputes.[75] Internal
disputes in fact raged on, but this time the adversaries came from
within the ranks of nurses and their supporters. The matters at issue
were standardized training and registration, and once again class
and gender played a role in the ensuing debates over the level and
range of knowledge, education, and even professionalism required
of nurses. The major adversaries in the debates over registration,
however, were all socially prominent women: Florence Nightingale,
who wanted nurses to come from the ranks of the lower-middle and
upper-servant classes, and Ethel Gordon Fenwick and the Princess
Christian – founders of the British Nurses' Association – who wanted
nursing to be a profession for educated ladies. The lady adversaries
at the heart of the debates, however, kept their bitterest antagonisms
out of the realm of public discourse[76] – perhaps because they were
women at a time when women were chary of publicity, or perhaps
because they had imbibed the lessons of the damaging debates of
the previous decade. Their public decorum did not mean, however,
that their dispute was enlightened or the result salutary. Brian Abel-
Smith concludes that the efforts of the "professionally-conscious
lady nurses" of the British Nurses' Association produced "unrealistic
policies" that resulted in a chronic nursing shortage.[77] Indeed, had
the public had greater opportunity to witness and assess the debates
over registration and to take part openly, the process of establishing culturally sanctioned parameters for standardizing the education

and registration of nurses in Britain would likely have been more expeditious, the nursing shortage of the early twentieth century less acute and protracted.

The ultimate casualty of the new system of nursing was the male nurse, whose interests had been lost in the charged debates over lady nurses. While having some supporters, the male nurse was not a figure that fired the public imagination. Without a strong champion within the active ranks of either medicine or nursing, and with no pressing issues of public interest at stake, there was no impetus to create or drive a public debate over male nurses, a group that had neither class status nor cultural cachet. While the public discussions cited earlier demonstrate a continuing openness to male nurses in Victorian culture, nursing journals indicate that there was no support for men from within the profession itself. Eva Gamarnikow notes that between 1889 and 1923, only four articles treated the topic of male nurses in the weeklies *Hospital* and *Nursing Mirror*. These articles defined male nursing roles as marginal to the profession – asylum nursing and tasks considered "inappropriate for women," such as shaving or catheterizing men.[78] The pressures of class and of class-based gender politics within nursing eventually marginalized these men so completely that they were excluded from the College of Nursing when it was established in 1916.[79] Male nurses remained a presence in military hospitals but were otherwise relegated to work in mental asylums; they were never accorded the prestige of the professional lady nurse of the period.

By the end of the nineteenth century, the character of nursing for generations to come had been determined, a public character defined in large part through public debate. The image of the Victorian nurse may always be the Lady with the Lamp; the professional ideal – equally as problematic and probably more influential – was fashioned in the cultural debates over hospital care and military hospitals at midcentury, fired in the heated controversies of the 1880s, standardized by the professional associations of the 1890s, and imprinted on the collective consciousness of a nation. She is a lady, well-trained, efficient, selfless, and tactful: "patient, though right-thinking; forgiving, though clear-sighted; judicious in advice, entreaty, and even reproof." She is, in other words, the realization of Whyte-Melville's "real strong-minded woman."

"Books Are Better Than That": The Representation of the Nurse in Victorian Fiction

"Our ideals of womanhood," an anonymous contributor to the *Woman's Herald* in 1892 contends, "are largely originated by heroines in real life, and by heroines in fiction, as well as by the unconscious but powerful interaction of these two factors. With the progress of time and civilisation all ideals undergo considerable variation." The progress of time and civilization, according to this writer, had brought about a radical change from the time that Victoria ascended the throne, a change from an ideal of womanhood that was aristocratic to one that was "unquestionably democratic," an ideal that had been influenced by the most prominent working lady of the era, Florence Nightingale. This progressive ideal of the late Victorian period demanded that women's "energies should extend far outside the comparatively restricted limits of the home circle" and that a woman's "body, mind, heart, and hand should alike receive education and training."[1] With a few exceptions, real-life middle-class working women as characterized in the periodical press are not full-fledged heroines, but they are nevertheless engaged in a heroic struggle to define themselves as full-fledged members of a social and economic system within a culture that preferred to limit them to the domestic realm. By contrast, their counterparts in fiction are for the most part very much thoroughgoing heroines, fully engaged both in working careers and in capturing the hearts of those in their fictional worlds. Fiction, moreover, provides authors – and their protagonists – with a venue in which the vexing tensions and difficulties that confronted real women trying to enter the working world could be addressed and overcome, without the intrusion of the ungovernable exigencies of real life. These thoroughgoing heroines accordingly present a blueprint, admittedly fictional, for a hopeful future for working women and, as well as capturing the hearts of those in their fictional worlds, they also capture the imaginations of the reading public, thereby developing the "unconscious but powerful interaction" of life and fiction crucial to the evolution of cultural and social ideals.

RUTH AND THE POWER OF WORK

This powerful interaction begins with a figure with whom many readers were sympathetic, but whom none would care to emulate – the eponymous heroine of Elizabeth Gaskell's *Ruth*, a novel that has conventionally been interpreted both by Victorian readers and by modern critics as being about sin and redemption.[2] Ruth's fall from virtue is undoubtedly what Gaskell had in mind when she expressed her fear that critical reaction to her novel would be negative, that the fallen woman would be viewed as "an unfit subject for fiction."[3] Critical and public responses to *Ruth* were, however, largely favourable. The story was judged touching and beautiful; the protagonist was deemed sympathetic, noble and good; and the author was hailed as resolute and courageous. Victorian readers were not about to embrace the Ruths of their world unreservedly, however; Ruth is still lumped with the outcasts and the disgraced. As one commentator observes, that while "atoned and glorified," "Ruth *must needs* perish."[4] And Ruth is contaminated in so many other ways than sexual transgression; many reviewers were outraged more by the lie that she and the Bensons concoct in order to gain her acceptance in respectable society. But Ruth is also contaminated by something that Victorian readers would have felt but not consciously recognized: Ruth is contaminated by work.

Ruth is of special significance in the fictional representation of women and work because it was published in 1853, just before Florence Nightingale travelled to the Crimea and redefined nursing forever, and before the most active debates about middle-class women and work appeared in the periodical press. *Ruth* was published at a time, in other words, when the issues that were to become so contentious as the century progressed were just beginning to surface, when ladies were starting to join nursing sisterhoods, and when the message of the census data about the superfluity of women in Britain was prompting at least a few prescient observers to sound an

alarm.⁵ *Ruth*, as a result, is shaped in part by the changing perceptions of women and work that were beginning to circulate by 1850,
perceptions that influenced the moral and practical issues driving
the novel's plot. Certainly Ruth Hilton faces a host of moral and
practical problems, and she finds the solutions to those problems in
work. In every phase of her life, Ruth must work, an activity that is
not central to the lives of most Victorian heroines. But while Ruth
is contaminated by work, she is in the end also redeemed by work,
a paradox that exemplifies the cultural anxieties and conflicts developing over the emerging problem of superfluous women and their
need to support themselves.

The paradox begins with the contradictions in the characterization
of Ruth herself, the first being that she is an innocent and virtuous
fallen woman. While Victorian conventions would dictate that any
fallen woman would be by definition shameful and sinful, Gaskell
is at pains to construct Ruth as a sympathetic character who does
not fit the cultural paradigm. Ruth exudes innocence and virtue and
she eludes easy categorization. Victorian readers seemed prepared
to accept this set of contradictions (hence the positive reviews of
the novel), but only if Ruth dies – she "needs must perish."⁶ Ruth's
class position is also indeterminate. She presents in the novel as a
middle-class woman, in that she is constructed with conventional
middle-class characteristics, but she is so problematically middle
class that an unwary critic defining her as such without extensive
qualifications would surely invite ridicule. A middle-class woman
circa 1850 would have to be deemed a lady, and Ruth has neither the
requisite education nor the accomplishments for such a designation.
Ruth nevertheless has a number of more or less credible middle-class
credentials that do add up. Her father was a "respectable farmer,"
the narrator tells us – the respectable tag indicating that he was not
himself a labourer. Her mother was the "daughter of a poor curate"
– meaning that she was very respectable indeed, and while an impoverished curate would barely have a toehold in the middle class, the
narrator describes Ruth's mother as "a delicate, fine lady," a description that suggests middle-class education and refinement.⁷ Ruth, in
other words, inherits the personal characteristics of a middle-class
lady from her mother, and she also fits the novelistic conventions of
the virginal middle-class heroine. She is graceful, kind, and sweet-
natured. She is domestic, longing for her old home, and affectionate
and gracious with the old family servants when she manages to visit

them. She is beautiful but modest and she is obedient and respectful of those in positions of power over her, which – again paradoxically – is part of her downfall. She trusts the feckless Bellingham because he is a gentleman; she believes in his social and moral superiority because she is innocent.

Ruth's identity is also protean. She embodies a series of conventional Victorian feminine identities in the novel – vulnerable virginal orphan, exploited seamstress, fallen woman, mother, governess, nurse, and, ultimately, self-sacrificing quasi saint. Once she realizes that she is pregnant, she also assumes the role of widow to avoid public exposure of her past. Despite her problematic status as middle class, made even more dubious by her sexual fall from grace, Ruth develops one middle-class characteristic after another as her story progresses. As her son grows, she works on her own education to equip herself to begin his education, thus turning herself into the ideal of the Victorian mother. Because of her innate personal refinement and her acquired knowledge, she is hired to be the governess of the leading family in her community – a position suitable only to a woman from a middle-class background.

What makes Ruth most problematic as a quasi-middle-class lady is also what makes her most noteworthy as a character, and that is that she works to earn her living. Not only does she work, but she works in some of the most culturally symbolic employments available to women at the time, employments that span the class spectrum: seamstress, governess, and nurse. The seamstress embodied a host of cultural contradictions. She was a sympathetic figure in the cultural imagination because her skill – sewing – was one shared by women at all levels of the social scale. Sewing was domestic and ladylike. The seamstress was also the paradigmatic exploited woman worker, a victim of one of the most notorious of the sweated trades, her sad fate celebrated in poetry and in the visual and plastic arts.[8] Governessing was, by contrast, considered respectable and suitable for middle-class women without families to support them, but, as many novels from the nineteenth century and many subsequent critical assessments demonstrate, to be a governess was to be socially displaced, to be neither one of the family nor one of the servants, a potentially disruptive figure in the domestic milieu.[9] Whatever its disadvantages, however, the position of governess was genteel and could offer domestic advantages, especially in an affluent family such as the Bradshaws.

It is particularly significant that Ruth ultimately adopts the role of nurse once she is exposed as a fallen woman who has deceived her community and her employers. *Ruth*'s publication occurred at that moment in history when nursing was in the early stage of being transformed from an occupation deemed suitable only for women in the lowest levels of the working class into one that genteel ladies were undertaking. Nursing at midcentury was still plagued by dominant popular assumptions that associated the nurse with degradation, poverty, and even drunkenness. At this point it was not Ruth, but Dickens's disreputable, gin-sodden Sairey Gamp who remained the figure that epitomized nursing in the Victorian imagination. That Ruth becomes a nurse is accordingly a social demotion. Nursing may carry with it associations with domesticity and nurturing – fine feminine qualities – but at the time it is also a form of domestic service, and a distasteful one at that. As a consequence, her only remaining supporter in the Bradshaw family, Jemima, is appalled at the idea of Ruth becoming a nurse, insisting that she is "fitted for something better." Jemima goes on to observe that Ruth is better educated than she is herself and cautions her: "All your taste and refinement will be in your way, and will unfit you" (Gaskell, 314). In Jemima's eyes, even Ruth's compromised virtue does not reduce her to the level of nurses.

Ruth is nevertheless able to redeem herself through nursing for two reasons. The first is the evolving work ethic that is quintessentially Victorian, an ethic that is best captured in the benevolent rantings of that Victorian prophet of work, Thomas Carlyle (1795–1881). For Carlyle, work was the source of all personal fulfillment, all personal satisfaction. Work, moreover, is ennobling. "All work," according to Carlyle, "even cotton-spinning, is noble; work alone is noble." Work is indeed what brings us closest to heaven: "All true Work is sacred; in all true Work, were it but true hand-labour, there is something of divineness. Labour, wide as the Earth, has its summit in Heaven."[10] If Victorian reviewers and readers found Ruth to be noble, which they did, it was in no small part because she worked, and her work, like the nursing of the ladies in the early sisterhoods, carried with it the character of philanthropy. Ruth works with the kind of devotion to work envisioned by Carlyle, ennobling what was seen as the degrading position of nurse with her absolute commitment and dedication. And while Ruth may need the money, however meagre, that nursing supplies, her level of devotion and exertion raises her efforts beyond just work because she labours less for her own good than she does in order to benefit others. In doing so, she redeems herself and advances the idea of the working lady. Ruth anticipates, in both her words and her actions, the model of nursing that will eventually win over the naysayers in Victorian culture to the idea that ladies could and should be nurses. She responds to Jemima's misgivings by asserting that she will find use of "any *true* refinement" (emphasis added) and poses a question that presents the contrast between the Gamp and the lady nurse: "Would you not rather be nursed by a person who spoke gently and moved quietly about than by a loud bustling woman?" (Gaskell, 314).

What ultimately redeems Ruth is what ultimately redeems nursing – the willingness to risk death trying to save others. Ruth agrees to be the matron of the fever hospital, not just despite, but because of a deadly typhus epidemic. The ultimate irony is that she catches typhus, not from her impoverished patients in the hospital, but from the man who seduced her; he lives, but she "needs must perish." Ruth is apotheosized in the novel for her selflessness, just as the lady nurses who died caring for the poor during the cholera epidemic of 1866 were memorialized and praised in the Victorian press for their self-sacrifice. And like them, she "did not talk much about religion," one of the major assumed defects of the lady nurse, but instead provided intelligent and able nursing care (316).

Elizabeth Gaskell set out to write a story about sin and redemption. She produced a story that is also about a young woman who stooped to work – stooped to conquer, in a sense. Ruth's fall begins even before she is seduced and abandoned by Bellingham; it begins when she sinks to the expedient of working to support herself. Work and compromised virtue are, in a disturbingly real sense, mutually constitutive for the middle-class Victorian woman. To work is to be tainted, to be a social outcast; being sexually compromised is to be forced to work, to be self-supporting. And both the fallen woman and the working woman were deemed unwomanly. Ruth, then, can be interpreted as embodying the plight of the middle-class single woman who is forced to work because she is left without a male protector – without a father, brother, or other male to provide her with a home. It is then apposite that Ruth's death results from nursing her seducer, not, as some commentators have bemoaned, because she must expiate her sin, but because the taint of work and the taint of fallenness are so closely bound in Victorian concepts of womanhood. And if Ruth's qualifications for her diverse occupations are as dubious as her credentials as a middle-class lady, then her situation accords with that of the superfluous women trapped by the constraints of Victorian domestic and gender ideologies. There is no stable place for Ruth, just as there is none for the superfluous woman, in the only social world they know; there is no secure and viable identity that they can adopt.

EARLY NURSING STORIES AND THE NURSE AS *RACONTEUSE* (1850s–1890s)

Ruth is a contradictory figure – the fallen woman who embodies innocence, the tainted working woman who is redeemed by work and who in turn ennobles that work. And while Ruth embodies all the potential of the real and fictional working ladies who will follow the moral and practical trail she blazes, in 1852 she is something of a voice crying in the wilderness. Stories about nurses (rather than about the nursing that women do as part of their domestic role as wives, mothers, or daughters) do appear from the 1850s to the 1870s, although infrequently, and these are typically presented as factual – as memoirs or stories based on fact. The growing interest in the nurse as the subject of a narrative, or as the teller of a tale, is suggested by the republication of *Remembrances of a Monthly Nurse* in 1852, more than a decade after the original serial publication of the tales that comprise *Remembrances* in *Fraser's Magazine* and the *Monthly Magazine*. Three years later (January 1855), "The Hospital Nurse," a story subtitled "An Episode of the War: Founded on Fact," appeared in *Fraser's*, just a few months after Florence Nightingale arrived in Scutari with her team of nurses. These two examples of nursing tales establish several of the paradigms that define stories about nurses in the second half of the nineteenth century. Both claim to be factual, but these avowals are suspect, or at best very broad. The truth claims of "The Hospital Nurse" have no apparent basis beyond the fact that women did travel to Scutari to nurse. The 1852 "Advertisement" that prefaces the text of *Remembrances* acknowledges that they are not personal experiences but are nevertheless "founded upon facts which had come through various channels to the knowledge of the writer," who was "a lady ... who had previously much distinguished herself as a poetess of great power and feeling" and as an anonymous contributor to the *Monthly Magazine*.[11] The central character of *Remembrances* is, like Sairey Gamp, a monthly nurse – i.e., a woman brought in to care for a woman during confinement and delivery, and to attend to mother and baby in the first month postpartum.

Remembrances of a Monthly Nurse had initially predated Sairey Gamp's appearance, and its revival, some nine years after Dickens's character had stirred the imagination and the opprobrium of Victorian readers, suggests that the *Remembrances* were part of an attempt to restore the credibility of nursing.[12] The narrator of the tales certainly could not be more unlike Sairey. Moreover, the first-person narrator of *Remembrances* addresses some of the most salient issues about ladies, work, and independence that would appear in the press later in the century. As the widow of a military officer, she admits, she might "procure a situation as governess" or "become a companion to a lady of rank." As a woman with notable "family connexions," she could have accepted a pension from her "proud and noble relatives." She scorns all such expedients as stooping "to eat the bread of dependence." Recognizing that working as a monthly nurse would be regarded as "descend[ing] ... many steps in life's ladder," she hides her identity by changing her name and "place of abode," determined to "at least preserve ... [her] self-respect and become a useful member of society."[13] She then goes about reinventing herself as "Mrs. Griffiths," the monthly nurse, by reading up on midwifery and offering her services to a celebrated *accoucheur*, who immediately sends her off to care for the young wife of an earl.

That "Mrs. Griffiths" has the education and breeding that her previous position in society has afforded her is undoubtedly what enables her to be as commanding a figure as she clearly is, which accords with the claims of lady nurses some years later as they tried to establish themselves as professional workers whose personal attributes would make them superior caregivers for the sick. And "Mrs. Griffiths," who so "detested dependence," interprets the role of monthly nurse not in terms of its supposed lowly social standing, but in terms of the authority she possesses in her specialized knowledge:

Now, a monthly nurse in my opinion is a very great personage. She generally rules the whole house where she is an inmate, from the master downwards. What can exceed her authority for her brief four weeks? Even the medical gentlemen often defer to her opinion and are anxious for her approbation. The lady of the mansion is her entire slave; the domestics tremble at her frown;

the children of the family dare not enter their mother's chamber without her permission; and as for the baby! – I have never repented of the choice I made. (v)

Unlike a subservient governess or companion, "Mrs. Griffiths" "rules the whole house" – master, mistress, servants, and even the attendant "medical gentleman." And while this portrayal of a lady of social standing becoming an assertive and successful nurse could be read as a salutary endorsement of lady nurses, "Mrs. Griffiths" is just the sort of practitioner of medical services that Florence Nightingale disdained – the lady with no training who assumes that she is innately suited to specialized work. "Mrs. Griffiths" admits that she had "no recommendations, no experience." Her sole initial qualification is "common sense" and while she claims to have made herself "mistress of ... [her] profession by reading and inquiry," her ability to secure her first position seems to be based as much on her appearance and deportment as on any professional expertise. She outfits herself in "a rich black silk dress, bought for the occasion, with a very handsome India shawl," and drives to the door of the man "considered the first accoucheur in London" in a hired carriage, and is engaged on the spot (vi). It is perhaps not surprising then that *Remembrances* relates very little in the way of actual nursing, focusing instead on the narrator's relations to members of the household and on the intimate details she acquires about the lives and loves of her employers in her role as confidante and advisor.

Nightingale's professional values are again undermined in "The Hospital Nurse," whose protagonist, Mary Vaughan, volunteers to work in the hospital at Scutari. Mary has previously engaged in some genteel nursing by providing care for the victims of accidents in the coal-pits on her brother's estates, and for the victims of cholera from among his tenants; she has not, however, had any formal training or hospital experience. Her experience caring for these victims, the narrator asserts, "had rendered it unnecessary for her to prepare herself for the work before her by a course of instruction in a London hospital," an opinion with which Nightingale would undoubtedly have differed.[14] As in *Remembrances*, neither the practice of nursing nor the training of nurses is addressed, while the dress, the deportment, and the imagined suitability of the protagonist for her profession are outlined in detail. In both texts, the protagonist is a woman without a husband – Mary's fiancé died mere days before their wedding – and neither is without family resources to support her. As possible exemplars of the working lady, both protagonists present work not as an unfortunate necessity and fall from middle-class grace, but as a choice, based on a desire for independence on the part of "Mrs. Griffiths," and on an aspiration to do good works, on the part of Mary Vaughan. Similar motives drove many of their real-life counterparts, and while they often did not have the luxury of choosing whether or not to work, they did value the freedom to choose what work they would do. Many of the real women of the period also imagined that they had the capability to take on work for which they had not trained, but the real world of work was not as easily mastered as the fictional one, to which the many periodical articles about the need for women to obtain sound education and training attest.

Remembrances and "The Hospital Nurse" establish some of the conventions of representation that will define fictional Victorian working ladies for decades. If a working woman is to be the central character of a story, she must have the credentials of any Victorian heroine – she must be desirable and domestic, either married or marriageable, which typically means that she is either a widow or a young woman whose intentions to marry have been thwarted, by death or by some other force beyond the control of the lovers. The choice to work cannot be a choice not to marry, although the choice to work may lead to marriage, as when a tender young nurse catches the attention of a noble young doctor, as frequently happens in stories later in the century. In *Remembrances* and "The Hospital Nurse," it is evident that neither protagonist would have made the choice to work if her husband or fiancé were still alive. Mary is especially clear – if rather maudlin – about the relation between her quasi-widowed state and her calling to nurse. "The sunshine of my life is over," she reminds her brother-in-law, who tries to dissuade her from going to Scutari, "and you know it is long since I was made to know that henceforth I must try to live for the many instead of devoting myself only to *one*" ("The Hospital Nurse," 98). *Remembrances* and "The Hospital Nurse" also lay the foundation for two dominant categories of nursing stories – the texts in which the nurse is not the subject but the source of the stories, and the texts in which the nurse is the heroine of an adventure tale, a love story, or possibly both. For the Victorian reader, the real interest of *Remembrances* lies in the stories of the secret lives of the prominent families for whom "Mrs. Griffiths" has worked. Mary Vaughan's sad love story is literally at the centre of "The Hospital Nurse," imbedded in the narrative between her discussion with her brother-in-law about her decision to go to Scutari and her poignant leave-taking of her family at Christmas.

Perhaps not surprisingly, since at midcentury nursing was still not widely endorsed as a suitable employment for genteel women, the based-on-fact fictionalized nurse is often represented as working class. These nurses are not, however, ignorant or disreputable, suggesting that there was a general desire to rescue the working-class nurse from the spectre of Sairey Gamp. One such monthly nurse appears in a story in the *Dublin University Magazine* in 1862 that incorporates the cultural prejudices against monthly nurses, only to refute them. The narrator of the story is a lady, an officer's wife, who has taken a cottage on the Isle of Wight, where she gives birth to daughter and hires Nurse Brown to attend her. Initially suspicious that Nurse Brown's red face is "indicative ... of her being accustomed to her 'little comforts,'" the narrator eventually comes to realize that this nurse is in fact "sober and respectable." The focus of most of the narrative is once again the story that Nurse Brown relates about a child she had nursed years before, but in the process of telling the story, she reveals her true character, and her self-effacing kindliness and "humble talk" convince her genteel patient "that people are not the less sensible or sensitive for being poor; and that intuitive delicacy of feeling is by no means confined to the higher and educated classes."[15]

A similar attitude of mingled indulgence and respect emerges in an account of the reflections of a working-class hospital nurse that appeared in a series entitled "Women Who Work," published in *Cassell's Family Magazine* in 1874–75. The nurse's narrative of her experiences, presented as a garrulous set of responses to implied questions, reveals many of the drawbacks of nursing as a career, at least for those women without the advantage of class position. Although she trained in a hospital under the "new system," this nurse did not like hospital work, as it subjected her to the coarseness of disreputable and aggressive patients, whose "language and blasphemies" made her "wonder whether they're human beings at all, an' not animals possessed." Nursing in such conditions could be dangerous: she relates that one "great brute" bit "a nurse's wrist through" and that "a nurse was nigh strangled by a woman."[16] Hardly more appealing is private nursing in the homes of more affluent patients, where harsh and unpleasant conditions of work are the norm and where she is not treated with respect. The nurse eventually joins "one of those charitable institutions for nurses [i.e., a Sisterhood]," where she earns twenty pounds a year. She acknowledges the "great an' grave" drawbacks of these institutions – nurses do not have the power of choice in their assignments, they must live in the home, and they receive very little of the fee paid by the family – but she nevertheless expresses great respect for the administrators. "Those institutions," she attests, "are well managed and presided over by pious, charitable ladies and gentlemen, who take great care of 'em, [and] select the nurses with judgment" (49). She is simply grateful to have regular employment. This account is significant because it purports to represent the experiences of an ordinary working nurse, not a lady nurse attempting to raise the status of nursing. The presentation of the narrative in the voice of the nurse herself, however, does not ring true. The nature of the implied questions, the characterization of the nurse through dialect, and the deference for her social superiors she is represented as displaying smack of condescension on the part of the author. Nevertheless, this account serves to remind the reading public that working-class nurses are respectable and competent, having acquired expertise through training and experience. The nurse in this narrative is also aligned with her more genteel colleagues in nursing in that she, like them, turned to nursing after the death of her husband.

The fascination with the nurse as confidante and *raconteuse* continued to the end of the century, although the figure of the nurse eventually takes on middle-class characteristics; she speaks grammatical English, is self-assured and articulate, and has joined the ranks of a profession (even if the word profession is sometimes rendered in quotation marks in the text). The *Idler* published several nursing vignettes in the 1890s. In his "Novel Notes" column, Jerome K. Jerome relates "an incident told ... by a nurse." The nurse in question, "a quiet, demure little woman," is largely effaced by the stories she tells of her patients. She exists only as the observer and narrator of human nature, as one who sees "clearer into the souls of men and women than all the novelists" and recounts the intimate details of the cases she has nursed.[17] "Talks with a Nurse" appeared three years later, with Miss G__, "a lady well known in 'the profession' from one end of London to the other," relating her experiences, putatively in her "own words."[18] Miss G__ is a more defined presence than the quiet, demure woman in Jerome's "Novel Notes," and one who clearly represents the evolution of cultural attitudes towards nurses since the 1870s. "Twenty-five years ago," she observes, "nursing was not nearly so fashionable an amusement as it is now. When I say 'amusement,' I mean that people do not take the profession of a nurse seriously until they really get behind the scenes and discover the grim side of the work … Of course, my 'people' did not like a girl going in for this kind of work. At that time, only a few women of independent means took up nursing in earnest; and they had a halo round their heads immediately. Sairey Gamp ramped through the land, but good nurses were almost unknown" (329). The author is able to cram a host of cultural assumptions into these few sentences – early attitudes towards nurses as either Gamps or saintly ladies bountiful, parental resistance to young ladies becoming nurses, and limited current understanding of nursing as serious work rather than as a "fashionable mania." While Miss G__ does make general observations of this kind about nursing, the focus of the vignettes is still the intimate details of patients' lives. Miss G__ may assert that there "are tragic moments in a nurse's career," but those moments are not hers; they are, rather, "the experience of a poor man or woman's sin or sorrow" (423). As a lady who nurses the poor, Miss G__ continues to reflect the old tradition of the genteel philanthropic nurse and, as such, she functions as a respectable entrée into that most fascinating source of local colour to readers of 1890s journalism, the lives of the impoverished inhabitants of darkest London.

REVELATIONS OF HOSPITAL LIFE: FICTIONALIZED MEMOIRS AND BIOGRAPHY (1870–1880)

The response to cultural biases formulated in nursing stories became especially charged when debates about the role of lady nurses in hospitals surfaced between the mid-1870s and the mid-1880s.[19] As media coverage and public debate over the crises in several London hospitals heightened, the reputation of professionalized nursing and the relations between nursing and medical staff suffered significant damage. The mainstream press's coverage of these disputes in major hospitals inevitably created the sense of hostile relations between nurses and doctors. During this same time period, several versions of hospital memoirs appeared that either purposefully or inadvertently countered the prevailing representations of hostility among members of the medical and nursing staff that emerged in the press. Particularly pertinent to the study of the history of hospitals and of nursing is William Ernest Henley's "Hospital Outlines: Sketches and Portraits."[20] Henley (1849–1903), who became a prominent critic and poet (arguably best known for his stirring poem, "Invictus"), was hospitalized at the Royal Infirmary, Edinburgh for almost two years in the 1870s for treatment for tubercular bone disease. The record of his experiences of hospital life in "Hospital Outlines" is both raw and finely observed. The infirmary is "half workhouse and half jail" ("First Impressions," 120, line 14), the waiting room "stinks of drugs and dust" ("Waiting," 120, line 1), the ward is "the field where Science battles with Disease, / And Hope – sweet Hope – succumbs to Death alone" ("The Ward," 121, lines 13–14). Among the "Portraits" in this sonnet sequence are an old-style staff nurse, a new-style staff nurse, and a lady probationer. Since virtually all articles and stories about hospitals and nursing in the 1870s were authored by parties with vested interests in the debates over related medical and professional issues, Henley's view from the patient's perspective is especially illuminating and significant. His old-style nurse is reminiscent of Nurse Brown, a homely and unpretentious figure who speaks in a "broad Scots tongue" but who nevertheless carries herself with dignity, with "antique liveliness and ponderous grace" ("Staff-Nurse: Old Style," 125–6, lines 7, 4). She is valued and respected both for her character and for her thirty years' experience:

Patients and students hold her very dear.
  The doctors love her, tease her, use her skill.
    They say "The Chief" himself is half afraid of her. (Lines 12–14)

This old-style nurse accords with the version championed by the medical staff in the fraught public debates over hospital nursing services, and Henley's portrait of the new-style nurse does hint at the sense of superiority for which she was criticized in the press. She is "patrician to the last" and somewhat vain. Her gown and hair are impeccable, she discusses music and literature, and she "knows that she has exceeding pretty hands" ("Staff-Nurse: New Style," 126–7, lines 5, 11). She is nevertheless professional, capable, and very assured: she is "kindly and calm" and "gives at need, as one who understands, / A draught, a judgment, or an exhortation" (lines 5, 13–14).

Henley's versions of hospital nurses and staff are no doubt influenced to some extent by assumptions current at the time, but they share none of the ill will that coloured the hospital debates in the press from the mid-1870s to the mid-1880s. His old-style nurse is knowledgeable, kindly, and earthy; his new-style nurse is educated, professional, and somewhat patronizing; she does not, by contrast with her type as characterized by medical staff in the hospital debates, proselytize. The surgeon is almost god-like, embodying "faultless patience ... / Beautiful gentleness and splendid skill," worshipped by his patients as "another Herakles, / Warring with Custom, Prejudice, Disease, / As once the son of Zeus with Death and Hell" ("A Surgeon," 124–5, lines 6–7, 12–14). The medical student, by contrast, is a composite of human and professional flaws: "His traits? – resentful and suspicious vanity, / Showy dexterity, logical humanity, / Thin brilliance, commonplace intelligence," capped with "an egotism making these things great" ("A Student," 125, lines 9–11, 14). This last portrait is the one that accords most with the stereotypes of the time, the medical student having long been a figure widely satirized in comic sketches.[21] Henley's portrait of the lady probationer also appears to rely on shared cultural assumptions, as indicated by his appeal to the reader at the close of the sonnet to speculate about her past: "Do you not guess (with me) she has a history?" ("Lady Probationer," 126, line 14). The sonnet hints at the stereotypical failed romance. The lady probationer's "shy eyes" are "not unacquainted, it would seem, with tears" and she wears a mysterious "signet ring" ("Lady Probationer," 126, lines 3–4, 6). Like the other nurses in the "Portraits," however, she is professional and competent and indeed embodies the characteristics touted by reformers as being the most valuable assets of the genteel nurse. She maintains "a well bred silence" and is "quick, skilful, quiet, soft in speech and touch" ("Lady Probationer," lines 8, 12). Although his portraits draw on characteristics of existing cultural stereotypes, Henley presents all versions of the nurse as qualified and committed to their vocation. There is, however, a subtle difference between the old-style nurse and newer versions. In common with those of the surgeon and the medical student, the portrait of the old-style nurse does not hint at a life outside the hospital or at a back-story that explains her presence on the ward. There are no traces of secret tears, nor is she, like the new-style nurse, a "bright ... face ... waning fast / Into the sere of virginal decay" ("Staff-Nurse: New Style," 126, lines 1–2). However skilled and professional, the new incarnations of the genteel nurse, both in reality and in art, provoked speculation about her motives and about her identity as a woman, about why a middle-class lady would choose to work at all, let alone as a hospital nurse.

A more pointed counter to prevailing assumptions about the character of hospital staff and their mutually hostile relations appeared in *Work and Leisure* in 1880 in the guise of a serialized memoir of "A Nurse." The serial, entitled "Hours in a Hospital," recounts the supposedly true-life experiences of a probationer.[22] This memoir is clearly intended to influence readers' perceptions of the relations between medical and nursing staff by emphasizing the shared values of humanitarianism and cooperation between doctors and nurses and by presenting nurses as self-aware and constructively critical of their own practices. Actors in the stories are fairly stock incarnations of popular stereotypes – the martinet ward sister with the heart of gold, the young probationer both orphaned and disappointed in love, demanding and thoughtless doctors and medical students. Situations conveniently illustrate issues relevant to the current debates about nurses' conduct – conversations (presented as verbatim dialogue) about the suitability of some young women for the profession, descriptions of the nurses' religious observances (here represented as low-key and routine rather than ritualized), and accounts of interactions between doctors and nurses during patient rounds.

One of the most contentious issues of the hospital debates – the interaction or lack thereof between medical and nursing staff during doctors' ward visits – is presented in the memoir in terms that emphasize the dutiful subservience of the nurses, with just a hint of the level of ego of some medical staff.

> At a certain time the surgeon or physician, whose turn it was to visit, arrived, accompanied by his resident officer and a group of attendant students. The great man was waited on by Sister, carrying an inkstand, and by several anxious probationers ready to run in all directions for whatever might be wanted ... Occasionally these doctors' visits lasted as long as two hours, and at the conclusion it cost the nurses a good deal of labour to restore the ward to its ordinary state of neatness. (38–9)

There is implicit criticism here of the medical staff; its members come across as egocentric and thoughtless, taking the servitude of a bevy of nurses as their due and showing no awareness of the disruption they cause to the ward and its routines. Overt criticism, however, is restricted to the nurses themselves. The ward sister acknowledges that she has "no doubt that most of the Sisters of Queen's [a fictional hospital] are tyrannical" (78), but this tyranny is limited to the treatment of other nurses. Nevertheless, the author also acknowledges a more general lack of "self-forgetfulness" among nurses, somewhat similar to the doctors' complaint of their lack of tact. "Were the knowledge and skill of trained nurses acquired only in this spirit [i.e. of self-forgetfulness], were vanity and love of exercise of power excluded as far as is possible in human creatures from this highest of woman's work, we should hear less of those painful struggles for precedence and supremacy between doctors and nurses which bring such discredit on both professions" (111). There is enough shame and blame to go around in this version of the disputes. In an allusion to the public debate between medical practitioners and nurses, the author makes reference to "letters from doctors, written in anything but the generous and liberal spirit which should characterise members of so noble a profession; answers to these breathing everything save meekness" (111–12). Incorporated into the criticism is a glimpse of the ideal: the skilled but nevertheless self-forgetful trained nurse; the generous and noble doctor.

The memoir concludes, however, with another ideal that is less complimentary to doctors – the characterization of nursing as a calling morally superior to medicine, presented in the account of a conversation with James Hinton:

> An expression of surprise was once quoted in his [Hinton's] presence, "How any woman could condescend to be a doctor who had the chance of being a nurse." "Exactly so," he replied; "when a common-place young man says, 'I want to be a doctor,' I say, very well, because I dare say he will do well enough. And if a common-place girl wants to be a doctor, I take it for granted she will do well enough too. But if a girl says, 'I want to be a nurse,' I begin to consider whether she has the requisite qualifications; for the nurse's profession embraces all that is good in both the medical and the clerical professions, the positive elements of each without the negative elements of either. She has the doctor's science without his drugs, and the parson's religion without his dogmas." (114)

Although the memoir elides the class issue of nurse-doctor relations, in thus suggesting that commonplace young men or women would do for medical training while only exceptional young women would be suitable for nursing, the author subtly endorses the idea that nurses are ladies and ladies have personal qualities of refinement and judgment that commonplace individuals (here, presumably socially inferior doctors) lack.

The author of this memoir uses "Dora" as her character's name, clearly invoking the memory of Sister Dora, arguably the pattern for the self-forgetful trained nurse. Sister Dora – Dorothy Pattison – was one of the most famous and beloved nursing sisters of the nineteenth century. She had been the head of the Cottage Hospital at Walsall, where Margaret Lonsdale had been a probationer before going to Guy's Hospital. Sister Dora was highly regarded for her devotion to the lives and the peculiar needs of working men who were the victims of often horrendous industrial accidents in the foundries of Walsall. Lonsdale's hagiographic biography of her appeared in 1880, two years after Sister Dora's death and just before the controversy over nursing at Guy's became a public debate. Like the memoirs of "Dora Melville," the biography presents interactions between doctor and nurse as harmonious, as based on a common commitment to duty and to the welfare of the men and women entrusted to their care. Sister Dora does provide a certain amount of the not always welcome "moral restraint" that Lonsdale sees as one of lady nurses' most valuable contributions to hospital life. After a group of medical students indulge in "unseemly jokes and laughter" during a post-mortem, for example, Sister Dora summons the surgeon in charge into her private office and unleashes "a fury of anger" "not only at the discourtesy paid to herself, but at the disrespect shown to the presence of death." This potentially explosive incident results not in antagonism, but in accord, "in a mutual apology."[23] Sister Dora is also prepared to influence decisions about treatment. One of the most celebrated incidents in her career, referred to by the miners of Walsall as "Sister's arm," involves her intervention to prevent the amputation of a workman's badly mangled arm. Her intention is not to express any real reservation about the surgeon's decision, but to save the patient's livelihood: without his arm, he could not work. The doctor is furious and angrily consigns "the young man's death upon … [Sister Dora's] conscience." When both patient and arm survive after three weeks of constant attention from Sister Dora, the surgeon, "without whose leave," Lonsdale reminds us, Sister Dora could have done nothing, uses the case to illustrate to students what diligent care could accomplish (68–9).

While the focus in this biography is understandably on the accomplishments of its subject, the text also self-consciously presents the relations between doctor and nurse as based on mutual respect, both for their persons and for their skill. Lonsdale's vision here arguably represents her ideal of nurse-doctor relations, an ideal that not only was not realized during her experiences at Guy's but also was not shared by the doctors there. Octavius Sturges in fact cites the biography to denigrate the kind of nursing that Sister Dora represents, commenting that "no well-regulated hospital could have existed under such a rule."[24] The Cottage Hospital at Walsall not only survived, but was considered a model of its type.[25]

NURSING AND THE SEARCH FOR ADVENTURE (1870s–1890s)

The shifting cultural perceptions of the nurse in this period register quietly but perceptively in the fictional representations of genteel young women who struggle with the confines of the prescribed roles and expectations of mid-Victorian society. In the 1870s, fictional representations of nursing by ladies are still largely confined to the family sickroom, although hints about the appeal of hospital nursing can be striking. In Anne Thackeray Ritchie's novel *Old Kensington*, for example, the protagonist, Dorothea Vanborough (Dolly), struggles with misgivings about her engagement to marry and about the kind of hollow existence her life as the wife in an affluent household would be. Dolly envisions that life as "a sort of wheel of commonplace to which poor unquiet souls were to be bound, confined by platitudes and innumerable threads, restrictions, and silences." "Was this the life … [she] had dreamt of?" Dolly ponders, while the narrator affirms that her dreams of the future had sometimes been "of something more meaningful and truer, something responding to her own nature, a life coming straighter from the heart … – a life with a truth in it, and a genuine response and a nobler scheme than any she had hitherto realized."[26] The next evening, Dolly is seated at a society dinner beside a colonel – "an upright, rather stern, soldierly-looking man" – who is about to leave for the Crimea (303). When Dolly laments the passive role that women must play, he responds with a description of "a regiment of soldiers" he had seen that day, "in white caps and aprons, who fight with some very deadly enemies. They are under the command of my sister, my brother's widow. She is a hospital nurse, and has charge of a fever-ward at present" (305). The reference to the Crimean War and the characterization of nurses as soldiers recalls the nursing missions of Florence Nightingale and Lady Stanley to Scutari in 1858. These allusions suggest that nursing could be more than just work and more than just self-sacrifice. Nursing could mean travel, glamour, and adventure.

Nightingale had been particularly chary of ladies volunteering for the Scutari mission in search of just those ends, but the progress of the entourages of nurses travelling to the Crimea was followed closely by the British press, and the incursions of lady nurses into foreign war zones created a national sensation back home. The idealized and romantic representations of self-sacrifice on the part of lady nurses that appeared in the press had the predictable result of increasing public awareness of the potential for nursing to provide a career for respectable women, but they also had the unintended result of suggesting the possibility of foreign travel to sheltered young ladies in the middle and upper classes. Young men in the same social strata in Victorian Britain routinely made an extended continental tour as part of their education and coming of age. For their sisters, however, there had previously been no such opportunities; travel for them was restricted to intensely chaperoned and structured visits to limited destinations. Now there was the prospect of travelling under the protection, not of an intrusive chaperone, but of a professional designation. Work could be their ticket to ride.

Stories and putative memoirs subsequently appeared in periodicals that chronicled the experiences of women who travelled to the continent to nurse in conflict zones. Though not especially numerous, these accounts are revealing of attitudes towards women and travel. A particularly arresting example of this form of travel writing is a two-part narrative that appeared in *Blackwood's Magazine* in May and June of 1871, entitled "Under the Red Cross: A Narrative of Hospital-Life with the Prussians in France." As represented in this putative memoir, the designation of "under the red cross" functions as a form of travel visa. The first-person narration initially sets up all the conventional notions of the self-sacrificing young woman bent on aiding suffering soldiers. "I wished to devote myself to nursing the sick and wounded in the hospitals in France," the aspiring

Nightingale informs the Prussian envoy during a visit to Munich, a declaration that prompts him to offer the standard responses of the day to the idea of lady nurses, whether they worked in war zones or in London hospitals. "Doubtless it is a very noble mission you are undertaking," the envoy concedes, and "where ladies have been able to stand the work and privations, their nursing has been a very great help and comfort; but many don't know the hardships of such an undertaking, and turn out, notwithstanding their most praiseworthy intentions, helpless and useless."[27] This mingling of condescension and admonition provides a fairly typical paternalistic reaction to such a proposition, while the response of the English wife of the Prussian diplomat in charge of dispensing the Red Cross designation is revealing of another set of reservations about ladies who propose to nurse at the battlefront:

> You don't expect to get the Red Cross, do you? Because you had better give up that idea at once. It is next to impossible. They have refused scores ... Because ... there has been such unwarrantable abuse of the Red-Cross badge. Lots of people have gone ... with the idea that they would make a pleasant trip of it, see the country, write paying articles to the papers, and get their expenses gratis into the bargain! (636–7)

The memoirist's apparently unblushing response – "I don't want to write articles for newspapers – I should not know how to" – calls attention to the fact that this is exactly what she is doing. Admittedly, *Blackwood's* is not a newspaper and a memoir is not strictly speaking an article, but her experiences under the aegis of the Red Cross *are* producing paying publications, which creates an amusing, albeit somewhat troubling, irony.

"Under the Red Cross" is authored under the pseudonym "Vera," a moniker that implicitly affirms the veracity of her claims, both about her intentions and about the authenticity of her story as a memoir, both of which are dubious in the extreme. Vera's narrative is a lively pastiche of travel writing and politically partisan commentary. Vera is clearly recouping her travel expenses with her publication and, despite her protestations that she wants only to "nurse the sick and wounded at the seat of war" (636), she seems to have very limited contact with such things in her travels "under the Red Cross." To be fair, she does witness soldiers unloading coffins on the railway platform as she is about to set off on her official duties. The train taking her to the field hospital encounters a French military train "laden with wounded French and German" soldiers (645). Vera briefly describes the miserable condition of the wounded, and notes that, before turning to the German soldiers, the German medical team (including herself) attended to the needs of the French, whose condition was more wretched. She rather uncharitably notes, however, that the French Sisters accompanying the wounded chose to chant a litany rather than join the efforts to aid their countrymen, a blatantly political piece of reportage intended to highlight the humanitarian and efficient work of the medical and nursing staff from Protestant countries and reveal the incompetence of sisterhoods more bent on religious observance than on healing the sick. Once Vera arrives at a French convent that serves as one of the Red Cross hospitals, however, she seems respectful enough of the work of the mother superior and of a certain Sister Marie-Jésus, although the latter is represented more in terms of a seductress than a nun: "a pretty and charming woman, full of French ésprit, and not devoid of a certain coquetry even in her simple dress" (651).

Vera does relate her interactions with several sick or wounded soldiers and occasionally mentions the sound of cannon off in the distance. She even reproduces for her readers a facsimile of her Red Cross Legitimation Carte, all the more official looking for being in German (fig. 3.1). But the real force of Vera's narrative is in the way virtually every incident and every individual she encounters feeds into the prejudices, assumptions, and aspirations of a Victorian readership. The characters she encounters fit cherished stereotypes – the heroic young German soldier facing the amputation of his leg, the "poor light-hearted pleasure-seeking Frenchmen" (648), the impressively efficient English wife of the Prussian officer, the French nuns who are either mindlessly devout or unsuitably coquettish. Hospital life with the Prussians in France apparently has nothing to teach a young Englishwoman or her friends back home that they do not already know – except, of course, what it is like to travel on the continent in dangerous circumstances, what the local people and customs are like, and how plucky and resourceful a single young Englishwoman of sound education and breeding really can be. The bulk of Vera's narrative is accordingly devoted to the excitement and fascination of foreign travel. The significance of travel in and of itself is suggested by the very first

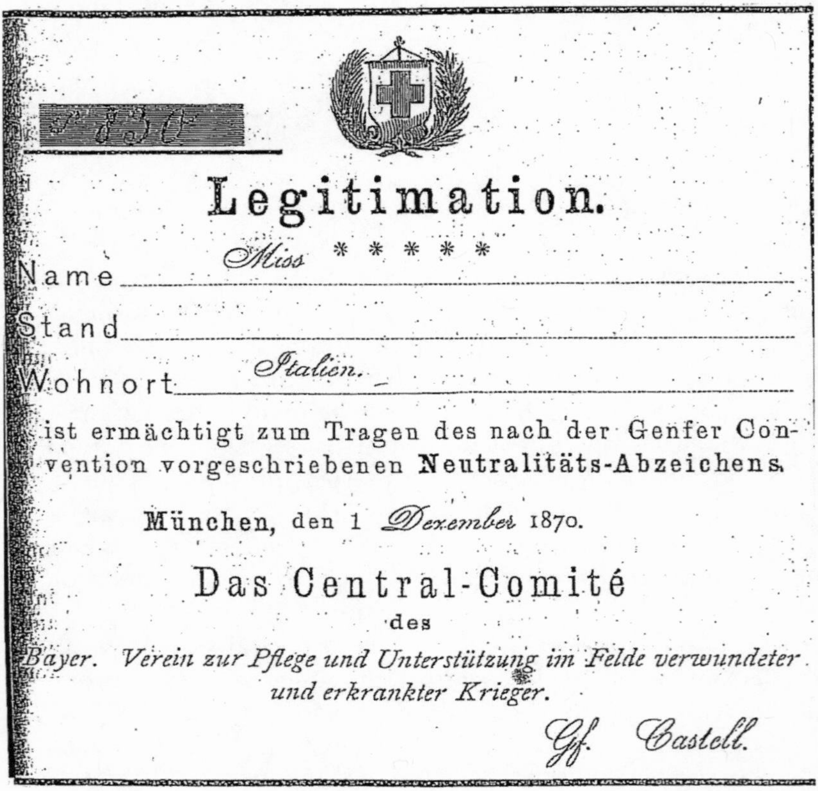

830

Legitimation.

Name *Miss* * * * * *

Stand

Wohnort *Italien.*

ist ermächtigt zum Tragen des nach der Genfer Convention vorgeschriebenen **Neutralitäts-Abzeichens.**

München, den 1 *Dezember* 1870.

Das Central-Comité

des

Bayer. Verein zur Pflege und Unterstützung im Felde verwundeter und erkrankter Krieger.

Gf. Castell.

Figure 3.1 Vera's Red Cross Legitimation Card. From "Under the Red Cross: A Narrative of Hospital-Life with the Prussians in France," *Blackwood's Magazine* 109 (1871): 639. © British Library Board

words of the text, which state that Vera has arrived in Munich from Italy (636). In between visits to officials to plead her case for a Red Cross badge, she attends the opera. Her nursing duties take her to several different locations (including a sojourn in Paris), and the journeys from place to place present the opportunity for her to recount various kinds of local colour – descriptions of food and lodging, quaint local characters and customs. When Vera does discuss actual "hospital-life," her descriptions involve very little in the way of personal experience but rather present the hospitals themselves as subjects of sociological scrutiny. When hospital duties do become part of her personal narrative, they highlight not her nursing skills, but her fearlessness. When the staff surgeon tells her that smallpox has broken out on their ward, she assures him that she has "not the slightest fear of infection." "You are not a bit afraid?" he asks, to which she replies with her usual conviction, "Not a bit" (701). And indeed the reader at this point is hardly surprised, since in the previous chapter, Vera and her travelling companion, the Prussian officer's wife, have threatened a couple of sabre-rattling ruffians with a revolver. (The sabre-rattling ruffians were members of the Bavarian cavalry – Bavarians apparently being less civilized than Prussians.) The lingering message of "Under the Red Cross" is that working ladies are capable and resourceful and that those among them who have the inclination to travel can finesse their credentials into opportunity and adventure.

If Vera's narrative elides much of the actual nursing in which she claims to have been engaged, *Recollections of a Nurse* (1889) ignores it almost completely, hardly mentioning medical staff or hospital organization, despite the wide range of experience catalogued by the narrator. Identified only as "E.D.," the narrator mentions training in the early 1870s, serving as a missionary in Africa from 1875 to 1877, going to South Africa in 1879 to nurse wounded soldiers, and undertaking private cases in Egypt, in Britain, and on the Continent from 1880 until returning to army nursing in 1885.[28] This narrative, too, is more travelogue than nursing memoir. What reference there is to nursing is limited to how men react rather than to what ails them. But while *Recollections of a Nurse* may have little to say about the experience of nursing itself, it is a more convincingly authentic reflection of reality than is "Under the Red Cross," which relates extravagant acts of bravado by the protagonist, such as wielding a revolver. The more frankly fictional the stories of nursing adventurers, it would seem, the more daring the protagonist.

Top honours in the category of daring nursing protagonist go to Hilda Wade, the eponymous heroine of Grant Allen's 1899 novel, subtitled *A Woman with Tenacity of Purpose*. Hilda's tenacity is evident in both her professional and personal life. She is, like Sister Dora, prepared to challenge the opinions of medical men – in Hilda's case, saving the life of a young woman who the surgeon insisted was doomed to die – and like any good Victorian daughter in the world of fiction, she honours her father implicitly. In Hilda's case, this means that she

HILDA WADE.

HILDA PEDALLED BRAVELY BY MY SIDE.

Figure 3.2 Hilda Wade in hospital uniform and rescuing a baby in a wild flight from marauding Matabele warriors in Rhodesia. Illustrations from Grant Allen, *Hilda Wade*, 5, 222. © British Library Board

is determined to clear the name of her dead father, a doctor who was framed for murder by his colleague, none other than the famous and pompous surgeon and researcher Professor Sebastian, with whom Hilda works at St Nathaniel's Hospital. Hilda has all the credentials of a fictional heroine: she is, in the words of Hubert Cumberledge, the admiring young doctor who narrates her story, "one of the prettiest, cheeriest, and most graceful girls" he had met, as well as being "bright, well-educated, sensible, winsome."[29] But Hilda is also characterized as something of a New Woman – intelligent, independent, and determined to fulfil her "Plan" to prove her father's innocence, an objective for which she is "resolved to sacrifice everything" (144). Hilda's plan eventually leads her into an unlikely series of adventures in Rhodesia, culminating in a wild flight across the veldt on a bicycle, with a baby tucked under her arm, pursued by a marauding band of Matabele warriors who have just murdered the child's parents (fig. 3.2). She then travels through India, serving along with Cumberledge as companions-cum-medical consultants for a wealthy English couple. There Hilda continues her cat-and-mouse pursuit of Sebastian, and outsmarts a group of murderous Buddhist monks who are part of his scheme to have her killed. On the voyage home, still on Sebastian's trail, Hilda saves herself and Sebastian from drowning when their ship founders.

With its cycling escapes from Matabele warriors and incongruously bloodthirsty Buddhist monks, Allen's novel is clearly comically hyperbolic. Nevertheless, Hilda Wade spends more time in the hospital and at sickbeds than do Vera or E.D., although her travels are associated less with nursing than with her much-vaunted "tenacity of purpose" fixed on vindicating her father. What being a nurse does for Hilda is provide her with a professional status that guarantees her independence and underwrites her capabilities. Hilda resides in a fictional world outside the realm of realism, but the association of nursing with exciting exploits in fiction persisted, and indeed nursing itself became the imaginative source, rather than the means, of adventure. This connection was significant for genteel young women whose lives, like Dolly Vanborough's back in the 1870s, promised nothing beyond the limitations of social intercourse, and the association of nursing with adventure became more explicit as the century progressed. The narrator of L.T. Meade's story, "The Little Old Lady" (1894), affirms that, having been a "private nurse for several years," she had "had, of course, many adventures."[30] Dinah Lethmore, the protagonist of "The Story of a Nurse," published in the *Graphic* (later in a collection entitled *Tales of the Children's Ward*, 1894), hungers for the "many adventures" that nursing promised to sheltered young ladies at the end of the Victorian period. Dinah expresses her frustrations with her confinement in the "tiny sphere" of social engagements when she announces her intention to enter nursing in an east-end hospital to her would-be suitor, Major Edis:

> "A boy can run away to sea, a man can travel, but a woman – ...
> well, it seems to me that the only way in which a woman is permitted to come into contact with the realities of life is to become a nurse."

"But you can travel" [Major Edis responds].

"In consort with my mother and my maid, staying everywhere at English hotels, and seeing only with the eyes of a paid courier. No, thank you; books are better than that."[31]

Part of what makes nursing more exciting than travel for Dinah is the hospital she has chosen in the east end, where the labouring-class patients and their families that she will work with will be to her as exotic as the inhabitants of a foreign country – something the eyes of a paid courier would never let her see.

The collection of stories that make up *Tales of the Children's Ward* accord with the idea of nurses providing readers with access into some kind of *terra incognita*, but "The Story of a Nurse" is indeed the story of a nurse, of her motives, of the challenges she faces, and of the work she does. Dinah struggles with the demanding and often menial work she must do, vowing "not [to] give in" as she toils "up and down the children's ward with swollen feet, aching head, and tired limbs" (35). She is nevertheless "deeply ... absorbed in the intensely interesting life of the hospital" (40). Many of Dinah's experiences parallel those of earlier nursing heroines, notably meeting with the resistance of family or friends and facing the dangers of caring for patients with highly contagious diseases. Like her fictional forerunners such as Ruth, Vera, and Hilda (who helps to care for Sebastian when he contracts the plague in India), Dinah willingly and fearlessly volunteers to risk her life in order to nurse infectious patients when a typhus epidemic breaks out (52). What Dinah's story offers that is lacking in other overtly fictionalized nursing narratives is a sense of the physical challenges faced by nurses in their day-to-day duties and the emotional intensity of their responsibilities. "A nurse comes face to face with the naked truth," the narrator observes; "man cannot clothe himself with conventionalities when on a sick-bed, nor control his natural impulses when fever has burnt all his strength away ... The nurse knows the mysteries of birth, she recognises the cry of agony, she sees the eternal parting between friends and foes, she watches the shadow of death descend alike on the good and the evil" (45).

REALISM AND MORALIZING: NURSING STORIES IN THE *GIRL'S OWN PAPER* IN THE 1890S

While "The Story of a Nurse" does depict some of the trials faced by nurses, the hardships are nevertheless frequently romanticized in their very intensity, as for example in the narrator's dramatic claim that, for the nurse, "reality – bitter reality – is hers" (45). Rather less sensational, and indeed almost stark, representations of the strenuousness of nursing feature in a number of stories published in the *Girl's Own Paper* in the 1890s, which, given the paper's mission to guide and counsel the young, is not surprising. Although articles on work and responses to letters from readers enquiring about employment opportunities in this publication are generally matter of fact, informative, and encouraging, stories in which young women wish to work tend to moralize and to replicate conservative platitudes. In "Dorothy's Career," for example, a young woman with aspirations to be an artist is disabused of her conviction that art is a nobler career than marriage and motherhood.[32] Another story, entitled "A Modern Mistake," represents that mistake as ambition on the part of a young woman; she is depicted as foolish and self-centred until she comes to her senses and marries.[33] Given that the message underlying these and similar tales is woman's calling to self-sacrifice, nursing presented a less obvious target for admonitions against the folly of adopting a career because of its potential associations with selfless devotion to the sick and suffering. That nursing was also often tarnished with the implication of being a "fashionable mania" and that it was still trailing clouds of ignominy from its association with the Gamps of earlier generations nevertheless ensured considerable scope for admonitory tales about nurses and their profession. "In Warwick Ward," for example, is subtitled "A Story of Routine," an uninspiringly accurate adumbration of the round of menial tasks and the endless exhortations to obedience – the "bewildering rush of new instructions and arduous duties" – that make up the life of a hapless young probationer.[34] "On Monmouth Ward" presents an overwrought struggle on the part of a nurse to resist the urge to fall asleep on night duty, essentially turning a physiological need into an evil temptation that demands soul-searching and prayer. Subsequently fully alert to the requirements of absolute wakefulness, the nurse is able to care for the sick and dying with true womanly devotion.[35] The connections among obedience (both to ward rules and to God), self-sacrifice, and womanliness are everywhere evident in these and similar tales. These stories are overtly didactic and their clear message is that those young women who see in nursing the opportunity for romance or adventure, or who are interested in nothing more than earning a living, are not suited to the profession – a view at odds with many of the representations of nurses and nursing at the time. Even the *Girl's Own Paper* featured articles that adopt a pragmatic rather than visionary perspective on nursing. "The Life of a Nurse," ostensibly based on an interview with "one of the pioneers of the 'lady nurses,'" dismisses the notion of vocation and posits that "the average nurse" in fact takes up her career as a matter of course rather than as the result of a sense of calling and that she is more successful for being less devoted. In order to avoid being ravaged by the "ardour and interest" of intense vocational commitment, a "successful nurse must be a happy mean between over-sensitiveness on the one hand and callousness on the other."[36]

Most of the moralizing nursing stories in the *Girl's Own Paper* were written by the same author, H. Mary Wilson, who also produced novels with a similar ethos on other subjects for both the Christian Knowledge Society and the Religious Tract Society (publisher of both the *Girl's Own Paper* and the *Boy's Own Paper*). A longer, more detailed, and more balanced account of nursing appears in "The Wards of St. Margaret's," serialized from February through August of 1894.[37] The author is identified only as Sister Joan, suggesting that personal experience informs her version of hospital life, a version that replicates many of the standard misgivings and ideals about nurses. The cautions about "obedience, simple and entire" and about "husband-hunting" (511) are woven into the dialogue, as are calls to devotion, to "high aims and lofty purposes" that will rise above the "narrowness of mere earthly striving" (723). The narrative that Sister Joan relates, however, manages to transcend the narrowness of mere convention, both in terms of attitudes towards nurses and nursing and with respect to storytelling. Sister Joan does not relate an episode with a moral (as do shorter narratives about nurses in the paper), nor does she present the experiences of a young woman embarking on an exciting career, who is ultimately so admired for her work that an attractive hero falls in love with and marries her (as happens in most of the novels or stories about nurses in other venues). The protagonist of "The Wards of St. Margaret's," Constance Wilson, is a woman who becomes a nurse when she is young, but the narrative follows the entire thirty years of her career. She does not leave nursing to marry, but rather turns down two suitors – one before she begins her training and the other when she is a staff nurse. Constance is accordingly characterized as a desirable young woman who freely chooses work over marriage, independence over domestic security. And while she espouses the doctrine of "obedience, simple and entire," she is an astute critic of unsound medical practice. She indeed tells a colleague and the hospital chaplain, somewhat facetiously, that she would like to write a book and describe the incidents she has found particularly distressing, some of which she relates as examples (700).

The narrative of Constance's years of training includes experiences typical of any probationer who must come to terms with the demands of nursing duties and with a new way of life, but these incidents are presented simply as experiences, rather than as cautionary tales. Challenges and frustrations are balanced by achievements and fulfillment; the hospital is the locus not just of work but also of friendship and social interaction. The pros and cons of nursing as a vocation versus nursing as a means of employment are aired in discussions among the characters, as are the different areas of nursing that a new graduate might undertake – private nursing, district nursing, and hospital nursing (559). Constance's earnest desire is to be a military nurse, a career that takes her to exotic locales in Egypt and the Middle East – Gibraltar, Malta, Khartoum, and Cairo (606, 621, 646). The excitement and interest that these locations might stimulate are downplayed in the text – the cities are mentioned only as points of landing, embarkation, or geographical orientation as Constance travels to the more remote areas to which she is stationed. Unlike the memoirs of military nursing cited above, this story focuses on the life and work of the nurses.

"The Wards of St. Margaret's" could be assessed as an unsatisfactory piece of fiction. It has no narrative line other than that of a life, more specifically, of a work life. There is no real excitement, despite the years spent in outposts in Egypt. There is no high drama, other than that of ordinary life and death. There is no critical incident, no narrative climax and denouement. The title is entirely misleading, as Constance spends only the early years of her career in St Margaret's Hospital. The narrative starts with Constance about to begin her nurse's training and ends with her retiring to a picturesque cottage in a Devonshire village with her long-time friend and colleague, Hope. The quasi-allegorical names of these characters are the admittedly not very subtle key to the real successes of the story, which the author suggests in a moment of reflection on Constance and Hope's lives: "Surely, wherever these two go, though they may never make for themselves a name or win earthly honours, are they not following in the footsteps of the Master by quietly doing what they can, even though the work may be thought easy and common-place; possibly it is not so much the great deeds accomplished as the life itself" (701). Constance and Hope are here virtually beatified for their humble good works, but the story closes with a more secular celebration of the meaning and value of the lives of women who chose to live independent lives and who accordingly provide an answer to that vexing Victorian question, "what shall we do with our old maids?":

> The world often speaks slightingly of old maids ... but were the old maids one and all to vanish, methinks there would soon be a hue and a cry; for many a corner would be bereft of sunshine, many a sad heart would sigh for the friend and helper, many a home would be left desolate and dreary without the busy form and kind face of the old maiden aunt.
>
> Women who have fought their way through the world, not only for self-support, but in order to benefit those around them; who have loved as fondly and as deeply as many of the truest wives; who have suffered and learned by suffering how to sympathise as they have trodden the paths of life, whose hearts have not narrowed into selfishness, but grown and expanded in love towards the whole family of man. Such women may think lightly of the criticism of the world. They can afford to smile back on those who commiserate what they term their lonely lot. (747)

This passage modestly defines the retired working woman as an old maid, identifying her with traditional social definitions and values rather than with the more advanced ones represented by the Glorified Spinster. The old maid is an integral part of family and community life, here united in the concept of "the whole family of man." She represents the womanly ideals of sympathy and selflessness, but she is also brave and determined, having "fought ... [her] way through the world." Her experience, the passage implies, has been richer and deeper than that of even "the truest wives," and she is unscathed by the criticisms of an unenlightened world. With its unsensational account of useful lives lived, ending with this heartfelt commendation of the women who lived them, "The Wards of St. Margaret's" is one of the strongest endorsements of the independent working woman in the annals of the period.

THE INTRUSION OF LOVE (1870s–1890s)

Fictional tales of useful lives lived, however fascinating as windows into a historical moment, have limited appeal in the popular culture of the time, where the market for stories of adventure or for stories about love is likely to be vigorous. And while nursing in Victorian fiction represented adventure for many writers and readers, fictional nurses could be problematic as central characters. Constance and Hope are admirable figures, ones that young women might embrace as appropriate role models, but as fictional characters, they lack glamour. And in the Victorian period, a woman's glamour – or even just her claim for serious consideration – was conditioned by the continued dominance of the cultural ideal of domestic womanhood, an ideal defined by the necessity of women fulfilling their biological and sexual destiny as wives and mothers. However strong the interest in the working woman, there remained a conviction in the collective Victorian psyche that a woman who did not become a wife and mother was incomplete and uninteresting. Even in a story as focused on work as "The Wards of St. Margaret's," the protagonist's appeal is in part predicated on her characterization as desirable, indicated by her rejection of two suitors. Her life's work outside the domestic realm, moreover, is in the end justified through a favourable comparison of the career nurse with "the truest wives." Here and in other stories from the period, the tension between an ingrained cultural commitment to biological necessity and a growing fascination with the new career woman made the nurse heroine a tricky character to represent effectively – that is, as a figure who, in the eyes of contemporary readers, was simultaneously engaging and believable as both a woman and a worker.

As a result of the demands for a nurse protagonist to be a heroine rather than a hero – in other words to be feminine as well as professional – authors frequently relied on the expedient of having the nurse courted and eventually married off and consigned to the domestic sphere at the end of the story, as happens to Dinah Lethmore and Hilda Wade. In short stories, the romantic interest in the heroic nurse was often based on her mourning for a dead lover. As the century progressed and the career nurse became ubiquitous in

Victorian culture, she became more available to authors as a potentially sympathetic central character, rather than as an adventuress or
as a young woman temporarily expressing her independence before
settling into marriage. Novels and stories representing the career
nurse as the central character developed complex means of telling
a story about work and commitment that was nevertheless licensed
by romantic love. An early version of this phenomenon occurs in
Elisabeth Lysaght's 1877 novel, *A Long Madness*, which confronts
several issues of class prejudice, including the bias against genteel
ladies becoming nurses. The protagonist, Honor Deverill, is a rather
old-maidenish lady of thirty who decides to turn her back on the
frivolities of society to become a nurse. Despite being an unroman-
tic figure in the conventional sense, Honor is loved and courted by
her cousin, Sir Ruy Deverill, who disapproves of her career. In her
work in the hospital, Honor nurses a young stonemason, Hewitt
Fleetwood, who has been injured protecting her from an attack by
a local ruffian. Fleetwood is an autodidact of considerable aptitude,
and he and Honor discuss literature and religious philosophy; it is
clear that they are falling in love.[38]

As if to underscore Honor's desirability, despite the fact that she is
long past the youthful bloom that defines the love interests in most
Victorian novels, both the men who love her are younger than she
is: Sir Ruy is twenty-eight and Fleetwood is twenty-five. As the novel
progresses, it would indeed seem that the narrative trajectory will
be the resolution of the convoluted love story, which to some extent
it is. But just as the devotion of two men disproves conventional
assumptions about the desirability of a woman past the bloom of
youth, so too does Honor's adoption of the persona of the nurse
disprove conventional class assumptions about the demeaning and
coarsening influence of supposedly menial work. As she dons her
uniform for the first time she indeed becomes more youthful and
feminine in her bearing. "The soft, dim folds, of that hue which the
distant hills wear when the mist lies low on them, fell in demure,
restful ease and grace," the narrator observes; "and the white cap
... fitted so closely and soberly to the pleasant face, that had as yet
lost but little of the delicate colouring of youth, while it had gained
expression and character, and contrasted with the dark, smooth
hair, – so artistically, that Honor, after a glance at the mirror, felt
a quick, keen sense of something like gratified vanity" (I: 212–13).
Although the nurse's uniform would eventually be seen as becoming

and romantic, at this early stage in the development of the profession, uniforms and caps were associated with servants, and however gracefully the folds of the gown's fabric fell, it was still, unlike the apparel of a fashionable lady, plain and serviceable. Thus while the fit of the white cap, contrasting with her dark hair, may strike Honor as artistic and flattering, her more conventional friend, Mrs Fitzpatrick, considers it "odious" and the idea of Honor's becoming a hospital nurse "dreadful" (I: 212–13).

The representation of life and work in the hospital in *A Long Madness* is calculated to stress Honor's suitability for and commitment to her profession. The medical details of illness and injuries are limited, but descriptions of pain and suffering that are eased by Honor's sympathetic care abound. She finally has to respond, however, to the pressures of social expectations and to that other side of her character – the marriageable lady – and reluctantly agrees to marry Sir Ruy, only to admit later that she loves another man. In the denouement of the marriage plot, Sir Ruy is caught in a fire at the local inn and is rescued by Fleetwood, who is mortally injured in the attempt. As he lies dying in the hospital, Fleetwood tells Honor that he saved Sir Ruy for her, and she in turn tells Fleetwood that they will not marry after all. Honor and Fleetwood ultimately recognize, but do not openly declare, their mutual love. The marriage plot is resolved with Sir Ruy marrying another (whom he cannot love as he loved Honor) and with Honor validated as a true Victorian heroine by the unspoken bond of love with Fleetwood. Honor is then set free from the marriage plot and licensed to devote her life to nursing, which she does with great success. At the hospital, the narrator tells us, the "doctors look up to her with confidence and respect, for she is quick-handed, quick-witted, and always to be depended on" (III: 265). Although her fashionable relatives dismiss Honor as an old maid, the reader, who is privy to the story of her secret requited love, is, like Honor, released from the psychological bonds of the marriage plot and can applaud her professional success.

The determination of the author of *A Long Madness* to subvert the existing negative cultural assumptions about nurses and nursing is evident in the representation of another nurse in the text. Anne Goldmore acts as a foil for the main character, being virtually everything that Honor is not. Anne is young, attractive, and already a wife and mother when she enters nursing. She is also working class and, despite the fact that she has been "the slave and drudge of a man who was but a little higher than a beast" who has abandoned her, she is far from being a coarse Gamp. She is, rather, the ideal of Victorian womanhood, "made to be loved and honoured, pure and womanly, the best type of an English matron of her class" (I: 215–16). In thus representing the nurse in two radically different characters, Lysaght is able to portray nursing and nurses as consonant with all dimensions of admirable womanhood and culturally accepted feminine experience – with the woman who recognizes true love and ultimately refuses to consent to a merely advantageous union, with the intensely feminine woman who accepts her unhappy marriage, with the upper-class woman, with the working-class woman. Whatever one representative of the profession may lack, the other character supplies in order to render the figure of the nurse culturally unimpeachable.

This division in the characterization of the nurse becomes a relatively common strategy, especially late in the century, when nursing and, as a consequence, the nurse as represented in fiction are more highly professionalized. With the growing cultural emphasis on the necessity for middle-class women who enter the workforce to commit themselves fully to their work, the standard marriage plot that dominated Victorian fiction could less easily accommodate the figure of the nurse. The levels of uncompromising efficiency expected of the ideal nurse were, moreover, incompatible with the ideals of compliant femininity imagined in conventional Victorian fiction. The division of characterization sometimes occurs in two or more characters, as it does in *A Long Madness*, and sometimes in a single character whose role as nurse is separated from her role as conventional Victorian woman. This latter narrative strategy most typically has the protagonist-cum-love object work as a nurse for only a brief time. Her role in the marriage plot establishes her feminine identity, while her sojourn into nursing establishes one or more of a panoply of qualities or attainments that enhance her character.

This strategy may seem to be in part a falling back into older assumptions about nursing and its potential effects on feminine worth, but it nevertheless uses the idea of the professional nurse in positive terms, as an indicator of strength of character. "A Strange Revelation," a story in *London Society*, for example, opens with the first-person narrator stating, "I am a professional nurse, holding the position of sister of the Accident Ward in the Metropolitan Hospital," thus establishing her credentials as a woman who holds a position of responsibility in a large institution.[39] In the retrospective story she tells, she features as Patricia Langton, the young and innocent dupe of a bigamist who quickly abandons her. Unbeknownst to her at the time, the man who truly loved her has killed her false husband. The revelation becomes undeniably strange as the murderer, in a sort of Jekyll/Hyde transformation, comes to look like his victim – so much so that he is able to assume his victim's identity, return to London after the death of the murdered man's first wife, and offer to marry Patricia in order to save her reputation. Although she hesitates, on the grounds that marriage to such a man – i.e. the bigamist she believes him to be – is too high a price to pay for mere honour, she finally agrees on the condition that they never meet again. Soon after the marriage and his departure for America, she becomes a probationer and, as she tells her story, has been devoted to her profession for eighteen years. At this point, the man who saved her turns up as a mortally injured accident victim on her ward and dies, leaving behind his confessional journal for her to read.

As the central character of this rather sordid tale, Patricia as wronged young woman would be able to inspire little beyond the pity of readers, but as the mature and dedicated professional nurse, she commands respect. She embodies the professional persona so completely that she has no name, and is referred to as Patricia Langton only in the dead patient's journal. The assurance of her tone, her ability initially to scorn the notion of marriage to a cad for the sake of honour, her status as a respected and productive member of society, and ultimately even her authority to relate her story are all predicated on her professional standing. Her status as a medical professional also allows her to present and confront the "inexplicable fact[s]" of her story in defiance of "the deductions of reason and science" (525).

"A Strange Revelation" is highly melodramatic, its affective core based on the belated recognition between lovers after long parting, as the man dies in the arms of the nurse who turns out to be the woman he loved. A similar plot device frames "A Nursing Sister of St. John's," which begins with a conversation among guests at a fashionable country hotel. The group includes a "sedate-looking Scotch lawyer," a distinguished-looking colonel, and the radiant and captivating Miss Escombe.[40] When she leaves with her seven-year-old pupil, Miss Escombe, though admired, is dismissed as "only a governess." "Love and marriage," the lawyer affirms, "are not for her" (381). Ten years later, a kind and wistful Nurse Agatha comes to care for a dying man. She is none other than Miss Escombe; the dying man is the colonel, who, unaware at first of who she is, tells her of his love for the beautiful young woman he knew many years before. He finally recognizes her when her cap falls off and the rays of the setting sun light up "her hair like a golden glory" (383). Of particular interest in this story is the denigration (however reluctant on the part of the men who admire her) of the governess and the respect afforded the nurse, reflected in the physician's reliance on her skill in the "hard fight" the dying patient presents for them (381). But the governess with her young charge nevertheless embodied a feminine domestic ideal that her reincarnation as a nurse does not, until her golden hair escapes from the cap that is the emblem of her professionalism. In telling Nurse Agatha about his lost love, the colonel implies that he did not pursue her because she was "so young and so beautiful" and he was "already far on the downhill of life," omitting any reference to her position as governess. The "grave, pale nurse," however, has gained the professional and concomitant personal substance to be the beloved of a man of distinction and, though united too late for marriage, to inherit his considerable fortune, which she spends on "works of charity" while she continues her profession (383).

The conventional Victorian symbolism of hair as a marker of femininity and sexuality in this story, the feature that confirms the identity of Nurse Agatha as the desirable Miss Escombe, is also central to a very short narrative entitled "Sister," which appeared in *Blackwood's Magazine* (1892). The narrator is a doctor recalling experiences at a military field hospital. He is generally uncomplimentary about the work of nurses near battlegrounds, claiming that they break down if they are mature women and "cause mischief" if they are young.[41] His disdain for these nurses makes his almost reverential respect for the sister of the story's title all the more impressive, as he recounts her interactions with a young soldier she is tending who had just arrived at the field hospital with horrific wounds, including the destruction of both his eyes. In his dying delirium, the soldier mistakes Sister for his girl back home and with utmost compassion and tenderness, she allows him to continue to do so. As he gently reaches for her, he notices that her hair is done up in "a silly cap," which he undoes, letting her hair fall "about her shoulders" (892–3). "I had never thought," the narrator comments, "that she might be carrying such glory quietly hidden beneath the simple nurse's cap" (893). The revelation of Sister's physical womanliness prefigures the subsequent revelation of the depth of her feminine nature and experience. In a scene that borders on the erotic, the dying man touches Sister's face, her shoulder, her breast. As the narrator watches, he sees "her eyes soften into such a wonderful tenderness" and he senses he is "looking on a part of Sister's life which was sacred." Ultimately he sees that her eyes are "dull with a new pain" and wonders "what memories that poor senseless wreck of a man was arousing in the woman's heart by his wandering touch" (893). In the soldier's dying moment, Sister's lips meet his: the soldier's "heart give[s] a great bound within his breast" and then is still. Overcome with emotion, the narrator busies himself with tending to the corpse and when he once more turns his gaze on Sister, she has resumed her professional bearing, "filling in the papers – her cap neatly tied – her golden hair hidden" (893). The potential chaos of emotion, unleashed by the erotic touch and flowing hair, is once more contained under the nurse's cap, but the respect that the narrator feels for Sister is deepened by his knowledge of her life outside of her professionalism, of the unarticulated love story intimated by her tenderness and look of pain, of the intimacy of touch awakening memories of an intimacy in her past. Sister's status as a nurse and as a Victorian woman is ultimately enhanced by the revelation of her dual identity. Her efficiency is clearly not the result of any lack of feminine feeling but of a professionalism that demands the separation of private and public life, of personal feeling and professional duty. Her womanliness is all the more alluring because her experience is so private – even rather mysterious – and her awareness of the emotional needs of the dying man is so acute. Her untold story of lost love gains poignancy as it is once more contained, like her golden hair, by the requirements of her professionalism.

A more convoluted division of characterization occurs in a story by L.T. Meade entitled "A Girl in Ten Thousand," serialized in the *Young Woman* from 1894 to 1895 and later published as a novel. The protagonist, Effie Staunton, a physician's daughter, becomes a nursing probationer after the initial resistance of her father who, as Effie acknowledges to her mother, "despises ladies who are nurses."[42] Being very young and girlish – "a dark-eyed girl … [who looks] as if she might be any age between seventeen and twenty" – Effie has more credentials as a romantic heroine than as a professional woman (2). In the course of the story, however, she is required to exhibit more fortitude and earning ability than could normally be expected of Victorian young ladies. She is forced to abandon her training and her dream of becoming a nurse when her father dies and the family is faced with humiliation and ruin over the malfeasance of her ne'er-do-well older brother, who has stolen in order to pay off gambling debts. In the stories mentioned above, the professionalism of the nurse forms the credentials for the Victorian woman's assertiveness, just as the feminine woman guarantees the nurse's womanliness. Effie's brief exposure to nursing at this stage of her narrative, however, is not enough to underwrite her early displays of initiative and leadership credibly were it not for her association with Dorothy Fraser, who is arguably the real hero of the story. In the opening segment of the narrative – almost a prologue to Effie's story – Dorothy, a hospital nurse of unparalleled efficiency and expertise, agrees to attend a child ill with scarlet fever and diphtheria, when urgently summoned to do so by Effie's father. Dr Staunton, distrustful of the fine "lady nurse ... not suited to the work," sees Dorothy as an emergency "stop-gap," until he can secure the services of someone he considers more appropriate (19, 25).

In the course of attending to the desperately sick child, Dorothy exhibits the attributes of the skilled professional nurse to an almost uncanny degree. Dr Staunton had earlier commented on the extent to which "doctors hate to see a lady nurse in possession of a case" because, he insisted, she would in fact off-load the more taxing chores onto the servants in the household (18). The "possession" suggests both the nurse's aura of command and her use of the case to her own convenience. Dorothy takes full possession of this case to an extent unimagined by Dr Staunton. Her ability to bring order to both the sickroom and the entire household is something that Dr Staunton comes to admire unreservedly. Once the child is out of danger, Staunton recounts Dorothy's efforts admiringly to his wife:

> I never came across such a woman. If you only saw, Mary, the state of hopeless confusion, of pandemonium – for it really amounted to that – of that wretched house the morning Miss Fraser arrived; if you could only have seen the condition of the sickroom, and then have gone into it two hours later – why, it was like stepping from the infernal regions into Paradise. The order of the sickroom seemed to affect the whole house. The servants ceased to be in a state of panic, the meals were properly cooked, the squire came back to his normal condition, and Mrs. Harvey became quite cheerful. (65–6)

There is no doubt that Dorothy, like any good lady nurse, takes full possession of the case, and indeed the household, but rather than exerting an oppressive authority, she imparts a calm that produces a healthful order. There is indeed something almost mystical about her ability to soothe and reassure the anxious parents and servants in the household; Dr Staunton repeatedly refers to her as angelic, as a "blessed angel," a "good soul," an "angel" (62, 66, 84); her skill is admired by all and spoken of in reverential tones by other characters. When Staunton first learned of the grave illness of little Freda Harvey, he made a solemn vow to Effie: "If mortal man can pull the child through, I will do it" (28). Mortal man is not up to the task, but Dorothy Fraser is. She is in a very real sense superior to Dr Staunton, who ultimately feels incapable of saving the child without her. His relative inefficacy is subsequently underscored by the fact that he contracts diphtheria himself and dies. It is true that Dorothy has attended to him in his illness as well, without success, but at the same time she projects invulnerability, as if bacteria could not penetrate the impermeable barrier of her superefficiency; she is not subject to illnesses that strike down mere mortal men.

As mentor and role model to Effie, Dorothy's main function in the story is to establish by proxy Effie's credentials for her heroic hard-headedness in the face of potential ruin. As a young woman aspiring to Dorothy's proficiency, Effie is constructed as having the potential for the full-fledged hospital nurse's capabilities she does not yet possess. Effie's nursing parallels Dorothy's, but on a lower plane; her professionalism is always tempered by domesticity. While Dorothy works the veritable miracle of saving both Freda Harvey and, it would seem, the entire Harvey household, Effie remains in the Staunton household, looking after her fragile mother and her younger siblings. Mrs Staunton's tribute to her as "a good nurse – the most considerate, the most thoughtful, the most kind and clever darling" sounds like nothing more than the appreciative murmurs of a fond mother, like faint praise when compared with Dr Staunton's effusive encomium in appreciation of Dorothy's heroic efforts (64). When the demands of her brother's malfeasance weigh upon the household, Effie neglects her nursing duties in favour of rescuing her family. When admonished by her nursing supervisor, who advises her that a nurse's "first duties consist in taking care of her patients and in learning her profession," Effie replies that "home duties will always be first with [her]" (212–13). Dorothy, by contrast, appears to have no intense attachment to family. She lives in and for St Joseph's Hospital and for her high calling.

The differences between the characterization of Dorothy and Effie and between the narrative lines of their stories indicate the continuing problem that late-Victorian writers had with the figure of the nurse as protagonist. Dorothy Fraser is the embodiment of the nurse as a culturally empowered figure, the embodiment, indeed, of her profession, but her excess of professionalism subverts her femininity and so disqualifies her for the role of the heroine of the story. Dorothy is not represented as unfeminine, but her appearance is austere and her person controlled. She is endlessly calm and even her sedate uniform – "gray dress, gray cloak, gray bonnet" – accords with her "earnest and reposeful face" (28). Effie, by contrast, wears a uniform consisting of a dress in "a pretty lilac check" and "a cap with a frill around it" (154); her qualifications are quintessentially feminine – she is "attentive, tactful, kind and considerate," she is "soft and gentle" (203, 210). Effie can remain highly feminine throughout the narrative because she is not yet a full-fledged hospital nurse. Once she has solved the problems racking her family, she returns to her training and eventually becomes superintendent of one of the wards in the hospital where she trained, a professional position parallel to Dorothy's. The reference to Effie's success in her career and her promotion at the end of the story, however, are proleptic and so do not interfere with her feminine characterization. Moreover, after the reference to her being a ward superintendent, there is a hint that she will probably marry one of the hospital's doctors – the conventional fallback to the standard romance plot. That the character of the professional nurse (Dorothy) and the feminine Victorian lady for whom "home duties will always come first" (Effie) nevertheless stand in for each other in this story is made clear in that each is the girl in ten thousand. In his "unconcealed admiration" for Dorothy and her professionalism while nursing Freda Harvey in the opening chapters, Dr Staunton is emphatic: "That girl is one in ten thousand" (39). In appreciation of her efforts and of her willingness to defer her dreams of being a nurse in order to save her family from ruin, Effie, too, is recognized as being "a girl in ten thousand" at the end of the narrative (273). The girl in ten thousand of the title is the amalgam of the professional nurse and the feminine woman.

An arguably more satisfying integration of femininity and nursing professionalism occurs in *Nurse Elisia*, published in 1892. What is perhaps most arresting about this text is its incorporation of a wide range of prejudicial cultural attitudes towards nursing that prevailed over the course of the nineteenth century and that persisted in many quarters. The nurse of the title is recommended by a London physician of some renown to care for Ralph Elthorne, the very crotchety patriarch of an affluent country family and father of Neil Elthrone, one of the physician's medical students. The responses of the servants and family to Nurse Elisia mingle suspicions of professionalism with outworn perceptions of nurses as Gamps. The disagreeable upper housemaid, Maria Bellows, asserts that Nurse Elisia is "always trying to play the fine lady nurse, and showing off." Maria does not "believe she's a lady at all." [43] Elthorne's daughter, Isabel, resents Elisia; his sister Anne declares that her "experience of nurses is that they are dreadful women, who drink and go to sleep in sickrooms" (90). Elthorne's sons, Alison and Neil, long expected to marry a pair of social-climbing horsey young ladies from the neighbourhood, predictably fall in love with Elisia instead. Elisia discourages the young men and remains patient and dignified despite the aspersion on her character, but Maria alleges that she is just "a common hospital nurse trying to lead ... [Neil] on" (36). Elthorne Sr deplores the infatuation with Elisia on the part of his older son, Alison, as "a contemptible flirtation with a woman serving as a menial in this house" (216). Elthorne nevertheless admits that he "owe[s] Nurse Elisia ... [his] life" and acknowledges that "she is to be treated with respect" (226). And indeed she is, for not only is she highly capable and professional, but Elisia (otherwise Lady Cecily) is also the daughter of the late Duke of Atheldene (291). Her class position turns many of the prejudices against her on their head. She is not "playing" the fine lady and she is not setting her cap at the son of a mere squire in order to gain status. When she does finally marry Neil, it is he who "marries up."

As the chronicle of these stories indicates, the revelation at the end of the narrative of the true identity of the nurse – whether as a long-lost love or as a fine lady taking up a profession under cover of a lower-status identity – is a common enough trope to seem trite. *Nurse Elisia*, however, is somewhat different. The story does not end with a marriage that sets the nurse protagonist on course as the romantic heroine, about to relinquish her professional identity for that of domesticated wife and mother. Marriage for Elisia means more emphatic dedication to nursing. She and Neil set off to establish a hospital in Black Port, on the west coast of Africa, to treat "the local disease, which is increasing fast" (164), a dangerous mission to which they commit for five years. After they return to England and see for the first time their little nephews, born while they were away to Alison and his wife, Neil, but not Elisia, clearly longs to have children of his own. Elisia, sensitive to his wishes but devoted to her profession, recalls him to their new mission in the slums of London. Their children, she reminds him, are "the poor, the suffering, and the weak." The language in which they couch their dedication to their calling adheres to the most clichéd gender norms of the time, as if to mitigate Elisia's determined professionalism and her rejection of the conventional Victorian commitment to motherhood. The poor, suffering, and weak, Elisia notes, are "waiting yonder ... under the black clouds of the great city – ... waiting, waiting for the healing touch of my dear husband's hand." And, her husband adds, "for their pillows to be smoothed by their tender nurse – true woman – dearest wife" (313). On the surface, the almost cloying sentimentality of these, the closing words of the novel, seems to diminish the role of the nurse from skilled practitioner who saves lives to subordinate and sympathetic attendant providing nonessential services. A "tender nurse" is not a healer but a comforter, a surrogate mother.

There is another and arguably more important message in *Nurse Elisia*. Elisia's role is in fact anything but subordinate. It is her inheritance that bankrolls the successful hospital in Africa. It is her prompting that affirms her and Neil's rejection of the truly conventional roles encouraged by his father – affluent country doctor, devoted wife and mother. What the text ultimate affirms is that nursing is an occupation that disqualifies her from neither the role of woman nor of wife. Elisia's story accordingly becomes the emphatic culmination of the cumulative narrative of the Victorian nurse, a figure that began in the 1850s with tainted characters, such as Ruth, or marginalized ones, such as Mrs Griffiths in *Remembrances of a Monthly Nurse*. By 1892, Elisia, the aristocratic and accomplished professional nurse, affirms the role of the working wife who loses none of her womanliness nor her marital credentials because she chooses a career over motherhood. The genteel Victorian lady could be a career woman without losing caste.

4

Work and the Challenges of Modernity:
The Victorian Typewriter

On a Tuesday morning in March 1873, the "usually quiet locality of Cannon Row," reports the *Civil Service Gazette*, "was the scene of an extraordinary excitement." Gathered in front of the offices of the Civil Service Commissioners were "vast crowds," estimated at between one thousand and fifteen hundred, although the *Gazette* correspondent considers the larger number to be "nearer the mark, if not considerably within it." The crowds blocked the steps and courtyard of the commissioners' offices and brought traffic on Cannon Row to a standstill; business in the area had to be suspended; police intervened to no avail. Occupants of adjacent buildings jostled for a view of the unfolding spectacle, giving "the various windows looking into Cannon Row ... an appearance only to be ordinarily witnessed in our principal thoroughfares on the occasion of some great procession." What was perhaps most extraordinary about this milling crowd was that it was peopled entirely by young women. But what could incite fifteen hundred young women to congregate in front of government offices? An inspiring orator? Some *cause célèbre*? It was, in fact, nothing more nor less than an advertisement for eleven positions for "junior counterwomen ... at various metropolitan post-offices." Applicants were asked to appear in person on Tuesday and Wednesday morning at the commissioners' office, and appear they did. Many hopeful young women, the *Gazette* reports, never made it to the steps of the office, turning back when they saw the crowd. Another five to six hundred appeared on the Wednesday morning. The *Gazette* estimates that two thousand young women came to the commissioners' office to compete for the positions, and reports that "the Commissioners did actually examine for these eleven vacancies over one thousand candidates."[1]

By the 1870s, the reality of middle-class women in the thousands
trying to enter the job market, made glaringly evident in this one
instance of a throng of young women clamouring for a mere eleven
low-level civil service jobs, had created new and more concrete problems for advocates of employment opportunities for middle-class
women. The demographic imbalance had driven these women into
the workforce, but now they faced another disparity – that of supply and demand in the labour market. The spectacle at the Civil
Service Commissioners' offices was, as the *Englishwoman's Review*
remarks, only one "instance of the immense number of women who
... [were] in search of employment."[2] And while being a low-level
clerk may not seem, to a twenty-first-century reader, particularly
appealing, such white-collar work was considered at least minimally
respectable and had, moreover, the prestige of having been previously restricted to men. In 1868, the *Saturday Review* lists counting
house clerk in the same category with doctor, lawyer, and parson, as
positions that were barred to women.[3] As an area of work that was
deemed respectable and that had only just been made available as
an option for women, white-collar work had a cachet that so-called
"women's work" did not. Those women who had no inclination to
teach or to work with children accordingly found white-collar work
attractive, especially since it offered a greater prospect for achieving
personal and economic independence than other types of employment suggested in the periodical press as options for impoverished
gentlewomen, such as decorative arts that could be done in the home.

The overwhelming response to the 1873 advertisement for eleven
low-level positions is nevertheless startling, given the brief history of women's employment in the civil service up to that time.
A very few women had worked as office clerks earlier – only 15
in 1851, according to the census, and 279 in 1861. By 1871, there
were 1,446, which, while indicating an increase of almost one hun-
dred-fold over twenty years, still represented only 1.1 per cent of
all clerks employed in England and Wales.[4] The clerical jobs made
available to women in the early 1870s were less significant for the
numbers of openings they provided than for the interest and publicity they produced. Government offices, of which the Post Office was
the vanguard, initiated a policy of hiring a limited number of women
as clerks in what was termed "an experiment." Initially, eligibility
for these positions was available only through nomination and only
women who were deemed "ladies" could be nominated.[5]

The performance of these ladies in their new arena of work proved to be exemplary and indeed superior to that of men in comparable situations. The positive outcomes of employing female clerks were widely reported in the press. The "very satisfactory results" of this "experiment" are noted in the *Civil Service Review* in 1876 and reprinted in both the *Englishwoman's Review* and the *Woman's Gazette.*[6] In 1875, "A Government Official" reports in *Fraser's Magazine* that the "experiment ... very soon showed such fruitful results that it was greatly extended"; female clerks were employed not only in more government offices but also in insurance companies and law offices.[7] Educated women were also hired as bookkeepers and were again praised for their performance; according to the *Birmingham Daily Post*, the work of female bookkeeping clerks "is done much more accurately than by male clerks, to say nothing of the greater neatness which is also displayed."[8] Similar praise for women's work was extensive. The *Times* comments on the successful results of various initiatives to introduce women into government offices, quoting the controller of the Returned Letter Office, which began employing women in 1873. The women working in his office, the controller reports, had "completely surpassed" expectations. "They are very accurate," he affirms, "and do a fair quantity of work; more so, in fact than many of the males who have been employed on the same duty."[9] An article in *Truth* attests to the professional bearing of female clerks, observing that, among clerks dealing with the public in post offices, the "men treat you as if you were their servants; the women as if they were servants of the public."[10] A correspondent of the *Northern Whig*, in response to letters "attacking the system under which employment has been given to [women]," insists that "the post office women clerks of London are as civil, as exact, and something smarter, than any clerks of any sex ... [he had] had to do with in rather an extended experience."[11] Authorities in government offices, according to Margaret Harkness, are "satisfied that nothing is wanting among ... [lady clerks] of quiet, business-like ways."[12] The London School Board deems its large number of female clerks "conscientious, industrious, and zealous."[13] According to the *Pall Mall Gazette*, women bookkeepers "are more reliable than men"; one employer observes that "embezzlements have never to her knowledge occurred where a woman kept the books."[14] Another employer claims that women "work quicker than the men, and they stick to their work. Let the half-educated men unfit for clerks emigrate," he suggests, "and let us fill their places with educated ladies."[15]

Despite the glowing testimonials of employers and supervisors confirming that women's performance in the clerical work assigned to them generally surpassed that of men, that women were more reliable, more courteous, more conscientious, and more honest than their male counterparts, the rhetoric and subtext of the media reports reveal a continuing cultural ambivalence about women working in government and commercial offices. The persistence of the rhetoric of experimentation indicates the tentativeness of the initiatives to open up clerical positions to women. Articles acknowledging the excellence of women's clerical work consistently damn that work with faint praise. The *Times* article quoted above repeatedly points out that women have been employed in low-level clerical work of "a simple character" only, the kind previously assigned to boy clerks. The author even admonishes readers with the astonishingly prejudicial and groundless supposition that they "must not forget that attempts *may possibly* have been made which have not proved so fruitful" (emphasis added). The *Times* even adds a misogynistic anecdote that makes its positive commentary on women's work seem grudging at best. With reference to women working in the Telegraph Clearing-house Branch, a government official comments that the work was "well within the capacity of a female staff" because "it consisted chiefly in fault-finding."[16] The *Civil Service Review*'s report diminishes the efforts of women working in governmental departments by referring to the "small duties of their small offices."[17] And even while the clerical "experiments" were being hailed as successes and women were being praised as businesslike, naysayers were claiming the contrary and were grumbling about "semi-educated, refined, and incompetent women" overcrowding the job market.[18] "Women starve," according to a *Times* correspondent, "not for want of employment, but, sad to say, from sheer inability to fit themselves for it."[19]

While undoubtedly the effect of what one commentator acknowledges as "pride and prejudice,"[20] the subtle – and sometimes not so subtle – denigration of women's work was in part driven by a need literally to devalue that work, to make women's labour cheap. Hiring women as clerks in government offices was a response not only to the realization that thousands of educated women were in need of a livelihood, but also to the promise of economic advantages for employers: desperate women could be employed for much lower salaries than those demanded by men. "The employment of females as clerks," *Herapath's Journal* notes in 1878, "is calculated to relieve railway companies of some part of the weight of work-ing expenses."[21] Margaret Harkness makes a similar observation in 1881, asserting that women were admitted to the civil service "for the express purpose of economising by cheap labour."[22] In other words, women had to struggle not only against traditional assump-tions about their physical, intellectual, and emotional susceptibilities but also against economic imperatives to degrade the market value of their work. Market pressures also worked against women, as Harkness attests. But while admitting that "necessity now compels large numbers of women to seek occupation," she also envisions a time when "there will be less pressure at any given point, and the fic-titious conditions will decrease under which the female worker finds herself forced to give her labour at a lower rate than it is intrinsically and comparatively worth." Harkness closes her overview of women in the civil service with an earnest appeal to women workers to com-mit themselves to facing the challenges of their situation. "Patience is all that is needed," she assures them, "and a bond of mutual help-fulness, binding together all women irrespective of class to meet the obstacles incident to changing social conditions of life."[23]

CHANGING THE HABIT OF THINKING ABOUT WOMEN AND WORK

Meeting the increasingly complex challenges presented by the chang-ing social conditions of women's lives would require more than pa-tience and solidarity, however; it would require that women work as they had not done yet, as the *English Woman's Journal* had enjoined in 1858, and that society – including women themselves – must change its habit of thinking, as James Hinton urged with specific reference to nursing in 1870.[24] The women who were admitted into the civil service in the initial "experiments" were nominated to compete for the positions, with an eye, apparently, both to the neediness of the ladies in question and to their suitability for the work. The number of women applying for civil service jobs continued to surge following the positive reports about women's performance in government offices and the termination of the nomination system. By 1881, competitive examinations for women's positions in the civil service were open to all qualified female applicants. The ratio of applicants to positions remained remarkable – 920 candidates in an 1882 competition for 40 positions, according to the *Times*, and 2,500 candidates in 1885 for

145 positions, according to the *Daily Telegraph*.[25] The *Englishwoman's Review*, as part of the vanguard for changing the habit of thinking about women and work, endorsed open competitive examinations for female civil servants, just as the *Queen* had supported the certification of teachers in 1876. There "is a healthy tone about any open labour market," according to the *Review*, and women's qualifications, like men's, should be "submitted as a matter of course, to the same practical test." Without such openness, the *Review* foresees that "the employment of women will remain in an atmosphere of hot-house forcing ... [that would be] very injurious to their independence." The *Review* also notes that "some ladies are afraid lest a lower class of employées should ... be brought into contact with themselves."[26]

The *Englishwoman's Review*'s commentary reveals some of the cross-currents of anxiety that shaped public feeling at the time: market pressures, implicit invidious comparisons of women's work with men's, doubts about women's abilities and the concomitant imperative to validate them – in this case through examinations – and status anxieties among those who wanted office work to remain the refuge of genteel women only. Unlike the *Englishwoman's Review*, the *Quarterly Review* expresses "regret" that the nomination system was giving way to competition "without any restrictions as to ... social position," citing the "awkwardness" that would ensue if women from different social classes "associated and worked at the same desk."[27] Market forces proved to be in conflict with both personal values and cultural value systems with regard to other areas of employment as well. Genteel women were reluctant to work in the semipublic forum of Board Schools, and nursing – still perceived as menial work by many – was not attracting enough middle-class women to meet market demands. At the same time, being a lady-help had surprising appeal for many desperate women. A correspondent to the *Times* in 1879 reports that his advertisement for "a gentlewoman as lady housekeeper" elicited "upwards of 1,100 letters in reply."[28] The continuing flood of women into the labour market, moreover, had the effect of seemingly justifying the prevailing general mistrust of women's work ethic and abilities, as needy women with limited skills and education attempted to join the workforce.

Despite the growing numbers of destitute single women, cultural resistance to the idea of middle-class women working under any circumstances persisted, requiring advocates of women's work to be circumspect in their treatments of greater employment opportunities.

In other words, they had to employ the principles of double address, as discussed in chapter 1. Of most concern to conservative thinkers in the 1870s and the 1880s is the appropriateness of work that brings women into the public sphere as opposed to work that maintains their domestic character. Suggestions about suitable work can, as a result, be mindlessly inclusive as authors try to appeal to socially conservative and socially progressive readers alike. An 1880 advice book "for Mothers and Daughters," for example, defines three kinds of work – work for duty, for pleasure, and for necessity. Acknowledging only that girls should not waste their lives for "want of a worthy purpose," this volume makes no other judgments about the merits of the activities it endorses, which range from reading to charitable work, from china painting to poultry farming, and from office work to medical work.[29]

In periodical publications, the variation in attitudes suggests some evolution to more progressive perspectives – in other words, to changing the habit of thinking over time. *Cassell's Family Magazine*'s promotion of middle-class women's employments, for example, alters significantly over the course of the 1870s and 1880s. In the mid-1870s, *Cassell's* features articles on being a companion, on being a lady-help, and on doing handicrafts – all of which would keep women in the sheltered environment of a home, whether their family's or their employer's ("The Companion," 1874, 248–51; "Domestic Service for Gentlewomen," and "What Is the Best Education for Girls?," 1875, 178–80 and 341–3 respectively). That being a lady-help is not deemed menial, while nursing often is, suggests the powerful influence of the ideal of domesticity in the Victorian psyche. In an 1877 article, however, *Cassell's* begins to shift its perspective in a discussion entitled "New Employments for Women." After a pro forma gesture to public opinion in favour of the "quiet, womanly woman," this article comes out in full support of the middle-class working woman, with an emphasis on the opportunities presented by office work.[30] An 1881 article, "The Employment of Girls," pays more attention to the apparent benefits of keeping girls occupied at home (mostly keeping their possessions in order), but closes with suggestions about what they might do later in terms of careers.[31] This tactic of playing both ends of the spectrum reaches its most shrewd in a debate in an 1882 series called "The Family Parliament" about "Home Life *versus* Public Life for Girls."[32] As was perhaps inevitable in a publication explicitly directed to family reading, home life wins out, but not before the magazine presents a cogent and forcible argument for public life, a position supported by letters to the editor. The letters endorse women's place in public life as both a social and a personal good for the women who venture out to work. "Does not public life need those refining influences which are so largely bestowed upon it through the services of woman in the public sphere?" asks the Reverend J.A. Mather.[33] Another correspondent, who identifies herself as "a girl who went into public life some time ago," asserts that "public life offers the most opportunities, best appliances, and healthiest conditions" and moreover "affords the only true, because the only impartial, gauge of worth and ability." In her personal experience, she affirms, she has "bodily benefited by enforced exercise" and has been "mentally stimulated and strengthened by punctuality, perseverance, and responsibility."[34] By 1883, *Cassell's* lays aside equivocation and, in a series entitled "Remunerative Employments for Gentlewomen," endorses several options, while emphasizing nursing and office work.[35]

The development of more progressive attitudes was, however, anything but linear. Many publications were, like *Cassell's*, measured in their treatment of women and work and cautious in their endorsement of women's rights with respect to work. Advocates stress women's urgent financial need rather than any desire for independence. Margaret Harkness's observation that "necessity now forces many women out into the world" underscores the reality that finding employment is not typically something middle-class women choose to do, but something they must do.[36] Emily Faithfull similarly notes that "many women are compelled to earn their own living."[37] Some publications could be controversial or deliberately provocative. One of the more inflammatory stratagems – used not infrequently by polemicists who wanted to attract the attention of conventional Victorians – was to question the probity of marriage or to equate marriage with, or compare it unfavourably to, prostitution, generally on the grounds of morals or economics. The *Westminster Review* was particularly daring, denouncing the "thraldom" of conventional "dogmas" in an article in 1884, and claiming that such dogmas "condemned every woman to be a wife and a mother, and stamped the unmarried with reproach."[38] Three years later, another *Westminster Review* article even more provocatively suggests that these dogmas defined the "dominant type of marriage" as being "like prostitution, founded on economical considerations."[39]

THE ADVENT OF THE TYPEWRITER

Despite continuing cultural discomfort with the idea of working ladies, by the early 1880s hard-working and capable middle-class women had nevertheless managed to gain a foothold in the offices of Victorian Britain. That they were ultimately able to secure their position permanently was the outcome of the advent of the typewriter. The new technologies of the nineteenth century played a significant role in providing new employment opportunities for women, in part because the jobs they produced were entirely new and accordingly had no established gender specificity. Women worked as telegraphists from the earliest days of commercial telegraphic use in the 1850s and later quickly dominated the field of telephone operators,[40] but it was the typewriter – the first ubiquitous business machine and arguably the greatest business innovation of its time – that enabled women to transform the business office from an almost exclusively male preserve and to define themselves and their role in the workplace in terms of occupation and skills, rather than in terms of gender.

Recent historical analyses of the emergence of women as typewriters, however, persist in imposing anachronistic gender stereotypes onto the nineteenth-century female typist. Christopher Keep, for example, argues that early advertising campaigns, which "invariably showed a fashionably-dressed and attractive young woman posing alongside a new machine ... helped produce the cultural 'fit' between the normative values of femininity and typing."[41] Much of the advertising he cites, however, postdates the introduction of typing offices in Britain by over a decade, a crucial decade in the evolution of attitudes towards the middle-class working woman. Historical narratives about the typewriter similarly misrepresent the role of the woman worker and credit men, market forces, or a combination of the two with enabling women's advancements in office work. In his influential *Discourse Networks*, for example, Friedrich Kittler asserts that "apart from Freud, it was [Philo] Remington [manufacturer of the first widely marketed typewriter] who 'granted the female sex access to the office.'"[42] Pamela Thurschwell quotes Christopher Latham Sholes, the American inventor of the Remington typewriter, to support her claim that "from its inception the typewriter was imagined as a technology that would be especially liberating for women."[43] But Sholes's comment, quoted by Thurschwell – "I do feel I have done something for the women who have always had to work so hard. This will enable them more easily to earn a living" – was an 1890 retrospective assessment of what had occurred, not a predictive formulation of hopes at the time of the typewriter's inception.[44] Early European and American prototypes of the typewriter (a term coined by Sholes) had in fact been conceived of as aids to blind readers.[45] When Remington started production of Sholes's model, the target market for the typewriter was not clear, as the first promotional announcement extolling it as "graceful and ornamental" and as a "beautiful piece of furniture for office, study or parlour" suggests.[46] The *Times*, reporting on its introduction in London, predicts that the Remington typewriter "cannot fail to be of service in public offices as well as in those of professional and mercantile men"; the report makes no mention of women.[47] The typewriter is initially characterized as both pragmatic and progressive. In 1874, the *Times* reprints a brief item from the *Augusta Chronicle* that hales the typewriter as "one of the greatest and most useful inventions of the age." In a more lengthy article in 1876 that details the mechanism and functioning of the typewriter, the *Times* concludes that it is "an ingenious and practical piece of machinery" that "is well worthy of inspection by all who are interested in mechanical progress."[48] This convergence of attributes of enterprise, mechanical ingenuity, and industrial utility in early media notices of the typewriter is far removed from Victorian cultural perceptions of womanliness.

The record that survives in newspaper and periodical accounts of actual women and their entrance into the commercial world as typists or as managers of typing services in the 1880s suggests something quite different from the sexualized typewriter girl of the "popular representations" and the "media image" that Keep defines as culturally formative.[49] These women, like other middle-class women trying to establish their occupational credentials, were focused on professionalism rather than on femininity, although it is true that images of typists in the women's press often do conform to stylized versions of femininity. A set of illustrations of "Women Workers" in the *Queen* in 1888, for example, represents typists as young and attractive, with simple hairstyles that nevertheless reveal the curls in their hair; their dresses are modestly high-necked, but the skirts are elaborate, with elegant draping in the front and very impractical bustles in the back (fig. 4.1). However, the largest and most prominent visual representation of a typist in the *Queen*, appearing on the cover of the 6 April 1893

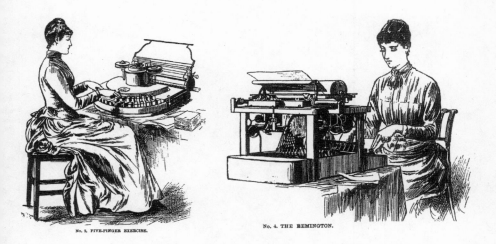

No. 3. FIVE-FINGER EXERCISE.   No. 4. THE REMINGTON.

Figure 4.1 "Women Workers: Female School of Shorthand and Typewriting," *The Queen, the Lady's Newspaper and Court Chronicle*, 20 October 1888, 481. © British Library Board

issue, is a decided contrast to the paper's conventional illustrations of ladies: the bespectacled typewriter wears a plain dress and has her hair tied back in a severe bun; she looks like a spinster schoolmarm, not an icon of fashionable femininity (fig. 4.2). Moreover, the femininity eventually associated with typing conforms less to normative Victorian values than it does to the edgier values of the independent New Woman.

Commentaries in the media that associate women workers with typewriters in the 1880s stress the promise of the work and the capabilities of the machines and operators, not the personal qualities of the women workers. One of the first references to typewriting as remunerative work for educated women appears in 1882 in the *Queen*, in a report, based on an article in the *New York Sun*, about the merits of the typing machine for use in law and commercial offices. "The swiftness and exactness with which the work is done," observes the author, "is marvelous."[50] The first notice of typewriting in the *Englishwoman's Review* in 1884 similarly focuses on the work itself and on the efficiency of the worker, remarking that typewriting "seems to promise a new field of employment to educated women" and that "an intelligent woman, who is energetic

Figure 4.2 "London Maids No. 3: The Type-Writer," *The Queen, the Lady's Newspaper and Court Chronicle*, 8 April 1893, 537. © British Library Board

and punctual[,] ought to be able to make a fair income by it."[51] And while the inventors and manufacturers of typewriters may have been men, women were not simply passive beneficiaries of male ingenuity and solicitude provided by Christopher Sholes and Philo Remington. Women were active in the development and proliferation of type-writing skills and in the adaptation of business practices to the opportunities typewriters presented. Wilfred Beeching reports that, in the United States, "the Young Women's Christian Association was one of the first organizations to foresee the possibilities of a new career for women."[52] The YWCA started a typing class for young women in 1881, an initiative that was, according to John Zellers, seen as folly, as "an obvious error in judgment." The women running the classes were deemed "well-meaning but misguided ladies" and the "female mind and constitution were not considered equal to a six months course in typing." It was the naysayers, however, not the supposedly misguided ladies, who misjudged the situation, as eight young women completed the initial course of training and the YWCA typing school continued.[53] Typing with all ten digits, as opposed to hunting and pecking with two fingers from each hand, was initially suggested at the First Annual International Congress of Shorthand Writers in 1882 by Margaret Longley, who, with her husband Elias, had established a shorthand and typing school in Cincinnati in the early 1880s.[54]

In Britain, as in America, women were active in the early development and dissemination of typing skills and services. In 1884 the Ladies Type-writing and General Copying Office in London – the first typing agency in Britain – opened under the auspices of the Society for Promoting the Employment of Women and under the management of Marian Marshall. This event is noted in both the *Englishwoman's Review* and heralded with great enthusiasm by *Work and Leisure*, whose editors "rejoice to chronicle this new and very promising department of work for women." The prospectus for this new business assures potential clients that all work will be "executed with care and promptitude."[55] Marshall was arguably the most accomplished and successful of the first wave of typists in Britain. Her London office flourished, according to the *Englishwoman's Review*, and she subsequently established the Cambridge University Type-writing Office, which specialized in providing services to the academic and medical communities. In response to the interests of this clientele, Marshall modified a typewriter to accommodate the Greek alphabet.[56] Marshall became something of a media luminary, being not only the subject of numerous articles in the women's press, but also a regular contributor to the *Queen* on issues related to women's employment, especially on the opportunities and demands of typing and office work and on the need for sound training.

The typewriter provided unprecedented professional opportunities for women, bringing them into the commercial world in large numbers and enabling enterprising individuals among them to set up typing services and training schools. Marshall's Ladies Type-writing Office was only the first of many similar establishments to open in Britain in the mid-1880s. From the beginning, these offices were conceived of as offering not only services to clients, but also on-the-job training for the operators of the machines. In its announcement of the opening of Marshall's London office in 1884,

the *Englishwoman's Review* reports that the office "not only affords
a means of earning a livelihood but also tends to educate, as every
manuscript must be thoroughly studied before being copied."[57]
Eventually, typewriting offices provided training courses for a fee. A
typewriting office opened in 1888 by Mary Day, for example, offered
a course of "classes for type-writing, shorthand and correspondence
or book-keeping ... for six guineas."[58] As the engagement of women
in the development of typing offices and schools demonstrates, the
typewriter not only figured prominently in the cultural reformulation of the middle-class woman worker, but also allowed women
to be active agents in defining a role for themselves in the commercial world. Women founded and administered these establishments,
worked and trained in them; women publicized the opening of new
offices and the success of trailblazers like Marian Marshall in their
newspapers and periodicals.[59] And women from prominent families
did not shy away from joining the ranks and offering typewriting
services; Charles Dickens's granddaughter established a successful
typewriting office on Wellington Street in London in the late 1880s.[60]
That the work initially was not gender specific also allowed women
to define themselves as workers with specialized technical skills.

WORK, TYPEWRITING, AND THE WOMEN'S PRESS

By the late 1880s, typewriting was well established as an occupation
for middle-class women in Britain. It also remained, temporarily at
least, at the forefront of occupations that allowed women workers
to resist gender stereotypes in their perceptions of themselves and
in their attitudes and approaches to their work. That the typewriter
had no initial associations with women or traditionally female en-
deavours (despite the fact that descriptions of early models compare
typewriters to sewing machines) also helped to maintain a distinction
between the female office worker's work and her womanliness. The
extent to which typewriting enabled women to maintain a division
between work and gender is suggested in the contrasting treatments
of typewriting and nursing in the women's press, most notably in the
Queen, which by the late 1880s had evolved into a reliable cultural barometer about middle-class women's work. Despite the respect
that nursing increasingly commanded in Victorian culture, media considerations of nursing are compromised by conventional notions of
femininity. In 1888, around the same time that nurses were trying to

form the British Nurses' Association, typists were trying to organize to set conditions of employment and pay.[61] Reports of the Typists' Society meetings reveal striking contrasts with those of the Nurses' Association, both in terms of the character of the meetings and of the reportage. The first annual meeting of the British Nurses' Association, the *Queen* reports, was chaired by Professor George Murray Humphrey, senior surgeon of Addenbrooke's Hospital and fellow of King's College, Cambridge, "who presided for the first time, he said, over a meeting of 'bonnets.'" "Bonnets" was perhaps a more suitable descriptor than a twenty-first-century critic would like to admit, for "the large number of nurses … from different parts of the country" in attendance played no more active a role at the meeting than did the hats on their heads. The executive committee admittedly included several hospital matrons and a female recording secretary, but it was the male honorary secretary, Dr Bedford Fenwick, who spoke on their behalf and described "the objects of the association" for the assembled members and observers. All motions reported by the *Queen* were put forward and seconded by men, some of whom added complimentary observations on the role of nurses and the aims of the association. The *Queen*'s reporter is untroubled by the condescension of these male patrons; she is indeed apparently charmed by Humphrey, finding his words "amusing" and characterizing "his kindly presence as chair … a pleasure and an inspiration to many nurses."[62]

Reportage on meetings of the Typists' Society, by contrast, is restrained and businesslike, as are the meetings themselves. No male patrons appear to give speeches or make supposedly winsome comments about the value of women's presence in sick rooms, offices, or wherever. The men who are at the meetings share in the work of the society, which is nevertheless dominated by women, with the central committee of the society comprising four women and one man.[63] At the meeting held on the same day as the first annual meeting of the British Nurses' Association (31 August 1889), the only nonmembers of the society present were Miss King, the secretary for the Society for Promoting the Employment of Women, and noted union activist Clementina Black. Like all of the typists' meetings, at which members efficiently pass motions, elect subcommittees, and move on to the next matter at hand, this one was all business.[64]

The *Woman's Herald*, a publication less likely than the *Queen* to endorse conventional gender assumptions, generally presents both typewriting and nursing in straightforward terms. A series of articles on "The Profession of Nursing" by Ethel Gordon Fenwick (Mrs Bedford Fenwick) nevertheless begins with a quotation from Sir Walter Scott's *Marmion* characterizing women as "ministering angel[s]" of the afflicted, and Fenwick affirms that "it has ever been held to be woman's highest mission to tend the sick and to soothe the suffering."[65] By contrast, while articles about typing sometimes make claims that "type-writing is an employment for which women are peculiarly fitted,"[66] that fitness is generally related to the skills that women have acquired in typing, such as their superior speed and accuracy, or to the satisfaction that government and commercial offices express about women's performance in the workplace. And women's success in securing office jobs was, as one columnist observes, not "from chivalry, not from a sense of justice, but simply because ... [the employer] could get a refined, educated woman to do the work of a common, uneducated man at the same wages."[67] Until the 1890s, reports about typewriting and typewriters in the women's press and the mainstream press alike are informational, noting the increased number of women entering this segment of the job market, reviewing lectures on and demonstrations of typewriters, and reporting on meetings of the Society of Typists.[68]

As the last decade of the nineteenth century approached, there was a cultural buzz about typewriting throughout the entire British Isles. The proliferation of the typewriter as business girl (as she was often called in America), typewriter girl, or female clerk, was both applauded and decried. The *Manchester Weekly Times* reported in 1889 that, in America, the typewriter "is everywhere ... and has taken her place among the institutions of the land."[69] The *Birmingham Daily Post* makes a similar but less sanguine observation about female clerks in England in 1892, noting that "a quarter of a century ago a female clerk was a rarity, but now they are to be found everywhere," intruding on male domains of employment.[70] In the same year, *Shafts* reports that "now nearly all the principal towns of England possess one, if not several," typewriting offices and that "there are now hundreds of typewriting offices, mostly run by women, in Great Britain and Ireland."[71] By 1895, typewriters were to be found "in every town in England," according the *Girl's Own Paper*, which went so far as to declare that "type-writing is rapidly becoming a power in the land."[72] National and regional papers report on lectures about and demonstrations of typewriters in cities and towns all over England, Wales, Scotland, and Ireland.[73] That these lectures, describing and demonstrating the most basic features of the mechanism and operation of typewriters, were so ubiquitous suggests how new and mystifying these machines were to most people.[74] The typewriter was cutting-edge technology at the time and typewriting was an area of employment whose cachet was its absolute modernity. Typewriting's association with city offices moreover carries with it the suggestion of the excitement and sophistication of urban life, "a suggestion of adventure, of departure from the ordinary routine."[75] The city's desirability as a venue for employment is evident, for example, in an article advocating rural district nursing as a career option; the author assures young women that "you can never be dull, for you will have as much to do as though you were working in a city hospital, shop, or typewriter's office."[76]

As characterized in the women's press, office work offers not just a means to make a living, but also a source of personal stimulation. Not only will the woman working in an office in the city never be dull, she will have a sense of achievement and pride, perhaps even of solidarity, as an article in *Young Woman* suggests. A conscientious and "good lady clerk," according to an article in that magazine, should strive to bring honour to "the proud name she is entitled to bear – that of a '*Working Woman*.'"[77] Typewriting, according to an article by Marian Marshall in *Shafts*, "is an occupation ennobling and improving in many ways," those ways being available through the professions, such as medicine and law, for which the typist may work. "Typewriters of intelligence and capacity," Marshall asserts, have "many opportunities for instruction and higher development."[78] The unfortunate corollary of this statement is that typewriters with limited capabilities working in positions providing little or no intellectual stimulation could be a drag on the prestige of an area of work that held such promise for educated women. The repeated insistence on the need for training, skill, and a high level of general education that appears in both the women's and the mainstream press indicates an intense anxiety about the erosion of the typewriter's status, and this loss in status certainly led to an erosion of earning power.

REVERSAL OF FORTUNES

The initial growth in demand for typewriters had been a boon for educated middle-class women, as the demand exceeded the supply. Throughout the 1880s, the media published hopeful notices promoting typewriting as a new and potentially fruitful area of work that seemed ideal for educated women. An early reference in the *Englishwoman's Review* heralds typewriting as promising "a new field of employment to educated women," a statement that assumes a level of general knowledge and learning.[79] *Work and Leisure*'s subtitle of a discussion of "Type-Writing" as "An Employment for Educated Women" similarly takes education as a given.[80] The *Queen* develops a comparable mindset as it increasingly takes up the promotion of typewriting as an appropriate employment for its readers, providing information and advice about training and jobs. Typewriters, according to the *Queen*, are not only educated, but are "for the most part ladies."[81] The *Queen* reports optimistically on some of the more intellectually demanding typewriting initiatives, such as Marian Marshall's office on the Strand that specialized in copying medical documents, requiring "operators thoroughly conversant with the technical terms, and possessing intelligent knowledge of the subject."[82]

The supply and demand relationship soon changed, however, and with a rapidity that was dizzying. The media reported a demand for typists in excess of supply in almost the same breath that they warned of a glut of undereducated and unskilled operators on the market. In 1888 and 1889, the media celebrated the growth of opportunities for skilled typewriters.[83] In February of 1889, the *Queen* reported "an immense demand in City houses for lady typewriters," but by June of the same year was decrying the pernicious consequences of competition and was urging women to "protect themselves against the present system of underselling" their services.[84] By 1890, the Society for Promoting the Employment of Women reported that "type-writing is already overcrowded, and that the competition is so fierce that in many offices they [typewriters] are underpaid."[85] The competition and underselling, all commentators agreed, was the result of undereducated and poorly trained young women flooding the market. "Typewriting is distinctly a profession and not a trade, requiring education, energy, and the other characteristics which make it essentially work for educated women," the *Englishwoman's Review* insists. The "mistaken system adopted by some offices of teaching a large number of illiterate young women" has stunted "the progress of the profession" by turning out "legions of incompetent workers."[86]

The relative cheapness of acquiring basic typing skills worked against efforts to maintain professional standards. "For twenty pounds a girl can become possessed of a typewriter and the knowledge to make herself proficient in its use, and that within three months," according to the *Western Mail*.[87] Observers were especially distressed that the government, once in the vanguard of promoting women's employment in civil service offices, was now in the vanguard of employers willing to exploit the oversupply of typists. The Society of Typists affirmed its object to prevent "the application of the sweating system to typist clerks" and government departments were criticized for capitalizing on "the competition to reduce the wages of the girls."[88] The *Woman's Herald* cited the government as "one of the worst sinners in the matter of sweating typists," while the *Queen* mocked government claims to be a "model employer" while paying "20 per cent. less than the rates of the Typists' Union."[89] Female typists in all sectors of the economy suffered a similar depression in wages. "A Girl Typewriter," writing to *Reynolds's Newspaper*, complained that her employer had reduced her wages from 30 shillings a week to 18 shillings because he could "get lots of girls ... for 10s. a week upwards." [90] As early as 1892, the income of "the purely mechanical typewriter" was used as the benchmark for marginal earnings in an article assessing the sweating of artists employed to paint reproductions for cheap picture dealers.[91] By the end of the century, typewriters were frequently equated with "restaurant-girls," or waitresses; *Chambers's Journal* went so far as to question "whether the restaurant-girl or typewriter is really better off than the servant in a reasonably good place."[92]

The work that had once held such promise for providing middle-class women with a comfortable independent life was fast gaining notoriety as an occupation debased by underselling among workers and by exploitation on the part of employers. There were even dark hints that employers might demand sexual favours. "Women clerks have the disadvantage of men," warns "A Girl Typewriter," "that they are often compelled, if they wish to keep a place, to sell not only their services, but their virtue."[93] The city, in this dispiriting version of the typewriter, is no longer the centre of excitement, but of isolation. "There is no loneliness like that in London," observes the London correspondent for the *Western Mail*, as he describes the straightened life of the daughter of a country clergyman earning her living as a typist and having "only her dark rooms to go to ... night after night." Under such conditions, according to this correspondent, "happy young girls are ... daily metamorphosed into care-worn, life-weary old women."[94] While this scenario may be overly melodramatic, at least in its foreshortened chronology, the problem of poverty and uncertain old age for the once happy young girls who entered the realm of clerical work was very real. Frances Low's "How Poor Ladies Live," cited in the *Western Mail* column referred to above, struck a sensitive cultural nerve when it appeared in the *Nineteenth Century* in 1897. Low assessed the "congested condition of the labour market for educated middle-class women, the competition that prevails therein" as "a condition of 'progress'" that tended to increase rather than to mitigate the distress of impoverished single women.[95] The "typewriting market," she noted, was "so overcrowded that, unless a girl be very expert, and in addition be an accomplished shorthand writer and French and German scholar" she would "make but the most wretched income" (406). Low here hit on one of the major reasons for the demise of typewriting as a promising option for educated women, the idea that knowledge and education beyond the mere mechanics of typing would not be assumed as part of the professional profile. Eliza Orme took Low to task for many of her suppositions, including this one which, Orme pointedly asserted, "only shows that inefficient work is badly paid. A thoroughly good typewriter," she continued, "with a tolerable knowledge of shorthand, and the ordinary education of a college graduate, has no difficulty in earning an excellent income."[96] Low's perspective, to be sure, was patrician, her main concern being impoverished gentlewomen of the old school, women who had been governesses or mistresses at girls' public schools, companions, or secretaries. (She was sniffy about Board Schools.) Low's dismissive placement of typewriting "in the lower ranks of 'skilled' labour" nevertheless reflected the unpleasant reality of the times, which left many young women making "a most wretched living," facing the kind of destitution that Low described among the aging single "gentlewomen" in "How Poor Ladies Live."

The sense that, for some young women trying to make their way in low-level typing jobs, life could be intolerable was corroborated by media reports of typists' suicides. Two such suicides in 1898 and 1899 were reported in the *Times* as well as in the *Western Mail*, in the first case, and in the *Illustrated Police News*, in the second. In both cases, the coroner's inquest brought in the conventional verdict of "suicide whilst of unsound mind," although curiously, in the second case, this verdict was elaborated to be "unsound mind brought on by influenza."[97] That both women were in their thirties is not incidental, as this would be the point at which they would be deemed no longer young, a point in the life of a late-Victorian woman when she would hope either to be married or to be settled in an occupation that offered her some sense of stability and some hope for the future. That one of the typewriters worked for that model employer, the Parliamentary Typewriting Association, was perhaps also not incidental.

The challenges of forging the new identity of the middle-class working woman led to significant progress in promoting women's employment, but the overly rapid development of the typewriter had led to some of the worst employment practices of women's sweated labour finding their way into this promising new area of endeavour. The consequent rapid devaluation of the woman office worker left many women facing relative poverty in the short run and the possibility of an uncertain future as one of the destitute aging women of Low's reckoning. But while even the most sanguine treatments of typewriting in the 1890s carry warnings about the adversities young women would face, the lure of independence continued to draw them into Victorian offices. The promise of freedom and excitement that office work represented lingered on. Work, however poor the remuneration, could still provide a woman with an independent identity.

5

"In Business to Stay":
The Typewriter in Victorian Fiction

Oh, here's to one type of the type-writer girl,
    Who comes to the office at ten,
Whose bleached Psyche twist terminates in curl,
    Whose thoughts are of marriage and men!
She sits on her feet in a soft easy chair,
    And prays that no business may come;
And reads Frenchy novels of love and despair—
    The while her jaws masticate gum.

And here's to her sister whose dresses are plain,
    Who is practical, earnest, and bright;
Who honors her work and would never disdain
    To labor from morning till night!
The former fair dreamer is out of her sphere,
    And is rapidly fading away;
While more of the latter are needed each year,
    For they are in business to stay.

Anonymous, "Two Type-Writer Types,"
Our Phonographic Poets, compiled by "Topsy Typist," 70–1.

The kind of cultural discomfort with the idea of the middle-class working woman that produced the divided characterization of the nurse in Victorian fiction similarly coloured the fictional representations of the typewriter. The typewriter presented very different representational problems, however. Unlike the figure of the middle-class nurse, she did not carry the baggage of preconceived notions from earlier incarnations; there were no images of Sairey Gamps to overcome. As a new cultural phenomenon, the typewriter offered not only untried employment opportunities, but also untried creative opportunities. The lack of cultural baggage, which might suggest that the challenges to characterization would be less daunting, in fact created representational conundrums. Emma Liggins quite rightly points out that "the independent lifestyle of the professional woman is variously represented in later Victorian fiction as a welcome [if often temporary] escape" from domestic duties,[1] and typewriting offered the promise of independence for middle-class women. Nevertheless, "independent woman" was oxymoronic to middle-class Victorian sensibilities, at least if the woman in question was to be considered properly womanly. The womanliness of a nurse, however professionalized she might be, could be preserved by her function as caregiver. The womanliness of an office worker was always under threat: high levels of efficiency and professionalism undermined Victorian concepts of femininity, but the only obvious womanly identity available for the female office worker was temptress, whether or not she was conscious of the role she was thus assigned. In the media, as we have seen, advocates for women's employment strove to define the new female office worker as a lady – as educated, decorous, and professional. Artistic representations, as the above poem suggests, advanced somewhat different perspectives. As the example above also indicates, there was a divide in cultural perceptions of what the typewriter might be like. To be sure, this early twentieth-century American version of that divide is stark, presenting only the options of an ill-bred, husband-hunting flibbertigibbet or a conscientious but colourless professional. Not only was the reality more complex than these options suggests, but so were the fictional representations in Victorian literature.

As unnuanced as these two representations of the typewriter are, they do reflect some of the painful truths about the state of employment for women office workers by the end of the nineteenth century. The traits of the "type of the type-writer girl" as represented in the first stanza are more characteristic of typists in Victorian cartoons and music hall sketches than those in Victorian business offices, but the suggestion of an undereducated and unskilled worker is not off the mark, as employers increasingly hired less educated women for lower and lower wages. The "plainly dressed" professional who is "in business to stay" must not only be "practical, earnest, and bright," but she must also be willing "to labor from morning till night." If you want to stay employed, the message would seem to be, you had better be agreeable to being exploited. As these two characterizations further suggest, there were difficulties in the cultural perception of the typewriter's sexual potential. The idea of attractive, accomplished, and marriageable young women working in close proximity to men – who are apparently always susceptible – produced high levels of anxiety in the overheated Victorian psyche.

The fundamental divide in the characterization of the fictional typewriter begins, then, with the clash between two sets of middle-class ideals – Victorian work ethics and Victorian femininity. The threat to the domestic ideal of femininity that created anxiety in the Victorian media also shapes early fictional representations of typewriters, one of the earliest appearing in a novel by James Payn entitled *Thicker Than Water* (originally serialized in the first volume of *Longman's Magazine* in 1883). The attitudes in the story run the gamut of those that appear in less abundant variety in individual narratives about typewriters for the next two decades, suggesting the inchoateness of cultural responses to both the machines and their operators at the time. Both the hope of independence and the discouragement of limited means colour the text; work is salvation, but also an unfortunate necessity for the protagonist; typewriting is characterized as both a profession and a trade.[2]

Shot through all this confusion of responses – and the thing that makes typewriting an interesting and appealing concept – is novelty. The typewriting machine is so new a phenomenon that the narrator feels impelled to describe it and its mechanism, on the assumption that "the great majority of ... readers are unacquainted with this ingenious invention"; certainly the characters seem quite taken aback by it. Though ingenious and even rather mysterious, the typewriter is nevertheless characterized as uniquely feminine. It may require laborious effort to learn to work the machine, but nevertheless, according to the narrator, "for women whose touch is delicate, and sight is keen, the task comes easy" (164).

For Mary Marvon, the protagonist of *Thicker Than Water*, work is a pressing issue. Orphaned as an infant, she was raised in boarding schools, her education and upbringing overseen by a benevolent but arms-length guardian who was an intimate friend of her late mother. All of the money left for Mary's future by her mother had been earmarked for an education that would "shield her ... from the pangs and pains of poverty ... and fit her as best might be for the battle of life," or in other words, to make her employable (10). As the result of her guardian's childhood friendship with a woman who married well and survived two wealthy husbands, Mary, upon finishing her education, was employed by this wealthy widow as a companion in perhaps the happiest circumstances of any young lady in Victorian fiction. The novel opens with Mary and her employer, Mrs Beckett, living on the best of terms in a luxurious house on Park Lane in London. Mary has become something more like Mrs Beckett's protégée, rather than just her companion, and not only does Mary enjoy comfortable surroundings, excellent food, and an engaging social life, but a generous salary as well. Her happy circumstances are clearly ascribed to her personal attributes, which have been enhanced by her sound education: she is beautiful, articulate, well-read, personable, and poised. As the narrator notes, "nature had not fitted her for the conventional *rôle* of a 'companion,'" which is perhaps why her days in that position are numbered (43). Unfortunately for Mary, she has attracted the attention of Edgar Dornay, the same eligible young man whom Mrs Beckett has decided to pursue, the age difference in her eyes being handsomely offset by her ability to pay his debts. While negotiating with Edgar for a marriage settlement, Mrs Beckett learns that he has proposed to Mary and promptly turns her out of the house with nothing. Now facing the "pangs and pains of poverty," Mary moves into a boarding house and must consider how to earn a living.

What saves Mary, at least temporarily, is her strong sense of self-worth and her willingness to work. She turns to that newest and most promising of technologies, the typewriter, to earn her living. She is befriended by Mrs Beckett's lawyer, Mr Rennie, who provides her with law-copying assignments, work that she can produce in her room at the boarding house. The story thus far sets up Mary, the typewriter, and typewriting, the occupation, in very particular ways. Mary, like the ideal aspirant to typewriting careers in the periodical literature of the time, is a lady; she is well-educated and refined.

Unlike her real-life counterparts, she is able to learn typing on her own, in the privacy of her boarding-house room. Although she, like them, is exceptionally diligent in learning and perfecting her typing skills, she is also apparently one of those women with delicate touch and keen sight for whom "the task comes easy." Moreover, in both learning the skills and putting them to use to earn her keep, Mary remains within the safe confines of the domestic sphere. If she no longer quite fits the mould of a middle-class domestic woman, she nevertheless avoids the taint of exposure to the public sphere. She does not have to leave her boarding house to pick up her law-copying work, as the documents are delivered to her through Mr Rennie, who admires and sympathizes with Mary. She also keeps her employment activities a secret from the other residents of the boarding house. Mary is accordingly able to avoid the split between the professional and feminine sides of the middle-class Victorian working woman, or so it would seem.

The union of femininity and a sort of nascent professionalism in Mary's character is further signalled throughout the text. She is characterized as having a "proud and independent spirit" (9); Mr Rennie judges her to exhibit "modesty without subservience, and an unflinching self-respect" (51). Mary herself repeatedly expresses, in thought, word, and deed, her desire for independence. Her excitement over "her new acquisition," her typewriter, for example, is that, "like Pandora's box, there was hope in it, and possibly independence" (164). But like Pandora's box, the typewriter and the independence it promises are anything but straightforward or unmixed blessings. The status of the work is indeterminate. In conversation with Charley Sotheran, her friend and son of her guardian, Mary boasts of her "new profession" and her ability "to earn quite a large income" (167). Charley, however, is pained that she must work and equates typewriting with seamstressing, aptly quoting the first two lines of Thomas Hood's "The Song of the Shirt" (1843) to characterize Mary's labour: "With fingers weary and worn, / With eyelids heavy and red" (167). In defence of the dignity of her new calling, Mary protests that "the type-writer is not a sewing-machine," but she then characterizes her work as a "trade," a significant downgrade from her earlier reference to her "new profession" (172, 167). Charley further applies some basic political economy to the future prospects of typewriting as a profitable line of business, pointing out the pitfalls of supply and demand. And while Mary bravely counters all of Charley's admonitions, she also anticipates the loneliness of the life on which she has embarked. At a time when typewriting was being celebrated in the media as the hope for independence for educated middle-class women, this brief fictional conversation presciently anticipates the challenges that young women working as typewriters will face by the end of the century and it throws a pall over Mary's sense of work as a kind of personal triumph that makes her feel "stronger to fight and fitter to endure whatever harsh Fate might have in store for her" (165).

While her ability to work may make Mary feel strong and fit to take on adversity, it ultimately does not have the power to protect her from the "pangs and pains of poverty," nor does it allow her true independence. Mary's conviction in her self-sufficiency gives her a sense of confidence that impresses others in her boarding house, one of whom marvels at her "courage and independence" (178), for, as the narrator notes, "the discovery that we are able to support ourselves, no matter how humbly, independent of outside assistance, is to the independent spirit a most solid grain of satisfaction" (190). But Mary soon discovers that her independence is a sham. To her dismay, she realizes that one of the pleadings that Mr Rennie gives her to type up is one she has done before, which makes her suspect that he is "sending her these pleadings, or some of them, out of mere charity, to keep her employed" (191). This realization drives her to attempt to find work on the open market, where she learns that, in addition to paying her for work she has already done, Mr Rennie is paying her at least twice the going rate. Despite the meagre income that she can legitimately earn, Mary is "resolutely, almost doggedly, resolved to gain her own living," although she has lost "the elasticity of mind with which she had commenced" (203). For all Mary's confidence, intelligence, and determination – much touted by narrator and characters alike – she is ultimately unable to cope with the rigours of independence. While she claims that toil is preferable to charity, she is so demoralized by her experience that, shortly after confronting the harsh realities of earning her living as a typewriter, Mary accepts another position as companion, an option that, to her mind, "promised peace and security" (208).

The ambivalence about the independent working woman in this story is striking. Mary has all the characteristics that should make her a success in the new field of typewriting, but the newness of this career option for women makes it problematic for what is a very conventional narrative. Mary remains essentially domestic, working in her boarding-house room secretively, admitting only to one other resident that she is actually typing to earn her keep. The only men who know her secret – Charley and Mr Rennie – are distressed about the need for Mary to work, expressing concern for her health and welfare and even, in the case of Rennie, providing charity disguised as employment. The author is unable to cast Mary as a fully professionalized woman, taking on the rigours of the public sphere by working in an office, making her way in the world without the help and support of sympathetic men. Mary's spiritedness makes her an attractive romantic heroine, as well as a candidate for independence, and it is always clear which option will win out. Until the plot delivers her to her inevitable union with Charley, Mary again secures an implausibly delightful position as companion in an affluent household where she is handsomely remunerated, treated like family, and included in the social life of her employer. If this story has a moral, it would seem to be that independence for a woman is an impossible dream – no matter how intelligent and motivated the woman might be. "There is, no doubt, a very genuine nobility about independence," the narrator observes, "[but] the process of gaining it is often not only rough and difficult but humiliating" (203). Domesticity, by contrast, is apparently always peaceful and secure.

At a time when even most fiction was more realistic about the dissatisfactions of life as a companion, and when nonfiction presented typewriting as one of the brightest hopes for middle-class women's economic independence, the mindset of *Thicker Than Water* seems to be out of touch with prevailing contemporary attitudes. Most fictional representations of typewriters in the early years of the rise of the woman office worker, however, had similar problems handling this genus of new woman. Unlike the nurse, she could not be conceived of in terms of caring and nurturing, traits that might give her professional role a veneer of conventional femininity. Almost inevitably, then, the typewriter's sexuality becomes an issue in fictional representations: she becomes the love interest or the temptress. While the nurse's competence is almost always important, the typewriter is commonly conceived of as being inept, which supposedly becomes part of her feminine charm, a kind of corollary to work being a misfortune for genteel young women.

JONES'S FAIR TYPEWRITER: SAVED BY THE UNDERSTUDY.

Mrs. Jones (who had a suspicion of jealousy of Jones's pretty typewriter) called on an opportune day to satisfy her curiosity. The understudy was at work.

Figure 5.1 "Jones's Fair Typewriter: Saved by the Understudy," *The Penny Illustrated Paper and Illustrated Times*, 25 July 1891, 51.
© British Library Board

COMIC REPRESENTATIONS OF THE TYPEWRITER: 1880s AND 1890s

In the late 1880s and early 1890s, the typewriter frequently figures in frankly sexist jokes and comic sketches. Employers are endlessly smitten by their pretty young secretaries; the employers' wives are endlessly jealous. In the comic poem "My Pretty Typewriter," for example, the "radiant, dashing young creature" of the title cannot punctuate or spell and "becomes tearful" when reprimanded, but is only dismissed when the speaker's wife sees her and is "filled ... with alarm."[3] A boy defines "angel" as "typewriter" for his Sunday School teacher because that is what he has heard his father call his typewriter.[4] The cartoon "Jones's Fair Typewriter: Saved by the Understudy" pictures the homely typewriting "understudy" at work when the boss's wife appears (fig. 5.1).[5] A pretty young secretary,

on accepting her employer's proposal of marriage, insists that she
be allowed to select her successor in the office.[6] Even stories with
more original comic premises still present the typewriter as either
dim-witted or alluring. A sketch with the title – at once revealing and
misleading – of "The Tantalising Typewriter" presents the typewriter
as the source of confusion that arises when an author tries to dictate
a play. The typewriter is "of all the girls the most amusing," according to this sketch. Given that the comic premise is the illogicalities
that occur when the playwright dictates without differentiating what
is dialogue, what is action, and what is punctuation, the confusion is
obviously not entirely the fault of the typewriter, although she is the
one represented as obtuse.[7]

The tables are turned to some extent in a short story entitled
"Hipple and the Fair Type Writer," in which the typewriter uses dictation to protect herself against the unwanted advances of a male
superior.[8] Alluring Mabel Fosdick is hired by the firm of Poplin and
Son to type the letters dictated by their "hypercritical correspondence clerk," Mr Hipple. The punctilious Hipple demands that Miss
Fosdick type precisely what he dictates, with "unvarying accuracy."
She is faultless in her performance – so much so that Hipple no longer
reviews the letters before having them mailed. Eventually one of the
firm's clients sends back a letter that alarms him. As the only means
available to her of revealing Hipple's harassment, Miss Fosdick has
typed the letter he dictated, complete with the personal and unwel-
come verbal advances to her that he interjects between phrases of
the business correspondence. Along with references to Miss Fosdick
being "a charming creature" with "ruby lips" and a "birdlike voice"
in these interjections are indications of outright sexual harassment.
"Why are you so cold to me?" Hipple asks, and then proceeds to
demand a kiss: "Give me just one kiss, Mabel, darling, won't you?
– one kiss now, I insist. What are you struggling for?" The upshot is
that Hipple is discharged, but the elder Mr Poplin, while expressing
anger that "a womanly and modest girl like Miss Fosdick should
be so grossly mistreated," also notes all her womanly charms and
decides to propose to her, only to discover that his son has beat him
to it. This unpleasant little story manages to insult both women and
lower-middle-class men. Hipple may be blameworthy, but the story
plays on mean-spirited prototypes of the small-minded clerk. Mabel
Fosdick may be capable, efficient, and smart – smart enough, in her
words, to "crush" the man who has persistently "annoyed … [her]

so much with his attentions and refused to desist" – but her real interest to her employers remains her physical charms. There is even a suggestion that she has played all the men to her advantage, securing for a husband the most desirable man in the firm. Mabel may be a faultless typewriter, but it is her role as femme fatale that truly defines her in this story.

Comic treatments of the marriageable typewriter girl in the 1890s frequently feature typewritten letters, texts, and the typewriting machine itself as conduits for proposals or as documentation of a relationship. A mock accounts ledger, for example, traces the evolution of the relationship between Mr Giddiboy and his typewriter, the listing in the entries starting with the cost of an advertisement for a girl to do typing, followed by the salary for the typewriter, which keeps going up sharply as her identity in the ledger changes from "typewriter," to Miss Berrington, to Daisy. Large sums for flowers, lunches, dinners, and the theatre further bloom. In between these entries are the apparent appeasements to Giddiboy's family, starting with modest outlays for "candy and bonbons for wife and children," progressing to expansive sums for a "sealskin for wife" and a "silk dress for wife's mother," and finally ending with the cost for an advertisement for a "young man to do typewriting."[9]

The trope of the typewriter as attractive young temptress and potential homewrecker underwrites this sketch, but other treatments present bachelors who simply fall for pretty typewriters and propose to them, and while the women are represented as young and attractive, they are also given other praiseworthy characteristics. A short poem recounts an incident in which an employer dictates a mock advertisement for a job, the position being wife. The advertisement, while sentimental in the extreme, nevertheless requires a young woman who is "both pretty and wise" who will be a "helpmate to save up the cash."[10] In a sketch entitled "Learning the Typewriter," Frank Wilson has "fallen in love with his pretty typewriter girl," Ruth Brent, and, "like many other men in similar positions, he was rather shy of making his tender declaration."[11] He opts for the expedient of asking Miss Brent to teach him how to use the typewriter, and once he has mastered the machine to the extent that he can manage a full sentence, types up a brief confession of love and proposal of marriage. While Miss Brent is "fair and sweet," which indeed occasions Wilson's shyness, she is also clearly skilled and patient as she teaches her undeclared suitor how to work her machine. That Wilson "goes about telling everybody that the typewriter is the most marvellous invention of the age" indeed suggests that she was not only a good teacher but has also proven to be an admirable wife.

There is, of course, great comic potential in having a shy or artless suitor use dictation or the distancing device of a mechanically produced proposal, but these clumsy manoeuvres also suggest the awkwardness of social interactions between men and women in the Victorian office, an awkwardness that is explored more fully in a story that appeared in the *Idler* in 1893. In "The Type-Written Letter," Richard Denham comes to the realization that he is rich and that he wants someone with whom to share his fortune. Having spent his life carefully building up his business, Denham is out of place anywhere but in his office. "He was familiar with the counting-room and its language," he realizes, "but the drawing-room was unexplored country to him, where an unknown tongue was spoken." [12] His typewriter, Margaret Gale, seems the obvious choice for a wife, being "the only woman in the world with whom he ... [is] on speaking terms" (599). In this story, it is the man who is inept, at least in terms of his personal life. He is "vaguely" aware that a business office is an inappropriate place to propose marriage, but he knows "he would be at a disadvantage anywhere else." The extent of his romantic assessment of Miss Gale is that she is "a modern girl" whose "light and nimble fingers played the business sonata ... on his office typewriter." He is nevertheless well aware of Miss Gale's eligibility and attractions. She is pretty but sensible, comes from a "good family who had come down in the world," and carries herself with an "independent air" that keeps mere clerks "at a distance" (599).

Since the only language Denham knows is that of the business office, he is unable to couch his proposal to Miss Gale in anything other than business terminology, and so approaches her to discuss "a business matter" (600). As it turns out, Miss Gale is fluent in the language of business, so as Denham proceeds to stumble through attempts to propose partnership, he is unable to satisfy her cautions about the other party not providing any capital or about the projected annual profits of the partnership. When Denham persists in refusing to take her advice about discussing this partnership with his chief clerk, she suggests he write a letter, which he dictates to her, she types up, and he mails. Miss Gale is alarmed about this "most unbusiness-like proposal" and further perplexed that Denham has apparently mistakenly mailed it to her home address. When he does so a second time, she fears that he is "losing his mind" (604). He suggests that she should answer the letter, that he wants her for his partner, and that he wants to marry her. She quits the offices and leaves a letter for him that begins in the same business style as his to her, stating that she is resigning her position to accept a better offer of "a partnership in the house of Richard Denham," and ends asking Denham why he had put her through "all that worry writing that stupid letter, when a few words would have saved ever so much bother?" (605).

Throughout this story, the language of business overlaps with or disrupts the language of marriage contracts – language about partnerships, (business) proposals, friendly versus business associations, and monetary considerations. The most salient disruption, however, is in the negotiations between Denham and Miss Gale over the partnership he is proposing and in her final response to his letter. While Denham recognizes his disadvantage in any milieu but the business office, Miss Gale appears to be able to negotiate both social and business interactions adroitly. She is clearly well-versed in the language of business and in office and business procedures; she cautions Denham about his "most unbusiness-like proposal" and helps him find the language to express his intentions, despite the disconnection between his presentation of those intentions and his actual goal. And while we never see Miss Gale outside of the office, her family background, her ability to keep the clerks in the office at a distance, and indeed her capacity to manoeuvre graciously and helpfully through the linguistic minefield of Denham's confusing proposal all suggest her social as well as her business finesse. Not only can she integrate the two worlds adeptly, but she also seems to be at least the equal of her employer in the business realm, as well as his superior outside of it. As she remarks to him at the conclusion of her letter of acceptance, "You evidently *need* a partner" (605).

In this story that appears at that magical moment when the typewriter was at her cultural zenith, about to tumble into the slough of overstocked markets and typewriter pools, Margaret Gale epitomizes the professionalized yet genteel middle-class woman worker. Although the text affirms that she has that essential gift of beauty without which female characters are seldom deemed interesting, her appearance is not a focus of her characterization. Except for a reference to her air of confidence, her appearance is not otherwise mentioned. Her characterization is based entirely on what she

says and on how she handles Denham and the awkward situation
in which he places her, and in this she is a perfect blend of genteel
decorum and business aplomb. She is both diplomatic and astute as
she points out the apparent problems in the business arrangements
of the partnership he proposes. Although she does ultimately accept
Denham's marriage proposal, threatening to fade into the domestic
realm, there is every indication that this union will be not be based
on sentiment. Although the story does not quite present marriage as
a business arrangement, it is nevertheless clear that Margaret Gale
will not fade out but will be at least on an equal footing in the house
of Denham, where the one thing needed is a capable partner.

A CHANGE IN PERSPECTIVE: THE TYPEWRITER'S POINT OF VIEW IN THE 1890S

In most stories and sketches from the 1880s and early 1890s – those
cited above and numerous others that appeared in the periodical
press and in provincial papers – the point of view is always that of
the male employers.[13] The reader of these narratives is made aware
of their assessments of the young women who are in their employ
and of the cultural assumptions about typewriters that these eval-
uations reflect. Even in the fairly well-defined characterization of
Margaret Gale, the closest the narrator comes to revealing her inte-
riority is to remark that she is "doubtless shocked" when Denham
uses the word "marry" in reference to the partnership he proposes
in his letter (605). As the 1890s progressed, however, stories that
present the point of view of the typewriters themselves became more
common, which resulted in representations of the women and the
work that were less romanticized and less dismissive. In "Found
by a Letter," for example, the first-person narrator is a typewriter
working in dreary circumstances.[14] While the story ends up being
bathetically sentimental – the typewriter is reunited with her old lost
love when he appears in her office wanting someone to write a letter
for him to send to his "old mother," his right hand having been lost
in an industrial accident – the situation of the typewriter is grimly
realistic. She is alone on Christmas Eve, unable to go home to her
family in the country. She works in a cold, dingy office for ten hours
a day; she is weary; her fingers and her eyes ache. Even the machine
on which she types is characterized as "cranky" and "petulant." The
world around her seems busy, but she is isolated. In this admittedly

banal narrative, the typewriter's alienation from the working world is a none-too-subtle foil for the promise of quiet domestic life with her lost love back in the country, but it nevertheless does represent a more interesting take on the typewriter and her work than that in the previous texts above. This typewriter is something other than a fixture in the Victorian office and a temptation to her male co-workers. Her work, moreover, has meaning for *her*. In this case, it is the drudgery she tolerates in order to earn a living. There is indeed nothing in the narrative about her employer or about coworkers; her work exists only as work.

Work is a central issue in what is arguably the most progressive fictional treatment of typewriting as an employment for educated women in George Gissing's *The Odd Women* (1893). The most active of the working women in the novel, Rhoda Nunn and Mary Barfoot, are themselves no longer working as typewriters, but as the administrators and instructors of a ladies' business training school that provides capable young women with the skills to earn an independent living. In addition to instruction in typewriting, Rhoda and Mary educate their students in the feminist principles of independence and of resistance to conventional ideals of femininity, in particular to the idea of restricting educated young women's employment options to accepted norms. Even nursing's hard-won respectability carries no weight with their severely progressive agenda, as Mary Barfoot makes clear in a lecture to the students. "An excellent governess, a perfect hospital nurse, do work which is invaluable; but for our cause of emancipation they are no good," Mary asserts; "nay, they are harmful. Men point to them, and say: Imitate these, keep to your proper world. – Our proper world is the world of intelligence, of honest effort, of moral strength. The old types of womanly perfection are no longer helpful to us."[15]

The focus of much of the novel is indeed on intelligence, honest effort, and moral strength, and while work is an integral part of this world, the narrative reveals very little about women's experience of work. There are some details about the circumstances of Monica Madden's situation as a shopgirl at Scotcher's, as well as about the living arrangements in the shop's dormitory, but these details are provided only to reveal how young working women are exploited and to emphasize the importance of opening up more appropriate employment opportunities for educated women. There is also some information about the arrangements of Mary and Rhoda's business school, but little about their daily working life. Work, in *The Odd Women*, functions as an idea and an ideal that promises a new but as yet unrealized world for women, a world beyond domestic and quasi-domestic realms. "There must be a new type of woman, active in every sphere of life," Mary further admonishes her students in her lecture: "A new worker out in the world, a new ruler of the home" (153).

We see very little of Mary and Rhoda as new workers, but the effects of the independence their working life enables are everywhere apparent, especially in what could be seen as new rule in the home. They live and work together, providing mutual domestic and professional support. They clearly have sufficient disposable income to enjoy a very comfortable life, although this is partly because Mary received a moderate inheritance that allowed her to establish her school. Nevertheless, the success of their school is the result of their hard work and abilities. Indeed Mary, the narrator affirms, "could have managed a large and complicated business, could have filled a place on a board of directors, have taken a part in municipal government – nay, perhaps in national" (78). Their success, their advanced education, and their cultivated style of life make them fully rounded examples of the Glorified Spinster (although their advanced ideas accord with the Strong-Minded Woman).

Mary and Rhoda's ideas and their working and living arrangements are progressive for their time, but for the Victorian reader the discussions of marriage and sexuality in the novel, and indeed its narrative trajectory, would have seemed radical. The conventional marriage plot is frustrated at every turn, either by the determination of the principal characters to avoid marriage for the sake of the ideal of the independent woman or by the disastrous failures of the marriages that do occur. Rhoda fervently believes that the cause of women's independence demands "a strained ideal," a "widespread revolt against sexual instinct" – against both love and marriage. Like any great movement, she argues, this one "for women's emancipation must also have its ascetics" (84). Although she is temporarily lured away from her sterner principles in her romance with Everard Barfoot, she ultimately understands his limitations and refuses to marry him. With the exception of the Micklethwaites' union, the marriages in *The Odd Women* are painful failures, forms of entrapment for one or both parties. Better to be an odd woman like Rhoda or Mary, the novel implies, than trapped and emotionally tortured like Monica.

In the muted conclusion of the novel, as the older Madden sisters plan the establishment of their school and Rhoda holds Monica's now motherless baby girl and murmurs "poor little child," there appears to be little that is glorious about their spinsterhoods (332). And while their strength of mind would also seem attenuated, the novel's ending suggests that in fact very great strength of mind is demanded of those who have had to face the exigencies of what being an independent woman in 1890s Britain actually requires. Coming to terms with all the demands and emotional privations of independent living is daunting, which is perhaps why, like "Found by a Letter," other stories in which the narrative perspective is that of the typewriter do not as a rule completely escape the conventional marriage plot. Like one of the characters in *The Odd Women*, authors and readers alike apparently "feel a shameful delight" when they "hear of a girl getting married" (93). Although these stories may inevitably end in marriage, they nevertheless provide some insight into the experiences of young women in Victorian offices. The sentimental ending of "Found by a Letter" may cloy, but the descriptions of workaday drudgery ring true.

BACHELOR GIRLS IN LONDON: REALISM AND ROMANCE (1890s)

A more detailed exposition of the grind of everyday life for a young typewriter occurs in Geraldine Mitton's *A Bachelor Girl in London* (1893). Contemporary reviews note the realism of this account of the experiences of a young woman, Judith Danville, who has moved from a quiet home in the country to make her way in London. She has "secret literary aspirations – at once the hope and despair," the narrator observes, "of every girl whose mind is wider than her environment" – but being intelligent and practical, she learns shorthand and typewriting as a means to earn her living.[16] One reviewer assesses the novel as depicting "the trials and struggles of a young woman in a manner that suggests that of personal experience," another that this "entertainingly realistic" portrayal presents an "example ... [that] is scarcely encouraging."[17] The narrative certainly sets out all the challenges and discouragements that a young woman seeking employment in 1890s London might face – both the difficulty of finding work and the isolation and alienation of urban living. Judith sets out with "an eager determination" to succeed. She has the advantage of a small nest egg which, "with care, would last her five weeks," but after only three weeks of making "many weary pilgrimages after appointments relating to clerkships and type-writing," she comes to understand the realities of working life and the difficulties of finding employment. She feels "overwhelmed by discovering what herds of poverty-stricken, unattached women there were in the world ... [who] were all striving and scraping in order to live decently; some had grown old and wizened in the struggle, others went sullenly on day by day, doing work which was toilsome, uncongenial, and poorly paid, hating their lives, but seeing no hope, and uncomplaining from mere want of any surplus vitality" (Mitton, 9). Judith's situation is not as desperate as that of these herds of hopeless women she encounters in her initial search for employment, no doubt because she is yet young and still has reserves of vitality to sustain her, as well as "a mind ... wider than her environment" and a drive "to be, to do, not to stagnate" (8). She also has a family contact in London, her stepmother's sister, Mrs Amoore.

Mitton represents the vicissitudes of Judith's experiences – and the very strong emotions engendered by these experiences – with a clarity and an energy that does indeed suggest, if not actual personal knowledge, then at least deep awareness and close observation of the lives of young women in Judith's situation. Judith struggles with disappointment and despair when she is unable to find work, and while she is demoralized by her poverty and isolation, she nevertheless maintains her determination to be independent. Despite the monotony and insecurity of her situation as she searches unsuccessfully for work, Judith's "iron determination" grows stronger: rather than accept defeat, she would "sooner ... sell her clothes to hang on, in the chance of something turning up, or take a place as a servant"(60). She also gains useful knowledge through her experiences; she learns "the value of money" (58) and she develops "a good working knowledge of the main parts London" (59), a city whose siren call speaks to "the hot blood in her [that] craved excitement and adventure" (21). None of her experiences reach the height of scandal that such cravings might imply, although Judith's actions are daring enough for a respectable middle-class girl. She wanders through the city alone at night, finds "never-ending delight" in riding the omnibus (101), and enjoys conversing with the drivers and conductors. Judith indeed scoffs at conventional notions of respectability and congratulates herself for "doing something quite out of the common," believing that "many women ... ran in little ruts," ruts that were merely "the outward and visible sign of respectability" (21).

Judith's notions of both excitement and respectability are nevertheless often at odds with her experiences. She may "feel a slight stirring of emotion in the new experience of being out alone in London at night" (19), she may find the "very poverty" of the workers returning home from their labours "refreshing after the sickening trivialities" of women in middle-class society (20), but she is later mortified when a policeman treats her with contempt, even though she asserts that she is "a lady" (25). On another occasion, Judith is taunted by a beggar who tells her, with a leer, that since she is "young and good-looking," she "need never know want," a clear inducement to prostitution (59). Encounters such as these leave her feeling "sullied and worn" and "oppressed with a sense of moral leprosy" (30). In the wake of her fruitless search for employment and seemingly endless rebuffs, the city's diversions are increasingly beyond her reach. In order to economize, she must forego the pleasures of the omnibus; she is depressed by the "sense of isolation in the midst of crowds," by "the taste of her monotonous food," and by "the look of her badly-papered walls" (59–60). The precarity of the bachelor girl's existence accordingly encompasses her entire being, undermining her social position and class identity as well as her financial, physical, and emotional states.

Just as she reaches the end of her meagre resources, Judith is able to secure employment – a common narrative trope in late-nineteenth-century stories about young working women. And while the quotidian details of Judith's life may be realistic, her salvation is less so. She finds work through the intervention of a social contact, one of the frivolous women Judith disparages. Judith here has an advantage unavailable to most of the young women in her position in the real world, but the assertions of her new employer, silk-merchant Edward Dasent, that he has been "three weeks without a typist" and that he "had scores of girls applying" attest to Judith's abilities and credentials, underscoring the vagaries of an overstocked job market (62). What rings completely true, whether in fact or fiction, is Judith's response to the prospect of secure employment and steady income. Her modest income of thirty shillings a week means to her "riches, comfort, luxury," and she further delights in reckoning how she will manage her budget, determining what economies would still be necessary and what small extravagances she might allow herself.

"All these details were small, petty, and of inconsiderable importance," the narrator observes, "but to her fraught with momentous consequences. She felt already the working woman, the bachelor girl of the period who owed her bread to no one, but walked fearlessly and straight on her path" (63–4).

Judith's euphoria over being employed and independent blind her to her true position as an inexperienced young woman in an unfamiliar social milieu. Despite the fact that her employer has warned her that the office does not "have any ladies" and that "we are all working men and women," Judith persists in thinking of her value as an employee being her status as "a lady," as possessing the qualities of "honesty and loyalty" peculiar to that station (62, 64). She has also lost sight of the vulnerability of her position, having "nearly forgotten" the dark night when even the policeman regarded her as a vagrant and suspicious woman, a moment characterized by the narrator as one "when the barriers between herself and the rest of sinning humanity had been swept away, and she saw herself as frail and unreliable as the weakest" (64). While this characterization belongs to the narrator, it is clear that Judith shares this perspective, one that assigns the "barrier" of moral superiority to an individual because of her class, a perspective that has been part of her identity for her entire life.

While her success in finally securing employment temporarily re-establishes Judith's sense of self, her sense of class cachet now enhanced by the conviction of strength and independence, she is in fact as vulnerable as ever. Her income is not sufficient to allow a comfortable style of life; her occasional small extravagances force renewed constraints on her daily expenditures. She finds her work both monotonous and exhausting, leaving her with no time or energy to pursue outside interests or her desire to write, and withering her newly-restored confidence. "Once again it was borne on her," the narrator observes, "that she was only one of the crowd, nothing grander or more heroic than the toiling multitude amongst whom she lived; but the lesson would have to be repeated many times ere she knew it by heart" (89). Her loneliness leads her to establish a friendship with Lex, the charming but reprobate brother of the same socialite who helped her to find work. Judith confesses to Lex that she is "weary of the monotonous drab of every-day existence" (140), and it is this weariness with her straitened circumstances that leaves her vulnerable to Lex's manipulation. While feigning empathy with her situation – he, too, he asserts, must work in an office – he tempts her with the prospect of effortlessly obtaining £10. A friend of his, he claims, bet him that her employer Dasent makes over £2,000 a year, which could be proven if she could find evidence, through a letter or an invoice, that he received £50 in any one week (178).[18] Judith initially demurs, but, after several additional weeks of loneliness and penury, produces the required document, only to discover that there was no bet, but only a plan to obtain information about Dasent's business dealings. Dasent eventually figures out what has happened and Judith is "dismissed in disgrace" (282).

As the reviewer in the *Graphic* opined, Judith's experiences present an "example ... [that] is scarcely encouraging." Reflecting on her situation, Judith acknowledges that she has found work "soul-crushing" and "hard" (309), but what she finds most distressing is her susceptibility to dishonourable conduct. "How immeasurably had she fallen in one year!" she laments. "She had been bribed and betrayed her trust; had made bad companions; she had feared to tell her employer when his goods were in danger" (292). What stands out in these comments and in the story itself is the extent to which the bachelor girl pays for the independence and potential excitement of living on her own in the city. Even before her "fall," Judith confides to her sister that she has gained "worlds of experience ... in London," but at the expense of becoming "mean and narrow and sordid" and of losing "hope and heart." "I'm covered with smuts," she laments, "and I've lost things that I can never get back" (168). These references to a fall, to sordidness, and to irredeemable loss draw strong parallels between her experiences and sexual incontinence, as if her enjoyment of riding omnibuses and other minor pleasures of the city were scandalous responses to "the hot blood in her [that] craved excitement and adventure" (21). Judith comes to believe that independence, like sexual indiscretion, destroys the refined feminine character: "the strong-handed, capable woman of thick boots and short skirts, whose life was a burden to no one, must yield the gentler, finer qualities, the atmosphere of a graceful, refined elegance could not be distilled by her" (170–1). Near the end of the novel, Judith again expresses her sense of loss, confessing to Weston, the sympathetic and sensitive son of her stepmother's sister, "I am not half so good as when I came up to Town, I have lost things I can never regain – ideals, beliefs, and hopes and enthusiasms" (314).

These repeated allusions to the socially ruinous states of being lost or fallen and the "scarcely encouraging" tale of the experiences of a bachelor girl in which they are imbedded are no doubt at some level a set of warnings to any energetic and eager young women considering the option of independent urban life. Judith's story could indeed be read as an illustration of that cherished Victorian canard that work in the public sphere destroys a woman's refinement and femininity. With all the advantages of intelligence, diligence, and some family connections, Judith not only failed but was degraded by her experience. But the story does not end in her ruin. Judith, like almost all Victorian female protagonists, is destined for marriage, albeit one that embodies a particularly strained version of the ideal Victorian union of the masculine and the feminine. Her suitor, the mildly cynical Lawrence Pitt, who has previously lived a selfish life, and Judith, the woman who is sullied by the exigencies of independent life, miraculously restore each other's virtue, transformed by their mutual declaration of love: "The sordid, stained creature, whose reflection she had grown used to look for the in the mirror of her mind, had vanished, and she stood reincarnate once more, a strong, pure woman, sanctified by the privilege of her greatest gift, the power of raising and ennobling man" (339). But this egregiously bathetic ending, slavishly bound as it is to conventional Victorian notions of ideal sexual relations, cannot completely override the other messages woven through the story. The socialites in the novel repeatedly appear shallow by comparison with Judith, who is earnest and hard-working. Even the most frivolous of Judith's relatives and acquaintances recognize the commitment her independence entails. Weston, at one point, characterizes office work, as compared to superficial social engagement, as "something real" (74). And the worldly Lawrence Pitt, on seeing her some months after their first meeting shortly after her arrival in London, recognizes that "from a vigorous girl she had passed into a self-possessed woman" (243). Judith, in other words, has grown up, a fate from which the idealized Victorian girl is protected. In the end, for a "girl whose mind is wider than her environment" (8), and for all the other girls whose minds are similarly primed to escape the shackles of Victorian propriety, freedom is worth the cost of a few city smuts.

Grant Allen's version of the typewriter's marginality in *The Type-Writer Girl* (1897) makes light of the challenges faced by young women embarking on white-collar careers. Juliet Appleton, the twenty-two-year-old protagonist, embodies the conventional characteristics of her fictional type, i.e., a young woman embarking on an independent life. She is intelligent and well-educated, but she has been orphaned and left penniless. Like so many others in her position – whether in fact or fiction – she sets out with great hope and enthusiasm. She has "taken pains to learn shorthand and type-writing," not realizing that these skills had been mastered by "every girl in London."[19] The wages Juliet can command may be meagre, but her typewriter is nevertheless the instrument of her independence. When she finds the work dull and the atmosphere in the legal office in which she works misogynistic, her typewriter secures her freedom: she pawns it and joins an anarchist commune in the countryside. When she decides to return to London, she redeems the typewriter and resumes her role as typewriter girl.

Because Juliet's tale is comic, Allen is not at pains to depict the everyday drudgery of either her work or her domestic life. The drudgery merely supplies Juliet with opportunities for farcical attempts to shake off the "fustiness and mustiness" in the clerical world by, for example, enlivening the prose of legal documents with "a greater variety of graphic adjectives such as 'amethystine,' 'prismatic,' 'opalescent,' 'empyrean,' or even 'colossal'" (35, 33). In her first-person narrative, Juliet constructs her world imaginatively in the genres of high romance and adventure.[20] She characterizes the men and women who people her world as the heroes and villains of history, epics, and romances – Old Testament stories, tales of Oriental potentates, classical mythology, opera, and Shakespearean plays. The identities Juliet assigns to other characters indicate the extent to which they are part of her comic fantasies: the chief clerk in the first office in which she works is the Grand Vizier, her charming employer in the second office is Romeo. Juliet's story accordingly provides little insight into the limited life of a typewriter girl; Juliet is simply unconstrained by reality. The idea that a typewriter might be the agent of liberty, however, is central to her story. She admits to her poverty, but remains buoyed by her independence. And while she interprets her life through the lens of romance, she does not in the end succumb to the traditional romantic ending. Juliet neither dies for nor marries her Romeo, but leaves him to her rival in love and moves on to another office.

Juliet seems to exhibit none of the vulnerability that is the essence of Judith's inability to secure an entirely happy and successful independence as a bachelor girl. There is an intimation of potential trouble, however, when the "Oriental leer" of her employer drives her from the office and indeed from his employment (35). Juliet's security, like that of many young office workers, is vulnerable to the presumptions of male entitlement. Vulnerability as a young woman seeking employment and independence in London is similarly the fate of Ione March, the eponymous protagonist of an 1899 novel by Samuel Rutherford Crockett. Ione, too, is challenged by the inevitability of confronting personal frustrations and compromising circumstances, although her situation is quite different from either Judith's or Juliet's. Ione comes from a background of wealth, privilege, and influence and so has led a less restricted life than Judith or Juliet has. The only child of widowed American millionaire and diplomat Henry Quincy March, Ione moves to London after an extensive stay in a Swiss resort. Her spirit and self-confidence are established by her recent decision to break her engagement to a wealthy young man who has proved cowardly and dishonourable, a more prosaic form of freethinking credentials than Judith's literary aspirations, to be sure, but a telling challenge to Victorian matrimonial dictates nonetheless. Ione's driving desire is to escape a life "swaddled in cotton wool," a life she deems "dead" and "useless." Like Judith, Ione is determined to make her own living, even if it means being reduced to taking on menial tasks. "I would rather sell flowers on the street," she tells her father, "I would rather peddle candy on a train, than go on like this."[21]

Unlike *A Bachelor Girl in London*, *Ione March* could never be considered a realist novel. Ione herself is much too good to be true, able to turn her hand successfully to just about any task. She is at various times in the narrative an exemplary typewriting and shorthand clerk, a promising actress, a gifted floral arranger, and an efficient and sympathetic nurse, having trained for three months and having in addition "been through a season's cholera in an Italian city" (258). Ione's story and many of its details are, moreover, highly romanticized. Ione finds nothing but joy in work and wonders how her father could "know the happiness of work himself, and yet deny it to ... his only daughter" (91). Even as she realizes she must leave her first typewriting situation, she is nevertheless inspired by being part of the working world; she aestheticizes drudgery, finding that the "sounds and scents of this world of hard-working millions" are "like notes in a song to her" (112). When she is once more employed, the same routines that weary and discourage other young women work like a tonic on Ione. She puts on "fresh bloom and beauty" and the narrator goes so far as to compare her state of joy at having "a purpose and a career" to the "loveliness which comes to most women when they fall deeply … in love" (141). While this rather jarring comparison may be an adroit reversal of conventional expectations, it does not reflect the real experiences of young women at the time, although it does effectively set up the more common experiences of shattered hopes and dreams that confront Ione. And the shattering of these hopes and dreams is the result of the same difficulty faced by Judith and most real-life bachelor girls – vulnerability. Although Ione is characterized as more attuned than Judith to the commercial world – Judith laments the difficulty that "girls have no business training"[22] while Ione has "learned from her father that business is sacrosanct" (132) – she is nonetheless unprepared for the culture of the Victorian office and the pitfalls it presents.

Ione's progress through several working positions is generally implausible, but some of the individual situations have a disconcerting ring of truth. She finds her first position in a company from which she had previously ordered typewriters on behalf of her father and is naively untroubled by the fact that she is hired on the spot and immediately given a choice workspace, "seated beside a beautiful new machine, close by one of the largest windows of a wide City office" (90). Ione may not understand the implications of her apparent good luck, but her fellow typists do, and she must contend with the strained politics of the workplace, which are underwritten by the exigencies of the job market. The other girls clearly dislike her and call her a cuckoo because, as one of the other girls tartly explains to Ione,

> you have been "planted" upon us. Oh, we know all about it at the Gopher & Arlington. We've been there before. You don't earn your own living. A gentleman came and arranged about you with the manager. He, and not the company, pays your wages. That isn't any pound-a-week dress. These aren't pound-a-week shoes! No, nor what you have got at the end of that gold chain under your dress – that's no pound-a-week locket … If you are square, then you don't need the work. Or else you come to improve, so that you may undersell us, and cut our rates for the sake of a little extra pocket-money. You take the bread out of somebody's mouth – you that don't need it. (95)

Crockett presents here a not uncommon complaint against middle-class women who entered the workforce, and with a plainspoken vigour that captures the resentment and indeed the anger no doubt felt by many desperate young women who had no resources other than their ability to earn a meagre living. This incident captures, in other words, the pain of exploitation, both of Ione and of the impoverished young women with whom she works. The young typewriters are understandably outraged by what they see as Ione's deceit, her intrusion into their world as an imposter, and her appropriation of the limited resources so desperately needed by other young women like them. Ione is crushed by their vehemence and demoralized by the knowledge that it was her father's interference that secured her employment and even her wages, denying her the independence she so earnestly seeks. As with Mary Marvin in *Thicker Than Water*, whose employment and wages were provided by the kindly Mr Rennie, Ione's independence is a sham.

Ione's second position as a typewriter seems full of promise. She exchanges her expensive tweed suits for cheap serge (126) and seems to fit right into the workaday world. She is so absorbed by work – she can "think of nothing else" as she transforms dictated letters into "perfectly transcribed and typewritten" ones (142) – that she is oblivious to another form of exploitation developing in her new place of work. She fails to note the first subtle and then blatant sexual harassment to which she is subjected; the improper attention from the clerks or business callers in the office, the "glances and covert innuendoes, nods, winks, and wreathed smiles," which she heeds "no more than the noisy chaff of the street" (142). She is no more alarmed when her employer, Mr Shillabeer – referred to by his disrespectful clerks as Porky – also pays her attention. He extends the hours of work to be near her longer, "and if at times the hand of the master rested longer than was necessary beside her own, it affected her no more that if the speaking tube of the official phonograph had fallen momentarily across her arm. Both were the exigencies of business, accidents of independence" (142). Ione also does not object when Shillabeer asks her to work on Sunday, but his clerks, one of whom has found out about Ione's background and knows that her father and her former fiancé are trying to find her, suspect that their employer has ulterior motives. They develop a plan to spy on Shillabeer and Ione and, at the opportune moment, save her and deliver her to her family, who the clerks assume will pay them in gratitude. As they wait for some indication that Shillabeer will make a move on Ione, one of the clerks reminds the other that "this is only the first act. Porky is playing his own game for all it is worth. By-and-by he'll give himself away. He simply can't help it. You know Porky as well as I do! Then the lady will be 'insulted,' and fling up her job in a huff" (153). That the clerks "know Porky ... well," that they know the "game" he is playing and what will happen next, suggests that Porky has played this game before, that there is a pattern to his exploitation and to its results – a young woman being forced to give up her position and lose her livelihood. What actually ensues is that Shillabeer is so entranced by Ione that he proposes marriage, but the result is the same: she is forced to leave her position.

As with almost all the nubile young typewriters in Victorian fiction, Ione eventually finds happiness in marriage, and indeed it seems almost impossible for authors at the time to imagine a story that leaves a competent and likable young office worker single. A potential exception to this rule appears in *The Craftsman* (1897), in which twenty-eight-year-old Melita Frayne has worked contentedly for three years in "a self-supporting, business-like concern" run by benevolent and ladylike Miss Urquhart. Miss Urquhart appears to be a model employer to whom Melita is only "one of many" owing her "a quite limitless debt." For Melita, work is fulfillment – "to work at something had always been her ideal of happiness." And typewriting, moreover, is not drudgery for her; indeed, as the narrator affirms, it was "probably because it was so very lowly" an occupation that Melita "had found it satisfactory when it came to her. It had opened a vista of fresh ideas. She saw new faces every day, and to the observant this is in some sort an education of itself."[23]

Melita's situation echoes that of Monica Madden when she studied typewriting and business with Mary Barfoot and Rhoda Nunn, thereby obtaining, the narrator of *The Odd Women* asserts, the only "real education she had ever received" (Gissing, 183). One of the new faces Melita sees every day entrances her, however, and even though she also demurely assures him that she holds her "humble typing as ... [her] object in life," the narrator confesses that this is a "womanly lie [told] quite as if she believed it" (Grey, 48). Melita throws over her avowed "ideal of happiness" – work – for the conventional Victorian ideal of happiness – marriage – leaving the reader with only the shadowy Miss Urquhart as the symbol of female independence.

A more substantial version of the independent female appears in George Brown Burgin's *Settled Out of Court* (1898). This novel also presents the starkly dual characterizations of the typewriter that appears in the verses at the opening of this chapter – the flighty temptress and the earnest professional. Pretty but irresponsible Mary Martlock receives roses from Aylmer Chase, one of the partners in the firm in which both young women work, but she complains that, if he wants to dictate a letter, she must "trudge up and down those narrow stairs" and get her skirt "quite spoilt by brushing against the dirty walls."[24] Edna, by contrast, not only works diligently in the office, but devotes much of her spare time to typing at home in support of good causes, even at times pawning her typewriter "whenever she had no money, and people appealed to her for help" (78–9). Mary complains that Edna is "painfully industrious," while Edna is concerned only to "get this [typewriting piece work] done to-night" so that she "can redeem Mrs. Pat Gallagher's flannel petticoat" (107–8). While Chase courts Mary, he admires Edna. "You are good enough to redeem all the women who ever sinned," he tells her, but he nevertheless chooses Mary for his wife (321). The text makes clear that Edna is in love with Chase and must bury "in her pure breast the one romance of her life" when Chase and Mary are united (322). In terms of the conventional marriage plot, Edna's fate is gloomy, but in terms of celebrating the capable and productive professional woman, she is triumphant.

Despite Edna's success as a professional woman, her fate in terms of the narrative of *Settled Out of Court* remains affectively ambivalent for all but the most orthodox feminist readings. This difficulty with presenting the professional woman as truly womanly or as entirely fulfilled continues to bedevil representations of the typewriter as the nineteenth century comes to a close. Approval for Edna's professionalism is underwritten by the charitable objectives of her work outside of the office and by her unrequited feelings for Chase; the reader feels pity for Edna, which in itself feminizes her. Similar problems underlie virtually every version of the typewriter outlined above, but by the 1890s, a fairly consistent pattern has developed in which the typewriter conventionally personifies the complex of irreconcilable characteristics that the middle-class professional woman presents to Victorian sensibilities. If her merit in the professional realm has not revealed her as a woman worthy of marrying in the closing pages of her narrative, the typewriter must validate her womanliness by means of an unfulfilled or unrequited love, as Edna does. A similar fate awaits Linda Grey, the rather severe young typewriter in Dorothy Leighton's *Disillusion* (1894), who believes that "love is such a miserable, selfish thing; it absorbs people and destroys work."[25] She responds to the assertion of the male protagonist, Mark Sergison, that "love is humanity's best endeavour" with a curt "Work, Mark, is our creed" (I: 10). Linda is nonetheless in an enviable position. She works in the City; her hours are "regular and not over-long" and her evenings are "entirely her own" (I: 20). She is, moreover, "used to going about by herself, accustomed to being independent" (I: 48). However, when Mark's flighty and irresponsible wife abandons him and their young son, Leo, Linda agrees to take charge of his care with the result that the young woman who "was essentially a non-domestic woman" who "detested cooking or washing" (III: 45) develops intense maternal feelings for her young charge. On an evening when Mark and Linda are caring for the boy together, they share a passionate embrace and Linda's face is immediately "transfigured with a sudden joy that had melted all the lines and softened the features which usually looked hard and severe" (III: 169). Linda accordingly becomes a convert to conventional Victorian womanhood, now believing that "no woman was truly alive until she had known the ecstasy of human love" (III: 203). There is a noteworthy twist in this feminization of the professional working woman: when the wayward wife returns, it is not the loss of Mark's love that Linda mourns, but the loss of Leo, the "vision of maternal joys [that were] opened to her only to be destroyed again as soon as beheld" (III: 226).

Maternal feeling may trump romantic love as the more potent feminizing force in *Disillusion*, but both that novel and *Settled Out of Court* share a significant subtextual theme. In both works, the rejected working women are demonstrably superior to the wives the male protagonists choose; they are superior as workers and they are superior as Victorian women. Aylmer Chase and Mark Sergison clearly marry the wrong women. John Fulford's 1899 novel, *Some Unoffending Prisoners*, turns this premise on its head. Dorothy (Dolly) Hammond is a young woman from an undistinguished family who is engaged to Lawrence Rhodes, a man of birth and breeding. He subsequently falls in love with a woman whose background is similar to his own, but who is unhappily married to a Casaubonesque rector. Dolly is no match for her rival, Doris, in terms of intelligence, sophistication, and indeed womanliness, but she is nevertheless portrayed sympathetically. Dolly is in fact a fairly realistic representation of a young office worker near the end of the nineteenth century. The narrator sums up her situation succinctly in a single phrase: "Dolly was a type-writer," which condemns her to being "one of a class that must work rapidly and correctly, at once with hands and head, and hear the incessant repetition of a peculiarly irritating noise, with Stoic composure." She works long hours for little pay under the sharp eye of an employer who is "exacting in her demands upon her young employees." And while Dolly is not "particularly fond of her work," she does it conscientiously and is uncomplaining about her situation.[26] Whatever the strains of her work, Dolly identifies the standard attractions – it is "far better than being a governess" and there is "a certain independence about the life, despite the hard work and the long hours of close confinement" (31). And Dolly also exhibits stoic composure in her personal life, having been engaged for two years to Lawrence (273).

The by now standard mechanisms of work defeminizing the working woman and of love feminizing her do not apply in Dolly's case, or at least not in conventional ways. Dolly is both a type-writer and affianced at the outset of the narrative and she is never portrayed as unfeminine. She is, however, depleted and rendered less desirable because of her work, but not by the nature of the work itself. It is the physical circumstances of work, the long hours and the insalubrious conditions, that undermine her attractiveness and consequently her womanliness. Her youth and beauty are eroded by the effects "of indoor confinement and arduous duties," which result in "her face ... getting somewhat thin, her delicate features becoming, though ever so slightly, too accentuated for a girl of twenty." Her overall appearance and deportment are also marred by poor pay and working conditions: "Her dress ... [is] not only plain but shabby" and she walks "with the inelastic, rather lagging step of a person fatigued, or used to fatigue" (30). As her rival in love, Doris, affirms, there is "no false halo of romance, ideality, or illusion" about Dolly's working life, but Dolly's personal life is about to take on the features of romance and tragedy. Dolly and Doris have become acquainted through a chance encounter, and have no idea about their mutual interest in Lawrence until they both happen to call on him at the same time. They both reject him as a result, but Dolly then sees Doris and Lawrence together walking along Oxford Street. In despair, she throws herself in front of an omnibus. Although she recovers from her injuries, life for the three trapped in this love triangle quickly unravels. Lawrence feels obliged to marry Dolly, but becomes unhinged and assaults her. Lawrence is arrested, Dolly is bereft, and Doris has to return to her rector husband – all, it would seem, unoffending prisoners of fate.

THE TYPEWRITER AS CULTURAL SYMBOL

What is perhaps most curious about *Some Unoffending Prisoners* is Doris's initial reaction to meeting Dolly and visiting her place of work – that place of "no false halo of romance, ideality, or illusion" (67). Although always at least a bit condescending towards Dolly, Doris is curious about her profession. "Type-writing is only a name to me," she tells Dolly. "You must tell me a little bit about it." Doris then asserts that she is "so glad to have seen a real, live type-writer" (46). Doris's response suggests the general understanding of the typewriter at the time – familiarity with the phenomenon without any real awareness of what the work or the life of the typewriter entailed. The typewriter existed in the Victorian imagination as a kind of cultural symbol, the ubiquitous exemplum of a modern young woman, embarking on an independent (usually urban) life. This referential capacity of the typewriter is evident in fiction that appears near the end of the century. When three sisters, in *The Daughters of Job* (1894), determine to strike "against their fate" and free themselves from the oppression they feel in their father's home, that one of them supports herself through typewriting seems inevitable.[27] In Richard Marsh's *The House of Mystery* (1898), the profession of the protagonist, Madeleine Orme, is established in the opening pages of the narrative, before she is whisked away to strange adventures in a gothic house and a very gothic story, never to type again. Marsh represents the darkest version of the life of a typewriter. Madeleine is overworked, underpaid, and mistreated. As she affirms later in the story, she is "a typist, a girl somewhere on the same level as a seamstress … [whose] whole life has been a struggle for bread … [who suffered] insult and contumely, work and weariness, hunger and despair … [along] with hundreds and thousands of other girls, better and cleverer" than she.[28] While Madeleine is thus portrayed as impoverished and exploited, her identity as a typewriter nevertheless confirms her modernity, her capabilities, and even her relative independence. She not only demonstrates all the initiative required of a young lady in a gothic plot, but also affirms that being a typewriter in 1890s London still has attractions that being trapped in a gothic setting does not. "Outside," she comments, "I might have a chance to become the mistress of my own fate" (80).

In Ménie Muriel Dowie's *The Crook of the Bough* (1898), the typewriting machine itself comes to stand in for a set of cultural assumptions about the young women who operate them. The protagonist, Islay Netherdale, supports the work of her brother George, who is a member of Parliament, by working unofficially as his secretary. Islay is a "well-trained, well-educated girl" and an "unusually good student of French and German," whose typewriting becomes the emblem of women's professional work.[29] The reader never witnesses her typing, but the machine is a ubiquitous presence whose physical location and appearance alter, representing Islay's changing attitude towards work and independence. As Islay devolves from a serious and energetic working woman, knowledgeable in the political discourse she transcribes, into "merely a pretty English girl," her typewriter, although always present, figures less and less prominently in her physical surroundings (296). Even at its most conspicuous, however, the typewriter is never completely present, as if presaging Islay's eventual rejection of her working life. It is at first semivisible, "hooded in its ugly little desk" in her London rooms (27). Later, when Islay and George go on a diplomatic tour of Europe, the typewriter travels with them, along with their luggage, "hooded like a falcon" (38). As they travel farther from home, Islay's gradual defection from working life is signalled by her mounting disregard for the typewriter, which "continued to be hooded, and his suggestive ringing of his bell when moved from floor to chair and finally to the stovetop in Islay's bedroom, continued to be disregarded" (38–9). When Islay and George return to London, the typewriter is so disguised that George can no longer see it; Islay has consigned it to a small study and placed a gold lacquered pot over it. She sends her brother's work out to a local typewriting office.

The use of the language of falconry to characterize the typewriter in this text works as a curiously displaced version of professional work as defeminizing. The typewriter itself takes the place of the falcon, a bird of prey in the control of the falconer, the operator of the machine. While this analogy imaginatively confers mastery to the female typist, the machine over which she holds sway is a predator.

It is, moreover, aesthetically unpleasing, its hood ugly. While Islay continues to have command over the machine, in that she keeps it hooded and ignores the bell that announces its location, her studied neglect of the typewriter suggests fear of its power, a power that could be transformative and, ultimately, unfeminine; it is no accident that the typewriter is referred to throughout with masculine pronouns. The eventual banishment of the typewriter to a back room, its ugliness and potential utility masked by a gold lacquered pot, reifies Islay's retreat from professionalism and her embracing of conventional Victorian femininity as "merely a pretty English girl." Islay's attempt to disguise the typewriter, because, she tells her brother, it "is so very ugly, somehow," prompts him to advise her sardonically to "gold-lacquer him" (240). Islay is here and elsewhere in the closing chapters of the novel challenged and even openly criticized for her return to conventional womanliness. Her reaction is one with which many young women at the end of the nineteenth century likely struggled. "But which," Islay asks her friend Grahame (whose very name announces how thoroughly modern and professionalized a young woman *she* is) "is the real 'me'?" (298).

THOROUGHLY MODERN MINNIE AND THE THREAT OF PROGRESS (1900)

The lingering cultural uneasiness with the middle-class professional woman permeates *In the Crook of the Bough*. There is something like nostalgia for an outmoded version of womanliness, along with guarded admiration for professionalism. The uneasiness with the successful working woman colours a story published two years later in very different hues. "Beyond the Gray Gate," by Alice Dudeney, tells the story of Nat Chaytor, a City clerk, and his wife, Minnie. The narrator is a friend of Nat's who clearly dislikes Minnie, describing her as "one of those small, sharp-featured, rasping-voiced girls, with an ineffaceable sneer on her lips" – "one of those" implying that she is a type that is not uncommon.[30] The narrator represents Nat sympathetically, but it is obvious that he is lazy and ineffectual in his job and it is unsurprising that he is dismissed. He tries to write for periodicals, his lack of success blamed on Minnie; she has "carefully cleaned and oiled her typewriter" and taken in copying work, but the "quick clinkety-clank of the typewriter tormented Chaytor; he hated machinery." Minnie is perhaps understandably a bit testy about his objections, asking "where would he be if it were not for machines?" since it is her intense labour that sustains them (205–6).

Chaytor, the narrator observes, is not "really fit for this work-a-day world" (206). That Minnie is so makes her not just unsympathetic, but reprehensible, at least in the eyes of the narrator. Her working persona is driven and uncompromising and, in Victorian terms, unwomanly. But if Minnie has been defeminized, it has not been because of work but because of need. Her typewriter, like Islay's, is unseemly in the domestic setting; it is ugly to look at, its action distressing to hear. What really disturbs Chaytor and the narrator is progress. They long for the world "beyond the gray gate," an idyllic version of a pastoral past – a place "away from machines," without "even the shriek of a railway engine" – that Chaytor wanders into one April afternoon (215). Even Minnie is charmed by Chaytor's descriptions of this peaceful oasis he believes he has found, but which they are never able to locate again. The vilification of Minnie, underscored by this nostalgia for the past, denotes distrust or even fear of modernization. Chaytor's death, hastened by his despair over his inability to find the gray gate again, signals the irretrievability of the past and of an illusory arcadia. Minnie's subsequent return to modernity is represented in disparaging terms by the narrator, who notes that, after returning to work as a typist in a City office, she opportunistically marries her employer "in less than a year." "She was always the sort of girl to do well for herself," the narrator sneers; "her marriage with Chaytor was an aberration. She lives in a very swagger house at East Croydon, wears rather loud dresses, and talks persistently of 'my cook'" (230–1). This degraded version of the marriage plot implies the meanness of modernity. The "delicately tinted, coquettish girl" that Chaytor remembers courting was transformed into "a shrewish woman" by the demands of modern economics and has ended up as a vulgar and pretentious one (208). She is not, like the attractive typewriters before her, a nubile young woman to be rescued from the hardship of a marginal existence by marriage to her benevolent employer. She is, rather, used goods and she is on the make, marrying precipitously for security and position.

But what is it about Minnie that demands such a negative characterization? It is perhaps that she represents all the threatening potential of a competent professional woman. In many ways, she is revolutionary, in that she is able to move between the roles of working woman and wife. This is a new kind of social mobility, suggesting an even greater level of freedom for women than merely the ability to postpone or eschew marriage. Minnie's ability to work at home, not uncommon with other fictional typewriters, also carries a new threat in that she is undermining the sanctum sanctorum of Victorian culture, the marital home, disrupting its peace – literally – with "the quick clinkety-clank" of her typewriter (206). The angst of a culture on the brink of a new century, wary of change and pained by loss of a half-remembered past, is here off-loaded onto the slender back of the beleaguered typewriter.

At the end of the nineteenth century, gender trouble continues to plague the figure of the typewriter. She nevertheless remains the symbol of hope for an independent life for some young women, but only a constrained hope, tempered by the realities of a life that is sustained by meagre wages and that is threatened with insecurity. As a cultural figure, she remains caught between professionalism and womanliness, either too professional to be feminine or too feminine to be professional. If a typewriter has the womanliness to become a wife, she ceases to work. If she keeps working, she is either a shadowy figure like Miss Urquhart in *The Craftsman* or a sad and disappointed one, like Linda Grey in *Disillusion*. If she manages to remain working, and yet assert her femininity, she becomes a disruptive figure, an unfamiliar sexual type, like Rhoda Nunn, or a scorned scapegoat, like Minnie Chaytor.

"What Shall We Do with Our Daughters?": The Women's Press and the Mainstream Media in the 1890s

MARKETING THE WOMAN WORKER

The challenges of forging the new identity of the middle-class working woman in the Victorian period had led to significant progress in promoting women's employment. Nurses in particular had gained status, but the overly rapid development of the typewriter had led to some of the worst employment practices of women's sweated labour finding their way into this promising new area of endeavour. The consequent rapid devaluation of the woman office worker left many women facing relative poverty in the short run and the possibility of an uncertain future as one of the destitute aging women of Frances Low's reckoning, as outlined in her "How Poor Ladies Live."[1] The ideal of the successful career woman nevertheless prevailed in the women's press, which continued to support the cause of the middle-class working woman and to challenge negative cultural assumptions about women's roles and capabilities. At the forefront of these efforts to support the success of the woman worker was the *Queen*, which had developed into a strong advocate for middle- and upper-middle-class working women over the course of the 1870s, '80s, and '90s. The mounting interest in women's work in the culture at large had been reflected in the number of articles and reports that appeared in the *Queen* and in the sheer quantity of inquiries from readers, which prompted the paper's management to establish an Employment Department and to introduce the Women's Employment column in 1889. As well as articles on various kinds of work, this new column featured an extensive question and answer service, providing information and advice about work and training to readers.

The no-nonsense tenor of the entries in this column is in keeping with the troubling realities of the labour market for middle-class women at the dawn of the last decade of the nineteenth century; as with other organs of the women's press, the *Queen* never failed to recognize and emphasize the social urgency of these issues and the large numbers of women affected. The demand for education and commitment that had been the rallying call for women to professionalize so that they would be fit to work now became the rallying call to protect professionalized women from the devaluation of their work and their careers. Despite the diminishing prestige of typewriting, the *Queen* used its lingering associations with technology and skill to continue to represent the typist as an icon of professionalism, leading the list of "women of education" for whom "an employment bureau ... is emphatically needed" – "thoroughly trained women, such as type-writers, clerks, shorthand-writers, journalists, printers, saleswomen, &c."[2] The level of commitment to education and training advocated by Marian Marshall and other *Queen* correspondents indeed aligns typists with masculine rather than feminine values. Female typists and correspondence clerks "must prepare for their calling quite as earnestly as their brothers do for professions," Marshall urges, "by educating themselves and going through a business training."[3] Another *Queen* correspondent posits that in many cases, a "daughter is more likely to follow in the father's than in the mother's steps. ... The girl has, in fact, her way to make in the world, as her father had his."[4]

The rallying call for standards and professionalism was sounded repeatedly, along with favourable comparisons of women's work with men's, comparisons that were both implicit and explicit. Outstanding models of female professionalism, for example, were the focus of an 1893 series entitled "Professional Women on Their Professions," which features interviews with prominent women in careers ranging from nursing to male preserves such as stockbroking. The leader for 2 July 1898 argues that the "increase of women dependent on their own exertions renders their training for some remunerative occupation imperative." The editor observes that the "employment of women in various occupations has made the most astonishing progress during the last few decades," noting that women "hold their own with their competitors of the other sex" in typing and shorthand.[5] The endorsement of work and of masculine work ethics eventually produces a reevaluation of conventional

domesticity and gender roles by the *Queen*'s contributors and correspondents in the Employment column. Perhaps the most radical
position regarding women and work to appear in the pages of the
Queen was Margaret Bateson's in an 1899 article entitled "Marriage
and Occupation," in which she advocates that women continue to
work after marriage. "If the occupation pursued before marriage has
been a good one," Bateson argues, " – has been anything that might
be denoted as a liberal profession – surely married and family life
stand to gain enormously."[6]

The establishment of the Employment Department in 1889 was
a source of pride to the paper's management. This department, the
editor reflects in 1897 with great satisfaction, "was the first of its
kind in the newspaper world."[7] What generated this initiative and
sustained the column for the remainder of the nineteenth century
was the interest and needs of women throughout England, women
eager for help and advice and women eager to help those in need of
work. The employment editor acknowledges that she was "indebted
to readers of the *Queen*" for alerting her about "various openings
for employment which they think that women might fill."[8] The flow
of inquiries about work, according to the employment editor of the
Queen, was substantial and persistent. And while it is impossible
to know precisely what the numbers of inquiries actually were,[9]
the reality of the demand for information about work and for help
in finding work is indicated by the fact that several other ladies'
periodicals followed the *Queen*'s lead and weighed in on the discourse of work. Similar in both format and demographic to the
Queen, the *Lady's Pictorial* published articles on work directed to
the needs and interests of women in the middle classes and higher.
These articles, many of which appear in a regular column on wom-
en's work, present the same kinds of employments as suitable for
ladies, with nursing, teaching, and typewriting and other office
work offering the most viable options. The *Lady's Realm* showed
less interest in work, at least in employments that could provide
sufficient income to allow independence. The column "Incomes for
Ladies" seems directed to the dilettante – ladies who want to dab-
ble in the decorative arts, for example – rather than to the aspiring
professional, although articles on nursing and medicine do appear
at the end of the century. The *Englishwoman* espoused progressive attitudes towards education and women's rights, but initially
showed only sporadic interest in employment, with more emphasis

on "stage stars" rather than on work that might afford its readers an independent living. In a dramatic move in 1898, however, the *Englishwoman* launched a registration service, "calculated to facilitate communication between Employers and Ladies in search of employment."[10] Subsequent issues ran long lists of notices – in some cases with an accompanying photograph – from ladies offering their services, most typically as governess or secretary, as well as a series on "Occupations for Women." While the readership of these periodicals would have been predominantly middle class and higher on the social scale, the correspondence about work indicates that women from fairly modest backgrounds read and used the employment advice and services. The *Queen* remained at the forefront of efforts to champion the new career woman, the results of which were a source of gratification to the employment editor. "The extremely appreciative and grateful letters which correspondents have sent us have amply rewarded our efforts," she reports, "and have offered a more than sufficient stimulus to further exertion."[11] This further exertion was considerable – the establishment of the Employment Consultation Bureau (1897), which provided individual interviews to advise ladies seeking work.

The need for and ultimate success of the employment departments and bureaus sponsored by women's periodicals were driven by the engagement of ordinary women – the readers of the paper – trying to secure fulfilling and suitable employment. Market pressures of various kinds might be working against satisfactory employment opportunities for many women, but women were actively engaged in mutual efforts to mitigate the threats to their collective success as career women: those who needed help and advice were actively seeking it out and those who could provide support and assistance were doing so. Women had in a very real sense done what James Hinton had called on women in nursing to do a generation earlier – they had changed their habit of thinking, the habit of thinking about what they could accomplish and about how they could respond to their situation when faced with adversity.

"WHAT SHALL WE DO WITH OUR DAUGHTERS?"

While the employment columns and bureaus initiated through the women's press attempted to address the challenges faced by middle-class women trying to enter the workforce, the mainstream

DRAWN BY J. H. ROBERTS

A BACHELOR'S SOLUTION OF A PROBLEM OF THE DAY

WHAT SHALL WE DO WITH OUR DAUGHTERS?

Figure c.1 "A Bachelor's Solution of a Problem of the Day: What Shall We Do with Our Daughters?" *Graphic*, 19 October 1895, 492. © British Library Board

press fixed its attention on the importance of ensuring that a new generation of girls would be prepared to the face the exigencies of modern life – and work. The media debate about the future of England's daughters, which flared up on and off from 1888 until the mid-1890s, was prompted initially by an 1888 article by Walter Besant in *Longman's Magazine*. Both Besant's article, "The Endowment of the Daughter," and the ensuing public discussions demonstrated that, despite lingering misgivings about the new middle-class working woman, the habit of thinking in the culture at large had altered by the 1890s. The strong "prejudice against permitting women" to have access to an education that would make them employable, the attitude alluded to by the *Englishwoman's*

Review in 1870, no longer held complete sway.[12] At the same time, Victorian attitudes about womanliness died hard, and had certainly not disappeared. The cultural tensions, though less strained than they had been a generation earlier, clearly persisted. Besant's article resonated strongly with public concerns and opinions, and the public responded, initially in a series of letters in the *Daily Telegraph*, followed by articles and letters in other periodicals and newspapers across the country. The mix of publications addressing the fate of the nation's daughters was eclectic, to say the least, including the *Penny Illustrated Paper and Illustrated Times*, *Reynolds's Newspaper*, the *Bristol Mercury and Daily Post*, the *Liverpool Mercury*, the *Leeds Mercury*, the *Newcastle Weekly Courant*, the *Western Mail*, the *Manchester Weekly Times*, the *Daily News*, the *Graphic*, and the *Pall Mall Gazette*. Although the *Times* did not take part in the initial public debate, it weighed in during another flurry of media activity in 1894–95.

The broad cross-section of media involved in considering the problems faced by single women underscores the significance of these issues for the culture at large. The variety of treatments also suggests the ubiquity of public engagement. Approaches ranged from serious –which indeed most of them were – to silly. The latter approach was typical of the *Graphic*, which featured a cartoon entitled "A Bachelor's Solution of a Problem of the Day: What Shall We Do with Our Daughters?" in which the bachelor of the title sits in an open carriage drawn along a seaside promenade by a fashionably dressed young woman on a tricycle; the young woman's arms are tied with reins held by the bachelor, who is fanned by another young woman peddling behind (fig. c.1). This cartoon efficiently mocks several issues "of the day" – the craze for cycling, especially amongst trendy young women, the problem of finding work for young women who appear to be more interested in fashion than in professionalism, the sometimes absurd suggestions for possible areas of employment for women, and the smugness of self-satisfied men who accept the subservience of women as their right.[13] The complex of social issues addressed in a cartoon that appeared in a quintessentially pop culture publication indicates the extent to which concerns over the education and employment of women were imbedded in the public imagination. The assumption that the readership would get the joke also implies the pervasiveness of such concerns.

Besant's article epitomized the enduring confusions in the mindset of a culture that had come to recognize the need for greater opportunities in education and employment for women, but that still cherished outmoded ideals of womanhood. Besant affirms the change in cultural attitudes in bold terms, acknowledging "the complete revolution of opinion as regards women's work which has been effected in the course of a single generation." "All is changed," he avers. "The doors are thrown wide open. With a few exceptions ... a woman can enter upon any career she pleases."[14] As progressive as this position sounds, it is qualified by its author's neochivalric sensibilities (one newspaper correspondent called him "the chivalrous knight of the womanly woman and the sworn foe of the new one").[15] So while Besant argues that the "absolute duty of teaching girls who may at some future time have to depend upon themselves some trade, calling, or profession, seems a mere axiom," he also declares that "no woman should be forced to work at all" (611, 614). He further insists, "with complete confidence," that the "average woman ... hates compulsory work: she hates and loathes it" (615). In the end, according to Besant, "we [presumably men] fall back at last upon nature" – meaning "the sense in man that it is his duty to work for his wife, and the sense in woman that nothing is better for her than to receive the fruits of her husband's labour" (615). Besant's solution – the "endowment" that he urges the middle-class father to provide for his daughter – is not, as one might have hoped, the endowment of education, but rather an annuity that would provide her with the means to obtain training, if she chose to work, or to subsist – barely – if she did not.

The ensuing debate in the *Daily Telegraph*, under the heading of "Our Daughters," highlights the Victorian sense of duty that echoed throughout Besant's article, in particular the duty of parent to child. The sense of patriarchal concern and proprietary claim regarding "our" daughters is accentuated in the question posed by the editors: "What Shall *We* Do with *Our* Daughters?" (emphasis added). The sheer number of letters – "hundreds and thousands" – attests to the significance of the issues at stake to fathers, mothers, daughters, and potential husbands alike. The correspondence was, in the estimation of the editor, "one of the most copious as well as most able" that had appeared in the paper.[16] The numerous pseudonymous signatures, as well as the real ones, indicate the spectrum of interested and disinterested persons who felt impelled to weigh in – women's advocates and activists such as Margaret Bateson and Emily Faithfull spar with various "Fathers," almost as many "Daughters," a few "Mothers," several working ladies, and a smattering of young men hopeful of becoming husbands. Not surprisingly, given the diversity of correspondents, the ensuing exchanges mingle all the most progressive attitudes towards women's education and employment with the same lingering misgivings typical of the times.

The most intense underlying source of tension in the debates among correspondents was the issue of marriage. Many advocate marriage, not education and independence, as the answer to what to do with daughters. "One of 'Our Daughters'" insists that "it is every girl's duty and pleasure to marry," and advises parents to train their daughters to be "agreeable and good-tempered, sympathetic and loveable" in order to attract and keep a husband.[17] "An Unmarried Man" and a "Confirmed Bachelor" are of much the same opinion, and further blame the dearth of marriageable men on the surplus of women taking men's jobs. The former ("An Unmarried Man") is distressed over women's "trespassing upon men's already overstocked labour market," asserting that "a woman's 'field of labour' is, and always has been, at home."[18] "If women would stay at home and get domesticated, and so throw open thousands of berths for men," the latter ("Confirmed Bachelor") argues, "they would stand a good chance of doubling the present marriage rates."[19] "A Tradesman's Wife" contributes some folk wisdom: "There is an old proverb that a father who does not teach his son a trade teaches him to be a thief. I would say a man who does not teach his daughter a trade of some sort, by which she can earn her own living, teaches her to be a husband-catcher" – a very indecorous thing for a middle-class young lady to be.[20]

The vast majority of correspondents understand the pitfalls of limiting young women's futures to marriage and argued for the wisdom of education. "A Perplexed Father" advocates for the training of daughters for "some trade or profession which may be useful to them in after life ... Women," he continues, " ... ought, in this age, to be taught not to look to marriage as their only profession."[21] Another father answered the question of what should be done with daughters succinctly: "Give them a sound education, and bring them up to work for their own living."[22] One of the challenges that these fathers faced in providing that education was the cost involved, especially for families with several daughters, an issue that was raised and addressed from several quarters. "A Business Woman" points out

Figure c.2 "Our Daughters: The D. T. [Daily Telegraph] Pessimists Refuted," *Penny Illustrated Paper and Illustrated Times*, 14 April 1888, 237. © British Library Board that nevertheless "it is every father's duty to educate his daughters as well as his means will allow."[23] The redoubtable but ever pragmatic Margaret Bateson, recognizing the burden of the cost of education for families with limited means, provides a simple and logical guideline: "Whatever is done for the sons do equally for the daughters."[24] That a girl's education is as important as her brothers' was hard for many late-Victorians to accept, but over the course of the approximately two weeks of the open debate in the *Telegraph*, parents and daughters, as well as general readers, were schooled in the necessity of providing young women with the knowledge they needed to work and be independent. As the editor notes in the leader with which the paper reluctantly closed the debate, "the first and widest conclusion forced upon the mind by the correspondence, now ended, is that a definite, special, and substantial fitness, and preparedness for work, should be imparted to every young girl, whatever her station."[25]

This editorial observation by the *Telegraph* highlights the importance of public debate in both forming and informing public opinion. That the wisdom of preparing girls to work had been "forced upon the mind by the correspondence" suggests the resistance of at least a portion of the population and reflects the earnest engagement of the correspondents themselves in seeking sound judgments about the problem at hand. And while the *Telegraph* had closed the debate in its columns, newspapers across Britain had taken up the question and continued the public dialogue. The *Penny Illustrated Paper and Illustrated Times* invited readers to "bestow a glance upon ... [their] gallery of Sweet Girl graduates in the honourable walks of serviceable industry," which the paper outlines in both illustrations and text (fig. c.2).[26] *Reynolds's Newspaper*, the *Bristol Mercury and Daily Post*, and the *Western Mail* all published summaries and commentary on the *Daily Telegraph* debate and continued with sporadic considerations about the future of "our daughters" over the next few years. In 1891, "our daughters" again became a hot topic, this time in the *Daily News*, which printed a letter from Warner Snoad, president of the Women's Progressive Society, a publication that sparked almost as much attention as Besant's article in 1888:

It is but a very few years ago that a little band of brave reformers persistently forced upon the British public the fact that a girl was actually worth educating – nay, more, that her education should be as good in its way as a boy's; and the new doctrine was received, as new doctrines ever will be, with incredulity, ridicule, and censure. But time rolled on; the earnest promoters of higher education for women prevailed, as truth and earnestness always must prevail in the long run; and the scheme, instead of proving an ignominious collapse, amid a host of failures, became a steady success.[27]

Snoad's position was endorsed by numerous subsequent correspondents to the *Daily News* and to *Reynolds's Newspaper*, her "admirable letter" praised for its common sense.[28]

The *Daily News* correspondents, like those in the *Telegraph*, present both progressive and retrogressive arguments, one in the latter camp going so far as to declare the incursions of educated young women into the workforce as "immoral" because it harms the prospects of young men.[29] A more enlightened contributor refutes the conventional charge that training for employment was wasted on the majority of young women, who were still destined for marriage and motherhood. "No girl would, I am sure, become a worse wife or mother," notes this writer, "because she had been trained to become independent, if necessary, and had thus acquired method and self-reliance."[30] A regular contributor to *Reynolds's Newspaper* who signs himself "Northumbrian" provides a particularly biting commentary highlighting the generally unacknowledged undercurrents of class bias in treatments of women's work and education. "Go a degree lower," advises "Northumbrian," "and ask what the superior class of the British workman can do with his daughter?" "The troubles of female labour," he concludes, "arise from the fact that the lazy and ornamental look down upon the workers instead of looking up to them."[31]

The concern over "Our Daughters" was eventually taken up by the *Times*, which, as always, lent gravitas to the problems already circulating in the culture at large. For almost a year, from December 1894 until November of the following year, "Our Daughters" was a recurring topic in the letters to the editor of the *Times*. The interventions in the *Times* are considerably less democratic than those in the *Telegraph* or the provincial papers, focusing on the daughters of "gentlefolk" who "are obliged to work."[32] The only employment considered in depth is that of the country schoolmistress, about which there are some misconceptions, mostly about how much education a country schoolmistress would require. In some minds, the country schoolmistress appears to be a replacement for the option of governess – the logic being along the lines of "send your indifferently educated daughter to a safe and quiet retreat to earn a minimal existence, doing something vaguely lady-like." There is some concern about "loss of caste" in taking on the role of country schoolmistress, but the muted responses to office work suggest that being an urban typewriter would be much worse.[33] There is a letter from Jessie Boucherett addressing misconceptions about women taking well-paid jobs away from men and pointing out that women are in fact replacing poorly paid "German lads," which might not have helped promote the option of office work to this particular set of correspondents – none of whom, by the way, are mothers or daughters.[34] Country schoolmistresses are not "New Women," as one correspondent huffily points out, and, according to another, their work is "more pleasant and even more remunerative than type-writing or other analogous employments to which destitute ladies betake themselves with lamentable persistency."[35]

"A PRETTY UNANIMOUS CONCLUSION"

Even before the appearance of Besant's article and the interventions from newspapers across the nation, a letter to *Reynolds's Newspaper* asserts that society at large had "come to a pretty unanimous conclusion that we must find 'work for our daughters to do.'"[36] The letters and editorials that appeared in the papers around the country for the next six or seven years had come to a similar "pretty unanimous conclusion" and, further, had determined that sound education was the key to preparing young women for work. The tenor of this public debate was fundamentally different from what it had been in the 1850s and 1860s. The question was no longer "What Shall We Do with Our Old Maids?" but "What Is to Be Done with Our Girls?" The framing of both questions suggests a sense of social responsibility: "we" must do something with "our" old maids or "our" girls. Here the similarity ends. Old maids are a problem, a nuisance, a drag on the economic and social system. If one of them happened to be your spinster sister or maiden aunt, she would be an economic burden on the family until she died. She was a failure within a system that defined a woman's productive socio-economic role as wife and mother. In 1860, the answer to the question "what is to be done with our girls?" would have been to find her a suitable husband. By the 1890s, the answer was the one that forward thinkers had been insisting on for decades: educate her for employment.

Notes

INTRODUCTION

1 [James Hinton], "On Nursing as a Profession," *Cornhill Magazine* 22 (1870): 451–6; 451.
2 "Ideals of Womanhood," *Woman's Herald*, 24 September 1892, 3–4.
3 "Typewriter" referred both to the machine and its operator in the Victorian period. "Typist" did appear, especially in the later years of the 1890s, but "typewriter" was the more common term. There was some controversy by the end of the nineteenth century about using the term typewriter vs typist to designate the person operating a typewriting machine. In an 1892 essay, Clementina Black demands absolute precision in terminology, insisting that "the lady who works a type-writing machine … is not a type-writer. The type-writer is the machine; the 'operator' is a 'typist,' and the process of operating is typing" (Black, "Type-Writing and Journalism," 35). Black (1853–1922) was an author, journalist, and political activist who advocated for the rights of women and the working classes. R.V. Gill also finds "type-writer" a "misnomer," on the grounds that it is more properly the term for the machine. In Gill's estimation, however, "typist" is "a most objectionable title," and she urges "some fertile brain" to "create a suitable title" (R.V. Gill, "Is Type-Writing a Successful Occupation for Educated Ladies?" *Englishwoman's Review* [1891]: 80–7, 87). Since no fertile brain came forward with more suitable terminology, I have opted for the title most commonly used in the Victorian period throughout this study – typewriter.
4 Williams, *Marxism and Literature*, 112–13.
5 Poovey, *Uneven Developments*, 2.

6   Margaret Bateson was the doyenne of journalism on middle-class women's employment in the late nineteenth century. In addition to her regular column in the *Queen*, she published individual articles on employment in that paper, as well as in the *Girl's Own Paper* and the *Woman's Signal*. She also lectured extensively on women's employment issues.

7   Bateson, *Professional Women*. Subsequent references appear in the text by page number.

8   Women were not called to the bar in Britain until the 1920s. Women did practise law, however, "in all but the formalities" ("Lady Lawyers," *Uxbridge and West Drayton Gazette*, 8 July 1876, 6). In 1876, two women, Eliza Orme and Mary Richardson, placed first and third respectively in the Roman Law examination at the University of London and subsequently set up offices in Chancery Lane, focusing on conveyancing and patents (Howsam, "'Sound-Minded Women,'" 44–55). Orme was also a social activist and supporter of women's rights. Although the first woman was not admitted to the Institute of British Architects (established in 1834) until 1902, Lynne Walker dates the entrance of women into architecture to the 1880s (Walker, "Entry of Women into the Architectural Profession," 13, 15). In the 1891 census, nineteen women listed their occupation as architect ("Woman Up to Date," *Sheffield Evening Telegraph*, 29 November 1895, 2).

9   Reader, *Professional Men*, 1.

10   Ibid., 1–24. Surgeons and doctors without a university education were initially excluded from the ranks of medical professionals (i.e., the Royal College of Physicians), ibid., 16.

11   Ibid.; Perkin, *Rise of Professional Society*, 1–17, 78–101; Colón, *Professional Ideal*, 1–21.

12   Perkin, *Rise of Professional Society*, 17–21.

13   Reader, *Professional Men*, 172–3.

14   Fletcher, *Feminists and Bureaucrats*, 12–13; Sutherland, "Education," 146–9. See also de Bellaigue, *Educating Women* and the essays in Part Two of Hilton and Hirsch, eds., *Practical Visionaries*, 67–128.

15   Dyhouse, *Girls Growing Up*, 65.

16   Dyhouse, *No Distinction of Sex?* 14, 17.

17   Ibid., 17; Sutherland, "Education," 154.

18   For detailed histories of women's hard-won entry into medicine in England (in addition to numerous biographies available of Elizabeth Garrett Anderson, Sophia Jex-Blake, and Elizabeth Blackwell), see Brock, "*The Lancet*"; Dyhouse, "Driving Ambitions"; and Blake, *Charge of the Parasols*.

19   Frances Low, "How Poor Ladies Live," *Nineteenth Century* 41 (1897): 405–17; 406–7. Low (1862-1939) was a social activist and journalist.

20   See, for example, Baly, *Florence Nightingale*; Bostridge, *Florence Nightingale*; and Manton, *Sister Dora*.

21   See, for example, Moore, *Zeal for Responsibility*; Helmstadter and Goddin, *Nursing before Nightingale*; and Hawkins, *Nursing and Women's Labour*.

22   See, for example, Abel-Smith, *History of the Nursing Profession*; Davies, ed., *Rewriting Nursing History*; Summers, "Mysterious Demise"; and Maggs, *Origins of General Nursing*. See also Vicinus, *Independent Women*, which examines nursing as one of several new career options for middle-class women, and therefore as an opportunity to gain dignity and independence. As Vicinus points out, however, her "central focus is the emotional, spiritual, and social significance of women's separate institutions" (7–8) rather than the public/cultural perceptions of the nurse and other working women.

23   Hawkins, *Nursing and Women's Labour*, 1.

24   Nursing as domestic practice, by contrast, has been the subject of literary studies, most notably Judd's excellent *Bedside Seductions*.

25   Keep, "Cultural Work," 403.

26   Mullin, *Working Girls*, 30.

27   See, for example, Anderson, ed., *White-Blouse Revolution*; Zimmeck, "Jobs for the Girls"; and Price and Thurschwell, eds., *Literary Secretaries*.

28   Lowe, *Women in the Administrative Revolution*, 7.

29   Dohrn, "Pioneers," in Anderson, ed., *White-Blouse Revolution*.

30   Jordan, *Women's Movement*, 6–20.

31   Ibid., 18–20. Bronwyn Rivers makes a similar argument about the influence of discourse on attitudes about middle-class women and work, with a focus on the "ideologies and linguistic forms" and "the ideological work performed by … novels." Rivers, *Women at Work*, 12.

32   Honnor Morten, "Questions for Women," *Queen*, 28 January 1899, 131. Morten (1861–1913) was a nurse and journalist.

33   For a comprehensive examination of the Woman Question, see Helsinger et al., eds, *Woman Question*. As arguably the most controversial cultural figure of the late Victorian period, the New Woman has generated a plethora of studies, most of which analyze the New Woman as a literary-cum-cultural construct. Some of the classics in the field include Cunningham, *New Woman* (1978); Ardis, *New Women* (1990); Pykett, *"Improper" Feminine* (1992); and Ledger, *New Woman* (1997). More recent studies, such as Sutherland's *In Search of the New Woman*, have considered the New Woman in larger social terms.

34   Northumbrian, "To the Editor," *Reynolds's Newspaper*, 29 January 1888, 2.

CHAPTER ONE

1   Holcombe, *Victorian Ladies at Work*, 10; "The Employment of Women,"
    Queen, 22 September 1883, 261. Boucherett (1825–1905) later founded
    the *Englishwoman's Review*. Margaret Beetham, citing Sheila Herstein,
    maintains that the society "grew directly out of the register of work in the
    English Woman's Journal." Beetham, *Magazine of Her Own*, 139; see also
    Herstein, "*English Woman's Journal*." Martineau (1802–1876) was a
    prominent author and essayist, especially noted for her series of stories
    simplifying and popularizing political economy for the benefit of working-
    class readers.
2   Harriet Martineau, "Female Industry," *Edinburgh Review* 109 (1859):
    293–36; 151–73 in the American edition.
3   Caroline Norton (1808–1877), granddaughter of the renowned Irish play-
    wright, Richard Brinsley Sheridan, fled from the brutality of her husband,
    George Norton, in 1835, when she was twenty-seven. Norton denied her
    access to their three young children and claimed his right, as her husband,
    to all her possessions and inheritance. In response to her desperate situa-
    tion, and to the intransigence of the law with respect to any of her
    attempts to remediate her circumstances, Caroline Norton published num-
    erous pamphlets on the injustices of the British legal system with regard to
    married women, who had no autonomous status under the law, no rights
    to income or property, and no custody rights to their children. In large
    part as a result of her indefatigable efforts, the laws regarding child cus-
    tody, divorce, and women's property rights were eventually altered and
    rendered more humane. Caroline Norton was also well-known during her
    lifetime as a poet and novelist. See Reynolds, "Norton," in *Oxford
    Dictionary of National Biography*.
4   John William Kaye, "The Non-Existence of Women," *North British
    Review* 23 (1855): 536–62; 559.
5   "The Disputed Question," *English Woman's Journal* 1 (August 1858):
    361–7; 361.
6   John William Kaye, "The Employment of Women," *North British Review*
    26 (1857): 291–338; 333.
7   Levitan, *Cultural History*, 132.
8   Honnor Morten, "Questions for Women," *Queen*, 28 January 1899, 131.
9   Kaye, "The Employment of Women," 328.
10 "The Disputed Question," 361.
11 "Female Education in the Middle Classes," *English Woman's Journal* 1
    (June 1858): 217–27; 223.

12   "Female Labour," *Fraser's Magazine* 61 (1860): 359–7; 367, 369.

13   "Queen Bees or Working Bees?" *Saturday Review,* 12 November 1859, 575–6; 576.

14   Bessie Rayner Parkes (1829–1925) and Emily Faithfull (1835–1895) were among the early members of the Society for Promoting the Employment of Women (often referred to by the unfortunate acronym of SPEW). Parkes was a regular contributor to the *English Woman's Journal*; Faithfull established the Victoria Press to provide opportunities for women in publishing.

15   "The Market for Educated Female Labour," *Times,* 7 November 1859, 10. Parkes's lecture was printed in full in the *English Woman's Journal* 4, 21(1859): 145–52.

16   "It Must Have Been Felt by All," *Times,* 8 November 1859, 6.

17   "It Is a Common Practice with Moralists and Historians," *Times,* 17 November 1859, 6.

18   W.R. Greg, "Why Are Women Redundant?" *National Review* 14 (April 1862): 434–60; 452, 454. William Rathbone Greg (1809–1881) was a noted essayist and social commentator. His interpretation of the census statistics has been questioned, then as now, in discussions of middle-class women's emigration. See Diamond, *Emigration and Empire,* 65 and Wagner, "Victorian Failed Emigration." Some analyses of the campaign to emigrate middle-class spinsters express doubts about the surplus itself. Rita Kranidis, for example, cites Jean Jacques Van-Helten and Keith Williams's claim that "the so-called female 'surplus' was a deeply ideological notion" to support her contention that, in the Victorian period, "women were in fact not materially or practically excessive in relation to England's capacity to accommodate workers" (Kranidis, *Victorian Spinster,* 27). Van-Helten and Williams, however, were basing their claim on statistics for 1911 from the Dominions Royal Commission (Van-Helten and Williams, "'Crying Need of South Africa,'" 21). Reports on the census itself, then and now, agree on the existence of a surplus. See for example Martineau, "Female Industry" (then) and Levitan, *Cultural History* (now).

19   Frances Power Cobbe, "What Shall We Do with Our Old Maids?" *Fraser's Magazine* 66 (1862): 594–610; 594. Cobbe (1822–1904) was a journalist and women's rights advocate.

20   Bessie Rayner Parkes, "The Balance of Public Opinion in Regard to Woman's Work," *English Woman's Journal* 9, 53 (July 1862): 340–4; 342.

21   Sydney Smith, "(Review of) *Advice to Young Ladies on the Improvement of the Mind* by Thomas Broadhurst," *Edinburgh Review* 15 (January 1810): 299–315; 307, 306. When reproduced, this review is commonly

titled "Female Education." Smith was one of the founding editors of the *Edinburgh Review* and a prolific contributor on various topics.

22 "Female Education in the Middle Classes," *English Woman's Journal* 1 (June 1858): 222.

23 Kaye, "The Employment of Women," 305.

24 Millicent Garrett Fawcett, "The Education of Women in the Middle and Upper Classes," *Macmillan's Magazine* 17 (1868): 511–17; 512, 514. Millicent Garrett Fawcett (1847–1929) was an author and women's rights advocate.

25 A Belgravian Young Lady, "Two Girls of the Period: The Upper Side. Our Offence, Our Defence, and Our Petition," *Macmillan's Magazine* 19 (1869): 323–31; 327. Subsequent references are in the text as "Belgravian" and page number.

26 Daniel Rose Fearon, "The Ladies' Cry, Nothing To Do!" *Macmillan's Magazine* 19 (1869): 451–4; 454.

27 Johanna M. Smith, "Textual Encounters," 51.

28 Kaye, "The Non-Existence of Women," 558.

29 Millicent Garrett Fawcett, "The Education of Women in the Middle and Upper Classes," *Macmillan's Magazine* 17 (1868): 515.

30 "Professor Fawcett upon Education," *Times*, 8 January 1870, 4. Professor Fawcett notes that this argument is a common one. Sydney Smith adopted a similar position in his treatment of female education sixty years earlier: "The formation of character for the first seven or eight years of life seems to depend almost entirely upon ... [mothers]. It is certainly in the power of a sensible and well educated mother to inspire, within that period, such tastes and propensities as shall nearly decide the destiny of the future man" (Smith, "(Review of) *Advice to Young Ladies*," 310). While Smith wanted women to be educated to enhance their lives, rather than improve their chances of finding work, later supporters of women's employment similarly present education as essential to the development of the capacity to be an effective mother.

31 A.G., "Hospital Nurses," *Times*, 20 October 1871, 10.

32 "Occasional Notes," *Pall Mall Gazette*, 14 May 1870: 10–12. "Gentlewomen and Self-Help," *Englishwoman's Review* (July 1870): 164–71; 164, 165,168.

33 Susanna Meredith, "Disease and Laundrie," *Times*, 22 August 1877, 10.

34 "Nursing the Sick," *Englishwoman's Review* (July 1868): 497–8.

35 As reproduced in "Training of Nurses," *Englishwoman's Review* (October 1868): 41.

36 "Artistic Wood Carving: A Remunerative Employment for Women," *Queen*, 11 January 1879, 21. Harold Perkin notes the growth of "women's professional and white-collar occupations ... especially elementary school teachers, clerks and other office workers, particularly typists and telephonists" in the last decades of the nineteenth century, positions he classed as "lower professionals" (*Rise of Professional Society*, 79–80). Perkin also points to the importance of collective and qualifying organizations in establishing the standards and stature of professions (85–6). Teachers, nurses, and clerical workers all formed such organizations by the early twentieth century.

37 "Artistic Wood Carving," 21.

38 "Two Associations of Women," *Queen*, 11 May 1878, 337.

39 A Female Teacher, "Correspondence," *Englishwoman's Review* (January 1872): 146; "The Letter We Published on Tuesday," *Times*, 21 February 1878, 9.

40 Emily Faithfull, letter, "The Employment of Women," *Times*, 22 February 1878, 8.

41 For a history of the campaign to professionalize and unionize teachers, see Tropp, *The School Teachers*, 108–59. See also Wardle, *English Popular Education*, 100–7 and Copelman, *London's Women Teachers*, 68–72.

42 J. Traviss Lockwood, "Elementary School Mistresses," *Times*, 16 September 1873, 9.

43 "We Seem to Have Before Us Two Facts," *Times*, 20 June 1872, 11.

44 Emily Davies, "Girton College," *Times*, 21 August 1873, 8.

45 "Ladies as Elementary Teachers," *Englishwoman's Review* (January 1876): 38–9; "Governess or Schoolmistress?" *Queen*, 16 October 1875, 253.

46 "Governess or Schoolmistress?" 253.

47 Emily Faithfull, letter, "Distressed Gentlewomen," *Times*, 22 August 1873, 4; "The Difficulty Found in the Choice of a Profession," *Times*, 1 September 1873, 9.

48 A Lady School Manager, letter, "Ladies as Elementary Schoolmistresses," *Times*, 28 August 1873, 12.

49 Emma Liggins also points out the stress placed by Victorian advocates on honour with regard to work in order to make paid employment palatable to middle-class women (Liggins, *Odd Women?* 34).

50 Steinbach, *Women in England*, 43.

51 Prochaska, *Women and Philanthropy*, especially 175–81.

52 See Dingwall et al., *Social History of Nursing*, 27–9. See also Holcombe, *Victorian Ladies at Work*, 72–3; Baly, *Nursing and Social Change*, 46–9; and Moore, *Zeal for Responsibility*, 3–4.

53   That sisterhoods played an important role in the reform of the profession
     is a given in nursing histories. The most authoritative and comprehensive
     history of nursing is Abel-Smith, *History of the Nursing Profession*. Other
     standard texts include Davies, ed, *Rewriting Nursing History* and
     Dingwall et al., *Social History of Nursing*.

54   See, for example, "Volunteer Nursing," reprinted from the *Lancet*, *Times*,
     7 September 1866, 4 and "News in Brief: Liverpool," *Times*, 10 October
     1866, 7.

55   "Cholera in the Hospitals," *Times*, 8 September 1866, 12.

56   "Sisterhoods: From the 'Bishop of London's Charge,' December 1866,"
     Englishwoman's Review (January 1867): 99–100; 100. When cholera
     reappears in London in 1892, a letter to the *Times* reminds readers that
     the "skilled nursing of today" will mitigate the threat the disease might
     otherwise pose. J.H. Thomas, "To the Editors of the *Times*," 1 September
     1892, 4.

57   Quoted in "Nursing in London," *Englishwoman's Review* (September
     1875): 430.

58   "Liverpool Nurse's Training School," *Englishwoman's Review* (January
     1872): 74.

59   "Employment as Hospital Nurses," *Daily News*, reprinted in
     Englishwoman's Review (October 1875): 479.

60   "Events of the Month," *Englishwoman's Review* (August 1876): 364.

61   "Nursing the Sick," *Englishwoman's Review* (July 1868): 497–8; 498.

62   "A Few Hints to Young Candidates for the Nursing Profession," *Woman's
     Gazette*, 1877, 123. Quoted in Jordan, *Women's Movement*, 141.

63   "The Disputed Question," *English Woman's Journal* 1, 60 (August 1858):
     364.

64   "Training-Schools for Nurses," *Fraser's Magazine*, n.s., 10 (1874): 706–13;
     713.

65   N.H., "A Suggestion for the Employment of Ladies," *Queen*, 5 June 1875,
     383.

66   "Nurses for the Sick," *Queen*, 13 May 1876, 322.

67   [James Hinton], "On Nursing as a Profession," *Cornhill Magazine* 22
     (1870): 451–6; 451.

68   Charlotte Haddon, "Nursing as a Profession for Ladies," *Saint Paul's
     Magazine* 8 (1871): 458–61; 458.

69   Ibid. *Fraser's Magazine* also notes the greatly increased demand for skilled
     hospital nurses and argues for the recognition of nursing as a profession

as well as for adequate and secure remuneration. See "Training-Schools for Nurses," *Fraser's Magazine*, n.s., 10 (1874): 706–13.

70 See Helmstadter, "Doctors and Nurses," 176.

71 Maggs, *Origins of General Nursing*, 26.

72 Seymour J. Sharkey, "Doctors and Nurses II," *Nineteenth Century* 7 (1880): 1097–1104; 1097.

73 G.W.M. [George Whyte-Melville], "Strong-Minded Women," *Fraser's Magazine* 68 (1863): 667–78; 668, 673. Florence Nightingale was, of course, in reality not the gentle Lady with the Lamp revered in the public imagination, but a determined sanitary reformer and hard-headed administrator – even more strong-minded than Whyte-Melville acknowledges. Whyte-Melville (1821–1878) was a novelist and poet.

74 "Events of the Quarter," *Englishwoman's Review* (October 1872): 308. For a discussion of the *Queen*'s introduction of articles on social issues, see my "Ladies and Professionalism."

75 [Frances Martin], "The Glorified Spinster," *Macmillan's Magazine* 58 (1888): 371–6; 373, 374. Martin (1829–1922) was a teacher and advocate for women's education, especially for the working classes.

76 Walkowitz, *City of Dreadful Delight*, 63.

77 "The Disputed Question," *English Woman's Journal* 1, 60 (August 1858): 364.

78 Edith Simcox, "Ideals of Feminine Usefulness," *Fortnightly Review* 27 (1880): 656–71; 667. Simcox (1844–1901) was a political and social activist in support of the status of women.

79 Margaret E. Harkness, "Women as Civil Servants," *Nineteenth Century* 10 (1881): 369–81; 369, 381. Harkness (1854–1923) was a socialist activist, journalist, and novelist, sometimes publishing under the pseudonym John Law. She had a brief career in nursing, for which she had little aptitude, training at the Westminster Hospital in 1877 and working for a short time at Guy's Hospital. See Lucas, "Harkness, Margaret," in *Oxford Dictionary of National Biography*.

80 Reginald Brabazon, "A Woman's Work," *National Review* 4 (1884): 86–90; 86. Brabazon (1841–1929) was a British diplomat and philanthropist.

81 Gertrude Dix, "Hard Labour in the Hospitals," *Westminster Review* 140 (1893): 627–34; 627–8. Dix (1867–1950) was a socialist and New Woman novelist.

82 "A Privileged Profession," *Westminster Review* 135 (1891): 6–10; 6–7.

CHAPTER TWO

1   G.W.M. [George Whyte-Melville], "Strong-Minded Women," *Fraser's Magazine* 68 (1863): 667–78; 673.
2   After the serialization of *Martin Chuzzlewit* in the early 1840s, Sairey Gamp represented to the Victorian imagination the essence of what a nurse was and accordingly besmirched the reputation of nurses for decades. In his 1849 "Preface" to the cheap editions of his novel, Dickens describes Gamp as "a representation of the hired attendant on the poor in sickness." Dickens characterizes Sairey's friend and associate, the equally disreputable Betsey Prig, as "a fair specimen of a Hospital Nurse" (Dickens, *Martin Chuzzlewit*, 848). Although Prig was a hospital nurse and Gamp was hired to attend to the sick or perform midwifery duties, Gamp nevertheless became the icon of questionable nursing practice, both inside and outside hospital settings.
3   "The Nursing System at Guy's Hospital," *Queen,* 2 October 1880, 291.
4   For a detailed discussion of the nursing crises, see Moore, *Zeal for Responsibility.*
5   "Hospital Nurses," *Times,* 17 February 1848, 8.
6   Nightingale herself contributed to the essentialist construction of the ideal nurse as feminine by asserting that "every woman is a nurse" (*Notes on Nursing,* 3).
7   Furneaux, *Military Men,* 194–5.
8   A Medical Pupil, letter, "Surgeons and Nurses for Scutari," *Times,* 17 October 1854, 10.
9   R.T.C., "After the Battle," *Times,* 15 November 1854, 8.
10 The category of "nurse attendant in a hospital, lunatic asylum etc." included 1,651 men, 27 per cent of all nurses in that classification. The much larger category of "nurse not domestic servant" (numbering 24,821) is exclusively female, however. See Summers, "Mysterious Demise," 369. As Celia Davies observes, it is difficult to distinguish in this larger category between nursery nurses who cared for children and nurses who tended to the sick. Davies, "Making Sense of the Census," 598.
11 "Training-Schools for Nurses," *Fraser's Magazine,* n.s., 10 (1874): 709.
12 "Nursing Sisters," *Chambers's Journal,* 15 May 1875, 305–7; 307.
13 "A Nurse Is One of the Oldest and Most Necessary," *Times,* 14 April 1876, 7.
14 William Gull, "On the Nursing Crisis at Guy's Hospital I," *Nineteenth Century* 7 (1880): 884–91; 888.

15 For a comprehensive history of the evolution of medical training and the medical profession in the nineteenth century, see Peterson, *Medical Profession*, especially 60–89.

16 Leader, *Guy's Hospital Gazette*, 17 July 1877, 78–9; 78.

17 "The Art and Mystery of Nursing," *Lancet,* 17 September 1881, 516.

18 Prosser James, "Men as Nurses," *Westminster Review* 147 (March 1897): 309–10; 309.

19 Herbert W.A. Wilson, "The Moral Influence of the Trained Nurse," *Westminster Review* 148 (1897): 320–35; 331

20 (Lady) Eliza Priestley, "Nurses à la Mode," *Nineteenth Century* 41 (1897): 28–37; 32–3. Priestley published extensively about sanitary reform.

21 "Hospital Nursing," *Times*, 9 April 1866, 8.

22 Elizabeth Garrett, "Volunteer Hospital Nursing," *Macmillan's Magazine* 15 (1867): 494–9; 495. Garrett herself was not in favour of ladies working on a volunteer basis and, like Nightingale, advocated for intelligent women of the lower middle class as the best candidates for good nurses. Educated ladies, "trained and qualified," she argued, should be in the position of nursing supervisors only and should be paid according to their educational and class status, "not less than 150 *l.*" per annum (498–9). Garrett (later Garrett Anderson) (1836–1917) was a pioneer in women's medical training and the first woman to be admitted to the British Medical Association.

23 "Hospital Nursing," reprinted in the *Times,* 9 April 1866, 8.

24 M.D., letter, "Hospital Nursing," *Times,* 1 November 1869, 5.

25 George Barraclough, "On Nursing as a Career for Ladies," *Fraser's Magazine* 19 (1879): 468–79; 474, 477.

26 See, for example, Warrington Haward, "Ladies and Hospital Nursing," *Contemporary Review* 34 (1879): 490–503; 493n. See also Sister Grace, letter, "Sisters and Nurses," *Queen,* 3 April 1880, 311.

27 Sister Grace, letter, "Sisters and Nurses," *Queen,* 3 April 1880, 311.

28 According to Mary Poovey, "this self-proclaimed subordination" contributed to the success of professionalized nursing in the nineteenth century. *Uneven Developments,* 166.

29 See Mumm, *Stolen Daughters,* 35–9.

30 Cameron, *Mr. Guy's Hospital,* 205.

31 Two of the nursing crises took place at King's College Hospital, in 1874 and 1883, the latter leading to the termination of the contracts between the Sisterhood of St John's House and both King's College and Charing Cross Hospitals. A less serious one in 1885 involved the sisters of All Saints, who provided the nursing care at the University College Hospital.

For a detailed history of the nursing crises in London hospitals, see
Moore, *Zeal for Responsibility*. The crisis at Guy's has fostered a veritable
cottage industry for historians of nursing. See, for example, Waddington,
"Nursing Dispute"; Helmstadter, "Doctors and Nurses"; and Adrienne
Knight, "Great Nursing Dispute." Waddington concentrates on the doctors' perspective of the controversy; Helmstadter specifically addresses
some of the vexed class issues inherent in the dispute.

32   The anxiety of the medical staff was likely exacerbated by another feature
of late-Victorian culture – the crisis of masculinity. However, the main
drivers of the hospital disputes, and the ones that influenced attitudes
towards nurses, were class insecurities and deep-seated cultural misogyny.
For detailed discussions of Victorian masculinities, see Adams, *Dandies
and Desert Saints* and Tosh, *A Man's Place*. Vanessa Heggie points out
that there was also tension between women doctors and nurses in the
late-Victorian period, driven by the doctors' need to establish a "distinct
professional voice, an unapologetic self-identity as intelligent and ambi-
tious, in distinct comparison to the allegedly less academic nurse" (Heggie,
"Women Doctors and Lady Nurses," 270). Heggie's assessment of hospital
nurses seems to be coloured by the negative opinions maintained by the
women doctors, whose exposure to hospital nurses was limited to the
small women's hospitals in which women doctors at the time worked, and
by a reading of nursing history based on the assumption that Florence
Nightingale's "nurse training schemes" (277) were the main driver in nursing reform, a view that has been revised substantially by, among others,
Helmstadter and Goddin, *Nursing before Nightingale*.

33   Cameron, *Mr. Guy's Hospital*, 203–4.

34   Moore, "Sturges, Octavius" and "Moxon, Walter"; Bettany, "Habershon,
Samuel Osborne," all in *Oxford Dictionary of National Biography*;
Bettany and Wilks, *Biographical History of Guy's*, 280.

35   Hervey, "Gull, Sir William Withey," in *Oxford Dictionary of National
Biography*"; Bettany and Wilks, *Biographical History of Guy's*, 268.

36   Manton, *Sister Dora*, 256–7. "Nurses and Doctors," *Saturday Review*, 22
May 1880, 661–2; 661.

37   Margaret Lonsdale, "The Present Crisis at Guy's Hospital," *Nineteenth
Century* 7 (1880): 677–84; 683.

38   An analysis in the *Saturday Review* addresses this issue, expressing some
sympathy for Lonsdale's inexperience and commitment, as well as for her
criticism of the situation at Guy's, but regretting her tone and indiscretion.
The article is even more critical of Walter Moxon's response, however,
characterizing it as "verbose fulminations" whose misrepresentations are

"calculated to mislead." "Nurses and Doctors," *Saturday Review*, 22 May 1880, 661.

39 "Nursing Sisterhoods," *Lancet*, 6 November 1869, 650.

40 Lonsdale, "Present Crisis," 682.

41 Ibid.

42 "Lady Nurses," *Medical Times and Gazette*, 10 April 1880, 401–2; 402.

43 Samuel Habershon, "On the Nursing Crisis at Guy's Hospital II," *Nineteenth Century* 7 (1880): 892–901; 900.

44 Seymour J. Sharkey, "Doctors and Nurses II," *Nineteenth Century* 7 (1880): 1097–1104, 1099.

45 "Lady Nurses," *Medical Times and Gazette*, 8 May 1880, 506.

46 Octavius Sturges, "Doctors and Nurses I," *Nineteenth Century* 7 (1880): 1089–96; 1093–4.

47 Gull, "On the Nursing Crisis at Guy's Hospital I," 888.

48 Sharkey, "Doctors and Nurses II," 1103–4.

49 Samuel Wilks, letter, "Guy's Hospital," *Times*, 29 July 1880, 10.

50 Walter Moxon, "Miss Lonsdale on Guy's Hospital," *Contemporary Review* 37 (1880): 872–92; 887.

51 Lonsdale, "Present Crisis," 680.

52 Moxon, "Miss Lonsdale on Guy's Hospital," 880.

53 Sharkey, "Doctors and Nurses II," 1103–4.

54 Samuel Habershon, letter, "Guy's Hospital," *Times*, 24 July 1880, 10. A report from the governors of the hospital reprinted in the *Times* points out that the only new religious observances adopted by the new matron were "short family prayers ... read from a manual issued by the Christian Knowledge Society, at which the day nurses attend before they go to breakfast and to their morning duty, and after they come off in the evening. The night nurses also after coming off duty attend the short daily service in the chapel, which has always been held there." "Guy's Hospital," *Times*, 1 October 1880, 10.

55 Moxon, "Miss Lonsdale on Guy's Hospital," 876.

56 G.W.M. [George Whyte-Melville], "Strong-Minded Women," *Fraser's Magazine* 68 (1863): 668.

57 Haward, "Ladies and Hospital Nursing," 490.

58 Gull, "On the Nursing Crisis at Guy's Hospital I," 886.

59 Sturges, "Doctors and Nurses I," 1093.

60 Moxon, "Miss Lonsdale on Guy's Hospital," 886.

61 That there was indeed a decreased need for doctors is borne out by the recollections of a physician who graduated from Middlesex Hospital in 1893 and who "remembered the drop in dressers' fees when trained sisters

took charge of the dressings" and the consequent salutary effect on hospital budgets, a result that also explains why the new system of nursing appealed to hospital administrators. See Manton, *Sister Dora*, 265n32.

62 Helmstadter makes a similar point, stating that "while they used the rhetoric of gender, religion, and class in public, the real issue ... was the doctors' efforts to preserve the old ward system." Helmstadter does not analyze the public rhetoric itself (Helmstadter, "Doctors and Nurses," 170).

63 Sister Grace, letter, "Sisters and Nurses," *Queen*, 3 April 1880, 311.

64 Emily Hornby Evans, "Guy's Hospital," *Work and Leisure* (1880): 282–3.

65 "Erratum," *Work and Leisure* (1880): 314. Besides printing limited correspondence regarding the crisis at Guy's, *Work and Leisure* also serialized the supposedly true-life experiences of a probationer. This memoir emphasizes the shared values of humanitarianism and cooperation between doctors and nurses and presents nurses as self-aware and constructively critical of their own practices. A Nurse, "Hours in a Hospital," *Work and Leisure* (1880): 18–22, 36–40, 77–80, 110–14.

66 "Nurses and Sisters," *Queen*, 20 March 1880, 245.

67 "The New Nursing System," *Queen*, 7 August 1880, 113; "The Nursing System at Guy's Hospital," *Queen*, 2 October 1880, 291.

68 "The Nursing System at Guy's Hospital," 291.

69 The editor, Helen Lowe, was the daughter of the dean of Exeter, and was no doubt able to lay her hands on the list of governors because of her social connections. See Rappaport, *Shopping for Pleasure*, 113.

70 "The Governors of Guy's Hospital," *Queen*, 6 November 1880, 493.

71 Henry C. Burdett, "Hospital Nursing," *Fraser's Magazine* 22 (1880): 112–25; 117; "Erratum," *Work and Leisure*, 314. Burdett (1847–1920) began medical training at Guy's Hospital in 1874. He became an active and ardent hospital reformer. See Prochaska, "Burdett, Sir Henry Charles," in *Oxford Dictionary of National Biography*.

72 "Guy's Hospital," *Examiner*, 20 November 1880, 1306–7; 1306. The conviction of another nurse for causing the death of a patient through misconduct prompted the *Saturday Review* to rehearse the details of the original dispute and to accuse the nurses of "inhumanity and carelessness." "Guy's Hospital," *Saturday Review*, 30 October 1880, 546–7; 546.

73 Cameron, *Mr Guy's Hospital*, 218.

74 "The Future Historian of the Reign of Queen Victoria," *Times*, 27 February 1888, 9.

75 Emma L. Watson, "Some Remarks on Modern Nurses," *National Review* 28 (1896): 567–72; 567. See also Priestley, "Nurses à la Mode."

76 They did, however, air their grievances in professional publications. See Abel-Smith, *History of the Nursing Profession*, 61–80.

77 Ibid., 242, 239.

78 Gamarnikow, "Sexual Division of Labour," 114.

79 Abel-Smith, *History of the Nursing Profession*, 89.

CHAPTER THREE

1 "Ideals of Womanhood," *Woman's Herald*, 24 September 1892, 3–4.

2 Literary critics typically interpret Ruth as redeemed through motherhood and/or through her work as a nurse. See for example Judd, *Bedside Seductions*; Malton, "Illicit Inscriptions"; Hapke, "He Stoops to Conquer"; and Chishty-Mujahid, "Scarred and Healed Identities." Kristine Swenson, in *Medical Women*, more insightfully examines Ruth's hospital work in the context of middle-class sensibilities and of evolving reforms in nursing at the time. See Chapter 1, "Angels of Mercy," 13–51. Rachel Webster revisits the idea that Ruth "needs must die," interpreting her demise as the fulfillment of Gaskell's Unitarian belief in suffering and death as the ultimate redemption for sin (Webster, "Improper Woman"). Tim Dolin's thought-provoking analysis interprets Ruth as a reinvention of her Biblical namesake whose life and death allow her to emerge "as if in fulfillment of a mission, to unsettle ... [the social] order and to instate, in her son, a new order ... [thus enabling] authentic Christian attitudes and values ... once more [to] permeate the secular world" (Dolin, "Moabite among the Israelites," 77).

3 Elizabeth Gaskell, Letter to Anne Robson (January 1853), in Chapple and Pollard, eds., *Letters of Mrs Gaskell*, 220–2; 220.

4 Christian von Bunsen, letter, 3 February 1853, in Easson, ed., *Elizabeth Gaskell*, 242–3.

5 According to Anna Fenton-Hathaway, Gaskell incorporated what Fenton-Hathaway terms "literary redundancy" into the texts of *Ruth*, *Mary Barton*, and *Cranford* as a response to the public debates over redundancy that erupted over the census data of 1851. Gaskell, Fenton-Hathaway argues, targeted "the assumption that matrimony represented a triumphal point of narrative closure ... [and] then challenged the related claim that episodes and plotlines should work concertedly toward that end" (Fenton-Hathaway, "Gaskell's Detours," 235). Fenton-Hathaway concentrates on the incorporation of the stories of marginalized characters' lives – usually unmarried or widowed women –through literary digressions, rather than

on issues of women and work. In *Ruth*, she focuses on Sally, the
unmarried servant in the Benson household.

6 Some commentators at the time were distressed by Ruth's harsh fate, notably other women authors. See Charlotte Brontë, letter to Elizabeth Gaskell,
26 April 1852, in Easson, ed., *Elizabeth Gaskell,* 200, and Elizabeth Barrett
Browning, letter to Elizabeth Gaskell, 16 July 1853, in ibid., 315–16.

7 Gaskell, *Ruth,* 31. Subsequent references are indicated in the text by page
number.

8 Real cases of young seamstresses dying from overwork and starvation
became *causes célèbres* in the press in the mid-nineteenth century. But in
representing the fate of the exploited seamstress, artists idealized her,
imbued her with all the womanly grace and beauty that befits a lady, and
often a very pious lady at that. Ruth, in the early chapters of the novel, is
cast in the image of the idealized artistic representation of the seamstress
familiar in Victorian culture. For discussions of seamstresses, see the collection of essays in Harris, ed., *Famine and Fashion.*

9 See Poovey, *Uneven Developments,* 126–33.

10 Carlyle, *Past and Present,* 155, 201.

11 C.T.D., "Advertisement," in Harriet Downing, *Remembrances of a
Monthly Nurse,* iii. Harriet Downing, as the references to her power and
feeling suggest, was a Romantic poet who published four volumes of
poetry and who also produced stories for *Bentley's Miscellany.* See Brown
et al., eds., "Harriet Downing," *Orlando. Orlando*'s entry on Harriet
Downing does not acknowledge her second series of *Remembrances of a
Monthly Nurse,* first published in the *Monthly Magazine* in 1839. The first
series appeared in *Fraser's Magazine* in 1836.

12 *Remembrances* was reissued yet again in 1862 as volume 7 in the Shilling
Readable Novels series.

13 Downing, *Remembrances of a Monthly Nurse,* v. Subsequent references
are indicated in the text by page number.

14 "The Hospital Nurse: An Episode of the War: Founded on Fact," *Fraser's
Magazine* 51 (1855): 96–105; 98.

15 "Nurse Brown's Story," *Dublin University Magazine* 59 (1862): 361–71;
361, 364.

16 "Women Who Work: The Hospital Nurse," *Cassell's Family Magazine* 1
(1874): 47–9; 48. Subsequent references are indicated in the text by page
number.

17 Jerome K. Jerome, "Novel Notes," *Idler* 2 (1892): 497–509; 497. Jerome
(1859–1927) was coeditor of the *Idler* and the author of comic novels.

18 G.B. [George Brown] Burgin, "Talks with a Nurse," *Idler* 8 (1896): 329–36; 423–9; 329. Subsequent references are indicated in the text by page number. Burgin (1856–1944) was a novelist and coeditor of the *Idler*.

19 For a discussion of the debates about lady nurses and hospital administration, see Chapter 2.

20 William Ernest Henley, "Hospital Outlines: Sketches and Portraits," *Cornhill Magazine* 32 (July 1875): 120–8. Subsequent references to the sonnets in this series are indicated in the text by title, page, and line numbers. Henley revised the sequence of poems comprising "Hospital Outlines," which were published as "In Hospital: Rhymes and Rhythms" in his *Book of Verses*. Some of the poems, including "The Student," were removed in the revised sequence, others were added, and several were altered. Most of the added poems were no longer sonnets. The portraits of the nurses and of the surgeon (renamed as "The Chief") remained as sonnets and had only slight variations in wording. I have chosen the original versions of the poems to analyze here as they represent Henley's freshest impressions at a crucial time in nursing history.

21 For example, Bob Sawyer and Ben Allen in Charles Dickens's *Pickwick Papers*. Physicians and surgeons did not fare much better in Dickens's works. See J.C. Dana, "The Medical Profession as Seen by Charles Dickens," *Medical Libraries* 1, 4 (1898): 19–21, www.ncbi.nlm.nih.gov/pmc/articles/PMC2047411/pdf/medlib00048-0007.pdf.

22 A Nurse, "Hours in a Hospital," *Work and Leisure* (1880): 18–22; 36–40; 77–80; 110–14. Subsequent references are indicated in the text by page number.

23 Lonsdale, *Sister Dora*, 123. Subsequent references are indicated in the text by page number.

24 Octavius Sturges, "Doctors and Nurses I," *Nineteenth Century* 7 (1880): 1089–96; 1092.

25 Manton, *Sister Dora*, 220–1; 225, 249.

26 Ritchie, *Old Kensington*, 284–5. Subsequent references are indicated in the text by page number. Anne Thackeray Ritchie (1837–1919) was the daughter of novelist William Makepeace Thackeray.

27 Vera, "Under the Red Cross: A Narrative of Hospital-Life with the Prussians in France," *Blackwood's Magazine* 109 (1871): 636–59; 696–717; 636. Subsequent references are indicated in the text by page number.

28 E.D., *Recollections of a Nurse*.

29 Allen, *Hilda Wade*, 73–4. Subsequent references are indicated in the text by page number.

30   L.T. Meade [Elizabeth Thomasina Meade Toulmin Smith], "The Little Old Lady," Christmas issue, *Woman at Home* (December 1894): 2–13; 2. Meade (1844–1914) was a prolific contributor of stories and articles to British periodicals. She is best remembered as the author of novels and tales for young girls.

31   Morten and Gethen, "The Story of a Nurse," in *Tales of the Children's Ward*, 30. Subsequent references are indicated in the text by page number. Morten (1861–1913) was a nurse and journalist. H.F. Gethen wrote numerous school stories and novels for young readers.

32   "Dorothy's Career," *Girl's Own Paper* 15 (1893–94): 344–5, 362–3, 376–9.

33   Lily Watson, "A Modern Mistake: A Story Told in Letters," *Girl's Own Paper* 15 (1893–94): 760–2, 778–9, 796–7, 802–3, 821–2.

34   H. Mary Wilson, "In Warwick Ward: A Story of Routine," *Girl's Own Paper* 14 (1892–93): 232–5, 251–2; 235.

35   H. Mary Wilson, "On Monmouth Ward," *Girl's Own Paper* 18 (1896–97): 89–90, 108–10.

36   "The Life of a Nurse," *Girl's Own Paper* 21 (1899–1900): 299–301; 299.

37   Sister Joan, "The Wards of St. Margaret's," *Girl's Own Paper* 15 (1893–94): 321–3, 348–50, 366–7, 382–3, 385–7, 412–13, 428–9, 444–5, 449–51, 472–4, 481–2, 510–11, 513–15, 538–9, 558–9, 562–3, 577–9, 605–7, 620–2, 634–6, 646–7, 668–9, 686–7, 700–1, 709–10, 721–3, 747. Subsequent references are indicated in the text by page number.

38   Lysaght, *Long Madness*. Subsequent references are indicated in the text by volume and page numbers.

39   Pleydell North, "A Strange Revelation," *London Society* 61, 365 (1892): 509–25; 509. Subsequent references are indicated in the text by page number.

40   A.E. Glase, "A Nursing-Sister of St. John's," *Argosy* 62 (1896): 380–3; 380. Subsequent references are indicated in the text by page number.

41   Henry Seton Merriman [Hugh Stowell Scott], "Sister," *Blackwood's Magazine* 151 (1892): 888–93; 889. Subsequent references are indicated in the text by page number.

42   L.T. Meade [Elizabeth Thomasina Meade Toulmin Smith], *Girl in Ten Thousand*, 19. Subsequent references are indicated in the text by page number.

43   Fenn, *Nurse Elisia*, 28. Subsequent references are indicated in the text by page number.

CHAPTER FOUR

1   As reprinted in "Events of the Quarter," *Englishwoman's Review* (April 1873): 160–1. Also reprinted as "The Female Labour Market," *Times*, 15 March 1873, 6.

2   Ibid., 160.

3   "The Goose and the Gander," *Saturday Review*, 11 January 1868, 42–3; 42.

4   Silverstone, "Office Work for Women," 101; Holcombe, *Victorian Ladies at Work*, 210, app., table 4a. The numbers cited above for 1861 and 1871 are taken from Holcombe's table 4a. Silverstone's numbers differ for 1861 and 1871, placing the number of female clerks at 274 and 1,412 respectively.

5   Margaret E. Harkness, "Women as Civil Servants," *Nineteenth Century* 10 (1881): 369–81; 369, 374.

6   "Female Clerks," *Englishwoman's Review* (December 1876): 564; "Female Clerks," *Woman's Gazette* (August 1878):124.

7   A Government Official, "Ladies as Clerks," *Fraser's Magazine*, n.s., 12 (1875): 335–40; 335.

8   "Women Clerks at Railway Depots," *Birmingham Daily Post*, reprinted in *Englishwoman's Review* (February 1878): 86.

9   "Female Clerks," *Times*, 3 January 1882, 3.

10   Quoted in "Women in the Civil Service," *Englishwoman's Review* (September 1881): 420–1; 420.

11   Quoted in "Women Clerks," *Englishwoman's Review* (February 1882): 85.

12   Harkness, "Women as Civil Servants," 375.

13   "Female Clerks in the London School Board," *Englishwoman's Review* (December 1883): 570–1; 571.

14   "Women Who Work: Clerks and Bookkeepers," *Pall Mall Gazette,* 6 June 1884, 4. Quoted in "Book-keepers," *Englishwoman's Review* (June 1884): 293.

15   R. Meyrick, "Symposium: Women as Clerks," *Work and Leisure* (1886): 14–19; 18.

16   "Female Clerks," *Times*, 3 January 1882, 3.

17   Quoted in "Female Clerks," *Englishwoman's Review* (December 1876): 564 and "Female Clerks," *Woman's Gazette* (August 1878):124.

18   "Salary No Object," *Englishwoman's Review* (January 1878): 1–7; 1.

19   Common Sense, letter, "Employment for Women," *Times,* 27 February 1878, 6.

20   Alsager Hay Hill, "Middle Class Destitution, No. II," *University Magazine* 2 (1878): 358–62; 359. Hill (1839–1906) was a poet and social activist.

21 Quoted in "Female Clerks on Railways," *Englishwoman's Review* (March 1878): 126.

22 Harkness, "Women as Civil Servants," 376.

23 Ibid., 381.

24 "The Disputed Question," *English Woman's Journal* 1:60 (1858): 361; [James Hinton], "On Nursing as a Profession," *Cornhill Magazine* 22 (1870): 451.

25 "Female Clerks," *Times*, 3 January 1882, 3; Untitled news item, *Daily Telegraph*, 2 July 1885, 5.

26 "Competition *v.* Nomination," *Englishwoman's Review* (September 1880): 23–4; 23.

27 [Jeanette Manners], "Employment of Women in the Public Service," *Quarterly Review* 151 (January 1881): 181–200; 187.

28 Herbert Tibbits, letter, "The Employment of Women," *Times*, 8 October 1879, 12.

29 Phillis Browne [Sarah Sharp Hamer], *What Girls Can Do*, 2. Hamer (1839–1927), under the pseudonym of Phillis Browne, authored numerous cookbooks and books of household management for girls and young women.

30 "New Employments for Women," *Cassell's Family Magazine* (1877): 331–2; 331.

31 M.B.H. "The Employment of Girls," *Cassell's Family Magazine* (1881): 274–6.

32 "The Family Parliament: Home Life *versus* Public Life for Girls," *Cassell's Family Magazine* (1881): 50–2; 179–80; 248–9.

33 Reverend J.A. Mather, letter, in "The Family Parliament," 180.

34 Elizabeth Evans Macgilvray, letter, in "The Family Parliament," 248.

35 See A.S.P., "Remunerative Employments for Women," *Cassell's Family Magazine* (1883): 313–14 and (1887): 274–5.

36 Harkness, "Women as Civil Servants," 369.

37 Emily Faithfull, letter, "The Intellectual Status of Woman," *Times*, 26 September 1881, 11.

38 "The Future of Single Women," *Westminster Review* 121 (1884): 151–62; 152.

39 "The Changing Status of Women," *Westminster Review* 128 (1887): 818–28; 826–7. For a similar bold comparison between marriage and prostitution see Millicent Garrett Fawcett, "The Emancipation of Women," *Fortnightly Review* 56 (November 1891): 673–85. Garrett Fawcett presents the very common middle-class case of a young woman contemplating marriage for economic security as being "on a par with what goes on

between twelve and two every morning in the Haymarket and Piccadilly Circus" (679).

40 Holcombe, *Victorian Ladies at Work*, 165–6.
41 Keep, "Cultural Work," 405.
42 Kittler, *Discourse Networks*, 352.
43 Thurschwell, *Literature, Technology and Magical Thinking*, 87.
44 Another American inventor of a typewriting machine retrospectively claimed credit as "the inventor of the typewriter girl." Speaking in 1900, Lucien Stephen Crandall asserted that he had "invented a type-writing machine, and away back in 1874 ... employed a young women to write on the machine. She was undoubtedly the first typewriter girl in the world." "He Invented the Typewriter Girl," *Hampshire Telegraph and Naval Chronicle*, 18 August 1900, 10.
45 "The Type Writer," *Times*, 25 April 1876, 6.
46 Beeching, *Century of the Typewriter* as quoted in Fyfield-Shayler, "British Typewriter Museum," 220.
47 "The Type Writer," *Times*, 25 April 1876, 6.
48 "A Complete Letter-Writer," *Times*, 12 March 1874, 12; "The Type Writer," *Times*, 25 April 1876, 6.
49 Keep, "Cultural Work," 404, 422.
50 "Remunerative Work for Women," *Queen*, 4 November 1882, 413.
51 "Type Writing," *Englishwoman's Review* (June 1884): 290.
52 Beeching, *Century of the Typewriter*, 35.
53 Zellers, *Typewriter*, 13–14.
54 Longley, "Writing Machines," 14–16. Brown, *Ancestors and Descendants*, 47.
55 "Type Writing," *Englishwoman's Review* (October 1884): 480; "The Ladies Type-Writing and General Copying Office," *Work and Leisure* (1884): 421.
56 Madeleine Greenwood, "Obituary: Mrs. Sutton Marshall," *Englishwoman's Review* (July 1901): 219–20.
57 "Type Writing," *Englishwoman's Review* (October 1884): 480.
58 "Type-Writing," *Englishwoman's Review* (October 1888): 473.
59 In April of 1886 alone, for example, the *Englishwoman's Review* notes the opening of a typewriting office by "two ladies" who intend "to form a large staff of female clerks"; in November, the *Review* announces the establishment of an office in Oxford by a Miss Burnblum. "Type Writing," *Englishwoman's Review* (April 1886): 189; "Type Writing at Oxford," *Englishwoman's Review* (November 1886): 514.

60   "Women and Their Work: The Typist," *Nursing Record* (17 October
      1889): 230–1.

61   "A Trade Combination for Typists," *Queen,* 1 June 1889, 770.

62   "The British Nurses' Association," *Queen,* 10 August 1889, 188.

63   "A Trade Combination for Typists," 770.

64   "The Typists' Society," *Queen,* 17 August 1889, 246.

65   Mrs. Bedford Fenwick, "The Profession of Nursing," *Woman's Herald,* 18
      April 1891, 406. Ethel Gordon Manson (1857–1947) had a notably suc-
      cessful nursing career until her marriage to physician Bedford Fenwick in
      1887, after which she was active in advancing the professionalization of
      nursing and the formation of the British Nurses' Association.

66   E.J.B., "About Type-Writing," *Woman's Herald,* 24 January 1891, 214.

67   Lady Violet Greville, "Place aux Dames," *Graphic,* 15 September 1894,
      306. Greville (1842–1932) was a journalist and author.

68   See, for example, "The New Convenience of Civilization," *Pall Mall
      Gazette,* 5 May 1885, 6; Evelyn M. Burnblum, "Type-Writing Offices,"
      Women's Penny Paper, 17 November 1888, 6; Marian Marshall, "Type-
      Writing Speed Competition," *Queen,* 23 February 1889, 239; "Society of
      Typists," *Times,* 19 May 1890, 12.

69   "The Typewriter in America," supplement, *Manchester Weekly Times,* 8
      June 1889, 8.

70   "News of the Day," *Birmingham Daily Post,* 17 May 1892, 4.

71   Lilloise, "Type-Writing as an Employment for Women," *Shafts,* 12
      November 1892, 31; Marian Marshall, "On Shorthand and Typewriting"
      (paper read at the Alexandra Hall, Cambridge, 25 October 1892),
      reprinted in *Shafts,* 26 November 1892, 61–2.

72   "Something about Type-Writing and Typists," *Girl's Own Paper* 16 (1894–
      95): 228–30; 228.

73   See, for example, "A Big Type-Writing Feat," *South Wales Daily News,* 1
      October 1892, 7; "Lectures, Social Meetings, &c.," *Aberdeen Press and
      Journal,* 11 April 1893, 6; "Something New in Typewriters," *Western Mail,*
      17 May 1895, 7.

74   Stories from the period also indicate this sense of mystery. See, for
      example, "Mr. Twistleton's Type-Writer," *Cornhill Magazine,* n.s., 55, 8
      (1887): 62–71, and Bangs, *Enchanted Type-Writer.*

75   R. Meyrick, "Symposium: Women as Clerks," *Work and Leisure* (1886):
      17. The lure of the city as a locus of excitement and novelty for mid-
      dle-class women in the late-Victorian period has been well documented by
      cultural historians and literary critics. See Walkowitz, *City of Dreadful*

Delight; Nord, *Walking Victorian Streets*; and Rappaport, *Shopping for Pleasure*.

76 Onlooker, "Plots in the Employment Field: Rural District Nursing," *Queen*, 24 September 1892, 523.

77 O.P.V. "The Lady Clerk: What She Ought to Know, and What She Has to Do," *Young Woman* 1 (1892–93): 262–3; 263.

78 "A Sketch. Type Writers. Marian Marshall," *Shafts*, 25 February 1893, 260–1; 260.

79 "Type Writing," *Englishwoman's Review* (June 1884): 290.

80 "Type-Writing: As an Employment for Educated Women," *Work and Leisure* (1885): 226–7.

81 "A Trade Combination for Typewriters," *Queen*, 1 June 1889, 770.

82 "Type Writing," *Queen*, 25 August 1888, 222.

83 See, for example, Ardern Holt, "The Art of Type-Writing," *Cassell's Family Magazine* (1888): 659–60; "Women and Type-Writing," *Queen*, 10 March 1888, 273; L. Reynolds, "Typewriting," *Work and Leisure* (1889): 13–16; 14. Holt claims that women's dominance of typewriting offices represents a general recognition of "the value of the refinement and higher education of gentlewomen" (660).

84 M.A.B., "Typewriting," *Queen*, 2 February 1889, 155; "A Trade Combination for Typewriters," *Queen*, 1 June 1889, 770.

85 Society for Promoting the Employment of Women, "Thirty-First Annual Report," *Work and Leisure* (1890): 207–10; 209.

86 R.V. Gill, "Is Type-Writing a Successful Occupation for Educated Ladies?" *Englishwoman's Review* (1891): 80–7. Quoted in "Type-Writing," *Work and Leisure* (1891): 169–73; 170.

87 "Lady Warwick's Scheme for Women," *Western Mail*, 12 August 1899, 3. Daisy Greville, Countess of Warwick (1861–1938) advocated for better education and living conditions for the poor. She was also a notorious society belle. The *Western Mail*'s endorsement of typewriting is in opposition to Lady Warwick's scheme, which is to have ladies take up agriculture.

88 "The Society of Typists," *Times*, 2 July 1891, 10; "Our London Letter," *Liverpool Mercury*, 9 October 1894, 5.

89 "Editorial – The Society of Typists," *Woman's Herald*, 4 July 1891, 584; "The Government as 'Model Employer,'" *Queen*, 20 April 1895, 686.

90 A Girl Typewriter, letter, "Clerks, Male and Female," *Reynolds's Newspaper*, 18 March 1894, 3.

91 "The Cheap Picture Market," *Bristol Mercury and Daily Post*, 18 April 1892, 3.

92   E.D. Cuming, "Domestic Helps and Hindrances," *Chambers's Journal* 3, 106 (December 1899): 17–21, 17.

93   A Girl Typewriter, "Clerks, Male and Female," 3

94   Australis, "Our London Letter," supplement, *Western Mail*, 20 March 1897, 7.

95   Frances Low, "How Poor Ladies Live," *Nineteenth Century* 41 (1897): 405–17; 405.

96   Eliza Orme, "How Poor Ladies Live: A Reply," *Nineteenth Century* 41 (1897): 613–19; 614. Orme (1848–1937) was a lawyer, social activist, and journalist.

97   "Inquests," *Times*, 30 August 1898, 8; "A Typewriter's Suicide," *Western Mail*, 1 September 1898, 6; "The Suicide of a Girl on Wimbledon Common," *Illustrated Police News*, 8 April 1899, 9; "Inquests," *Times*, 30 March 1899, 4.

CHAPTER FIVE

1   Liggins, *George Gissing*, 68.

2   Payn, *Thicker Than Water*. Subsequent references are indicated in the text by page number. James Payn (1830–1898) was a novelist, journalist, and editor of *Chambers's Journal* and *Cornhill Magazine*.

3   F.H. Curtis, "My Pretty Typewriter," *Penny Illustrated Paper*, 19 October 1889, 334.

4   "The Boy Fiend," supplement, *Hampshire Telegraph and Sussex Chronicle*, 29 June 1889, 12.

5   "Jones's Fair Typewriter: Saved by the Understudy," *Penny Illustrated Paper and Illustrated Times*, 25 July 1891, 51.

6   "Proposals," supplement, *Hampshire Telegraph and Sussex Chronicle*, 31 October 1891, 9.

7   "The Tantalising Typewriter," supplement, *Manchester Weekly Times*, 25 March 1892, 7.

8   "Hipple and the Fair Type Writer," *Newcastle Weekly Courant*, 18 March 1893, 6, reprinted from *Smith, Gray, and Co.'s Monthly*.

9   "From Mr. Giddiboy's Memorandum Book," supplement, *Western Mail*, 16 June 1894, 1.

10   "My Typewriter," literary supplement, *Hampshire Telegraph and Sussex Chronicle*, 12 June 1897, n.p.

11   "Learning the Typewriter," supplement, *Hampshire Telegraph and Sussex Chronicle*, 22 May 1897, 12.

12 Robert Barr, "The Type-Written Letter," *Idler* 2 (August 1892–January 1893): 597–605; 598. Subsequent references are indicated in the text by page number.

13 See for example "The Little Typewriter," *Aberdeen Weekly Journal*, 27 April 1898, 2; "Budding Romance Crushed," *Manchester Weekly Times*, 29 April 1898, 16; Judge, "A Pretty Comedy," *Manchester Weekly Times*, 12 August 1898, 16; "A Family Affair," supplement, *Western Mail*, 24 September 1898, 2; "Solicitude for His Typewriter," *Pall Mall Gazette*, 4 August 1900, 8; Mary Angela Dickens, "His Great Chance," *Ipswich Journal*, 29 December 1900, 2. Several titles are reprints from America, where similar attitudes towards women working as typewriters prevailed.

14 William Wicks, "Found by a Letter," *Hampshire Telegraph and Sussex Chronicle*, 10 October 1891, 10.

15 Gissing, *Odd Women*, 152–3. Subsequent references are indicated in the text by page number.

16 Mitton, *Bachelor Girl*, 8. Subsequent references are indicated in the text by page number. Geraldine Edith Mitton (1868–1955) was a novelist, biographer, and travel writer.

17 "New Novels," *Dundee Courier*, 13 April 1898, 6; "New Novels: A Latch-Key Novel," *Graphic*, 4 June 1898, 736.

18 There is a problem with the logic of this "bet" and the need to find the documentation about income. If Lex's friend made the bet that Dasent earned a large income, finding the evidence for this would mean that Lex would owe the friend the £10. It is not clear if the inability to assess the illogic of Lex's proposition to earn £10 is Judith's or Mitton's.

19 Grant Allen [Olive Pratt Rayner, pseud.], *Type-Writer Girl*, 28. Subsequent references are indicated in the text by page number. Allen (1848–1899) was a novelist and a prolific essayist of scientific and philosophical articles. Many of his novels are mysteries, some of which have independently minded female protagonists. His most notorious work is *The Woman Who Did* (1895), the story of a woman who enters a free-love union and subsequently bears a child, and suffers the concomitant painful social consequences. Allen's ideas about women were advanced, but not always enlightened.

20 In her analytically sophisticated reading of *The Type-Writer Girl*, Leah Price argues that there is a provocative tension between Juliet's identity as a typewriter girl – specifically as the typewriter girl of her own first-person narration – and her role as a creative writer and pseudoautobiographer. While I acknowledge that Allen's novel is clever – replete with witty satirical barbs directed at late-Victorian cultural and literary practices – I

nevertheless find it less intellectually profound than Price's reading suggests. Price, "Grant Allen's Impersonal Secretaries."

21   Crockett, *Ione March*, 86. Subsequent references are indicated in the text by page number. Portions of the novel originally appeared as "The Woman of Fortune" in *The Woman at Home* in 1897. Samuel Rutherford Crockett (1859–1914) was a Scottish minister, journalist, and novelist.

22   Mitton, *Bachelor Girl*, 95.

23   Grey [Lilian Kate Rowland-Brown], *Craftsman*, 38.

24   Burgin, *Settled Out of Court*, 104. Subsequent references are indicated in the text by page number.

25   Leighton, *Disillusion*, I: 8. Subsequent references are indicated in the text by volume and page number.

26   Fulford, *Unoffending Prisoners*, 31. Subsequent references are indicated in the text by page number.

27   Dale [Francesca Maria Steele], *Daughters of Job*, 14. Originally published in *Belgravia: A London Magazine*, 1894.

28   Marsh, *House of Mystery*, 79. Subsequent references are indicated in the text by page number. Richard Marsh (1857–1915) was a prolific author of popular stories and novels, best known for his gothic tale, *The Beetle* (1897).

29   Dowie, *Crook of the Bough*, 9, 10. Subsequent references are indicated in the text by page number. Ménie Muriel Dowie (1866–1945) was a celebrated New Woman novelist.

30   Dudeney, "Beyond the Gray Gate," 204. Subsequent references are indicated in the text by page number. Alice Dudeney (1866–1945) was a prolific writer of the late-Victorian and Edwardian periods. She is not generally thought of as a New Woman novelist, but her tales frequently address vexing class and gender issues forthrightly.

CONCLUSION

1   Frances Low, "How Poor Ladies Live," *Nineteenth Century* 41 (1897): 405–17.

2   "Employment Memoranda," *Queen,* 5 September 1891, 396.

3   M.M. [Marian Marshall], "Type Writing and Shorthand as an Employment for Women," *Queen,* 17 January 1891, 113.

4   "Precepts for Professional Life," *Queen,* 19 January 1895, 129.

5   "The Employment of Untrained Women," *Queen,* 2 July 1898, 2.

6   Margaret Bateson, "Marriage and Occupation," *Queen,* 5 August 1899, 240.

7 "A Central Bureau for the Employment of Women," *Queen,* 20 November 1897, 977.

8 Employment Editor, "Openings," *Queen,* 24 September 1898, 514.

9 Richard Altick suggests that, in the "'family' papers meant for the indifferently educated reader … many of the queries [from readers] … were concocted in the editorial office" (360). While the *Queen* addressed a considerably more sophisticated audience than the "humble Victorian reader" imagined by Altick, his comment does denote the kind of problem that confronts critics assessing the relationship between editors and readers. See Altick, *English Common Reader,* 361. The large number of notices from women seeking work that appear in the *Englishwoman*'s employment registry suggests that the claims of the *Queen*'s employment editor are genuine.

10 "An Unique Offer," *Englishwoman* 8 (1898): 46.

11 "Our Employment Consultation Bureau," *Queen,* 2 January 1897, 40.

12 "Gentlewomen and Self-Help," *Englishwoman's Review* (July 1870): 164–71; 168.

13 J.H. Roberts, "A Bachelor's Solution of a Problem of the Day: What Shall We Do with Our Daughters?" *Graphic,* 19 October 1895, 492.

14 Walter Besant, "The Endowment of the Daughter," *Longman's Magazine* 11 (April 1888 [1887–88]): 604–15; 607–8. Subsequent references are indicated in the text by page number. Besant (1836–1901) was an author and prominent social critic.

15 Australis, "Our London Letter," supplement, *Western Mail,* 20 March 20, 1897, 7.

16 "Leader," *Daily Telegraph,* 11 April 1888, 5.

17 One of "Our Daughters," "Our Daughters," *Daily Telegraph,* 29 March 1888, 3.

18 An Unmarried Man, "Our Daughters," *Daily Telegraph,* 30 March 1888, 2.

19 Confirmed Bachelor, "Our Daughters," *Daily Telegraph,* 31 March 1888, 2.

20 A Tradesman's Wife, "Our Daughters," *Daily Telegraph,* 4 April 1888, 3.

21 A Perplexed Father, "Our Daughters," *Daily Telegraph,* 30 March 1888, 2.

22 A Father, "Our Daughters," *Daily Telegraph,* 30 March 1888, 2.

23 A Business Woman, "Our Daughters," *Daily Telegraph,* 29 March 1888, 3.

24 Margaret Bateson, "Our Daughters," *Daily Telegraph,* 29 March 1888, 3.

25 "Leader," *Daily Telegraph,* 11 April 1888, 5.

26 Codlin, "The Showman," *Penny Illustrated Paper and Illustrated Times,* 14 April 1888, 237–8; 238. Accompanying cartoon by H.M., "Our Daughters: The D. T. [*Daily Telegraph*] Pessimists Refuted," ibid., 237.

27 Warner Snoad, "Letters: Our Daughters," *Daily News,* 29 September 1891, 6.

28 A Happy Daughter, "Letters: Our Daughters," *Daily News,* 5 October
    1891, 6. See also C.E.R., "Letters: Our Daughters," *Daily News,* 29
    October 1891, 3.

29 A.L.H. "Our Daughters," *Daily News,* 20 October 1891, 3.

30 E.E.W., "Our Daughters," *Daily News,* 29 October 1891, 3.

31 "Our Daughters," *Reynolds's Newspaper,* 4 October 1891, 2.

32 Edward Steward, "Our Daughters," *Times,* 8 January 1895, 6. Steward
    was the principal of the Salisbury Training College for Schoolmistresses.

33 W.J. Boys, "Our Daughters," *Times,* 28 December 1894, 10.

34 Jessie Boucherett, "Our Daughters," *Times,* 10 January 1895, 6.

35 William Rogers, "Our Daughters," *Times,* 24 September 1895, 6; R.H.
    Cave, "Our Daughters," *Times,* 27 September 1895, 8. Rogers (1819–
    1896) was an education reformer and Church of England rector.

36 Northumbrian, "To the Editor," *Reynolds's Newspaper,* 29 January 1888, 2.

Bibliography

NINETEENTH-CENTURY NEWSPAPERS AND MAGAZINES

Aberdeen Press and Journal
Aberdeen Weekly Journal
Argosy (London)
Belgravia: A London Magazine
Bentley's Miscellany (London)
Birmingham Daily Post
Blackwood's Magazine (Edinburgh)
Bristol Mercury and Daily Post
Cassell's Family Magazine
   (London)
Chambers's Journal (London)
Contemporary Review (London)
Cornhill Magazine (London)
Daily News (London)
Daily Telegraph (London)
Dublin University Magazine
Dundee Courier
Edinburgh Review
English Woman's Journal (London)
Englishwoman (London)
Englishwoman's Review (London)
Examiner (London)
Fortnightly Review (London)

Fraser's Magazine (London)
Gentlewoman (London)
Girl's Own Paper (London)
Good Words (Edinburgh)
Graphic (London)
Guy's Hospital Gazette
Hampshire Telegraph and Naval
   Chronicle
Hampshire Telegraph and Sussex
   Chronicle
Idler (London)
Illustrated Police News (London)
Ipswich Journal
Lady (London)
Lady's Pictorial (London)
Lady's Realm (London)
Lancet (London)
Leeds Mercury
Liverpool Mercury
London Society: A Monthly
   Magazine of Light and Amusing
   Literature for the Hours of
   Recreation

Longman's Magazine (London)
Macmillan's Magazine (London)
Manchester Weekly Times
Medical Libraries (Denver, CO)
Medical Times and Gazette
   (London)
National Review (London)
Newcastle Weekly Courant
Nineteenth Century (London)
North British Review (London)
Nursing Record
Pall Mall Gazette
Penny Illustrated Paper and
   Illustrated Times (London)
Quarterly Review (London)
Queen, the Lady's Newspaper
   and Court Chronicle
   (London)
Reynolds's Newspaper (London)
Saint Paul's Magazine (London)
Saturday Review (London)

Shafts: A Paper for Women and the
   Working Classes (London)
Sheffield Evening Telegraph
Smith, Gray, and C.'s Monthly
South Wales Daily News
Times (London)
University Magazine (London)
Uxbridge and West Drayton Gazette
Western Mail (Cardiff)
Western Morning News (Plymouth,
   Devon)
Westminster Review
Woman at Home (London)
Woman's Gazette (London;
   superseded by *Work and Leisure*)
Woman's Herald (London)
Woman's Signal (London)
Women's Penny Paper (London;
   superseded by *Woman's Herald*)
Work and Leisure (London)
Young Woman (London)

OTHER PRIMARY AND SECONDARY SOURCES

Abel-Smith, Brian. *A History of the Nursing Profession.* London:
   Heinemann, 1960.
Adams, James Eli. *Dandies and Desert Saints: Styles of Victorian*
   Masculinity. Ithaca, NY: Cornell University Press, 1995.
Allen, Grant. *Hilda Wade: A Woman with Tenacity of Purpose.* New York
   and London: Putman's, 1900. https://archive.org/details/
   hildawadeawomanooallegoog.
– [Olive Pratt Rayner, pseud.] *The Type-Writer Girl.* Edited by Clarissa J.
   Suranyi. Peterborough, ON: Broadview, 2004.
Altick, Richard D. *The English Common Reader: A Social History of the*
   Mass Reading Public, 1800–1900. Chicago: University of Chicago
   Press, 1957.
Anderson, Gregory, ed. *The White-Blouse Revolution: Female Office*
   Workers since 1870. Manchester and New York: Manchester University
   Press, 1988.

Anonymous. "Two Type-Writer Types." In *Our Phonographic Poets: Written by Stenographers and Typists Upon Subjects Pertaining to Their Arts,* compiled by "Topsy Typist," 70–1. New York: Popular Publishing, 1904.

Ardis, Ann L. *New Women, New Novels: Feminism and Early Modernism.* New Brunswick, NJ: Rutgers University Press, 1990.

Baly, Monica. *Florence Nightingale and the Nursing Legacy.* 2nd edition. London: Whurr, 1997.

– *Nursing and Social Change.* 3rd edition. London and New York: Routledge, 1995.

Bangs, John Kendrick. *The Enchanted Type-Writer.* London and New York: Harper, 1899.

Bateson, Margaret. *Professional Women upon Their Professions: Conversations Recorded by Margaret Bateson.* London: Horace Cox, 1895.

Beeching, Wilfred A. *Century of the Typewriter.* London: Heinemann, 1974.

Beetham, Margaret. *A Magazine of Her Own? Domesticity and Desire in the Woman's Magazine, 1800–1914.* London and New York: Routledge, 1996.

Bettany, G.T. "Habershon, Samuel Osborne." Revised by Kaye Bagshaw. In *Oxford Dictionary of National Biography.* Oxford University Press, 2004; online ed., https://doi-org.uml.idm.oclc.org/10.1093/ref:odnb/11830.

Bettany, G.T., and Samuel Wilks. *A Biographical History of Guy's Hospital.* London: Ward, Lock & Bowden, 1892.

Black, Clementina. "Type-Writing and Journalism for Women." In *What to Do with Our Boys and Girls,* edited by John Watson, 33–45. London: Ward, Lock & Bowden, 1892.

Blake, Catriona. *The Charge of the Parasols: Women's Entry to the Medical Profession in Britain.* London: Women's Press, 1990.

Bostridge, Mark. *Florence Nightingale: The Woman and Her Legend.* London and New York: Viking, 2008.

Brock, Claire. "*The Lancet* and the Campaign against Women Doctors, 1860–1880." In *(Re)Creating Science in Nineteenth-Century Britain,* edited by Amanda Mordavsky Caleb, 130–45. Newcastle: Cambridge Scholars Publishing, 2007.

Brown, Henrietta Brady. *The Ancestors and Descendants of William Henry Venable.* Cincinnati, OH, 1954, 47. http://www.wallace-venable.name/Venable_Genealogy/Ancestors_&_Descendants_of_Wm_Henry_Venable.pdf.

Brown, Susan, Patricia Clements, and Isobel Grundy, eds. "Harriet Downing." In *Orlando: Women's Writing in the British Isles from the Beginnings to the Present.* Cambridge: Cambridge University Press Online, 2006. http://orlando.cambridge.org.uml.idm.oclc.org/.

Browne, Phillis [Sarah Sharp Hamer]. *What Girls Can Do: A Book for Mothers and Daughters.* London: Cassell, 1880.

Burgin, G.B. [George Brown]. *Settled Out of Court.* London: C.A. Pearson, 1898.

C.T.D. "Advertisement." In *Remembrances of a Monthly Nurse*, by Harriet Downing. London: Simms and M'Intyre, 1852. https://play.google.com/books/reader?id=KJ1bAAAAQAAJ&hl=en&pg=GBS.PR4.

Cameron, H.C. *Mr. Guy's Hospital, 1726–1948.* London: Longman's, 1954.

Carlyle, Thomas. *Past and Present.* Edited by Chris R. Vanden Bossche, Joel J. Brattin, and D.J. Trela. Berkeley, Los Angeles, and London: University of California Press, 2005.

Chapple, J.A.V., and Arthur Pollard, eds. *The Letters of Mrs Gaskell.* Cambridge, MA: Harvard University Press, 1967.

Chishty-Mujahid, Nadya. "Scarred and Healed Identities: Fallenness, Morality, and the Issue of Personal Autonomy in *Adam Bede* and *Ruth.*" *Victorian Review* 30, no. 2 (2004): 58–80.

Colón, Susan E. *The Professional Ideal in the Victorian Novel: The Works of Disraeli, Trollope, Gaskell, and Eliot.* Houndsmills and New York: Palgrave Macmillan, 2007.

Copelman, Dina M. *London's Women Teachers: Gender, Class and Feminism 1870–1930.* London and New York: Routledge, 1996.

Crockett, Samuel Rutherford. *Ione March.* New York: Dodd, Mead, 1899.

Cunningham, Gail. *The New Woman and the Victorian Novel.* New York: Barnes & Noble, 1978.

Dale, Darley [Francesca Maria Steele]. *The Daughters of Job.* London: Everett, 1902. Originally published in *Belgravia: A London Magazine*, 1894.

Davies, Celia. "Making Sense of the Census in Britain and the USA: The Changing Occupational Classification and the Position of Nurses." *Sociological Review* 28, no. 3 (1980): 581–609.

– ed. *Rewriting Nursing History.* London: Croom Helm, 1980.

de Bellaigue, Christina. *Educating Women: Schooling and Identity in England and France, 1800–1867.* Oxford: Oxford University Press, 2007.

Diamond, Marion. *Emigration and Empire: The Life of Maria S. Rye.* New York and London: Garland, 1999.

Dickens, Charles. "Appendix D: Prefaces to the Cheap and Later Editions." In *Martin Chuzzlewit*, edited by Margaret Cardwell, 846–8. Oxford: Clarendon, 1982.

Dingwall, Robert, Anne Marie Rafferty, and Charles Webster. *An Introduction to the Social History of Nursing*. London: Routledge, 1988.

Dohrn, Susanne. "Pioneers in a Dead-End Profession: The First Women Clerks in Banks and Insurance Companies." In *The White-Blouse Revolution: Female Office Workers since 1870*, edited by Gregory Anderson, 48–66. Manchester and New York: Manchester University Press, 1988.

Dolin, Tim. "A Moabite among the Israelites: *Ruth*, Religion, and the Victorian Social Novel," *Literature and Theology* 30, no. 1 (2016): 67–81. https://doi-org.uml.idm.oclc.org/10.1093/litthe/fru062.

Dowie, Ménie Muriel. *The Crook of the Bough*. London: Methuen, 1898. British Library, Historical Print Edition.

Downing, Harriet. *Remembrances of a Monthly Nurse*. London: Simms and M'Intyre, 1852. https://play.google.com/books/reader?id=K J1bAAAAQAAJ&hl=en&pg=GBS.PR4.

Dudeney, Alice. "Beyond the Gray Gate." In *Men of Marlowe's*, 201–31. New York: Henry Holt, 1900.

Dyhouse, Carol. "Driving Ambitions: Women in Pursuit of a Medical Education, 1890–1939." *Women's History Review* 7 (1998): 321–43.

– *Girls Growing Up in Late Victorian and Edwardian England*. London: Routledge, 1981.

– *No Distinction of Sex? Women in British Universities, 1870–1939*. London: University College of London Press, 1995.

Easson, Angus, ed. *Elizabeth Gaskell: The Critical Heritage*. London and New York: Routledge, 1991.

E.D. *Recollections of a Nurse*. London: Macmillan, 1889.

Fenn, G[eorge] Manville. *Nurse Elisia*. New York: Cassell, 1892. https://catalog.hathitrust.org/Record/100489368.

Fenton-Hathaway, Anna. "Gaskell's Detours: How *Mary Barton*, *Ruth*, and *Cranford* Redefined 'Redundancy.'" *Victorian Literature and Culture* 42, no. 2 (2014): 235–50. doi:10.1017/S1060150313000430.

Fletcher, Sheila. *Feminists and Bureaucrats: A Study in the Development of Girls' Education in the Nineteenth Century*. Cambridge: Cambridge University Press, 1980.

Fulford, John. *Some Unoffending Prisoners*. London: Jarrold, 1899.

Furneaux, Holly. *Military Men of Feeling: Emotion, Touch, and Masculinity in the Crimean War*. Oxford: Oxford University Press, 2016.

Fyfield-Shayler, B.A. "The British Typewriter Museum." *Industrial Archeology* 14, no. 3 (1979): 210–44.

Gamarnikow, Eva. "Sexual Division of Labour: The Case of Nursing." In *Feminism and Materialism: Women and Modes of Production*, edited by Annette Kuhn and AnnMarie Wolpe, 96–123. London: Routledge, 1978.

Gaskell, Elizabeth. *Ruth*. Edited by Tim Dolin. Oxford and New York: Oxford University Press, 2011.

Gissing, George. *The Odd Women*. Edited by Arlene Young. Peterborough, ON: Broadview, 1998.

Grey, Rowland [Lilian Kate Rowland-Brown]. *The Craftsman*. London: Ward and Lock, [1897].

Hapke, Laura. "He Stoops to Conquer: Redeeming the Fallen Woman in the Fiction of Dickens, Gaskell and their Contemporaries." *Victorian Newsletter* 69 (1986): 16–22.

Harris, Beth, ed. *Famine and Fashion: Needlewomen in the Nineteenth Century*. Aldershot, HPH, and Burlington, VT: Ashgate, 2005.

Hawkins, Sue. *Nursing and Women's Labour in the Nineteenth Century: The Quest for Independence*. London and New York: Routledge, 2010.

Heggie, Vanessa. "Women Doctors and Lady Nurses: Class, Education, and the Professional Victorian Woman." *Bulletin of the History of Medicine* 89, no. 2 (2015): 267–92. https://muse.jhu.edu/.

Helmstadter, Carol. "Doctors and Nurses in London Teaching Hospitals: Class, Gender, Religion, and Professional Expertise, 1850–1890." *Nursing History Review* 5 (1997): 161–97.

Helmstadter, Carol, and Judith Goddin. *Nursing before Nightingale, 1815–1899*. Farnham, Surrey, and Burlington, VT: Ashgate, 2011.

Helsinger, Elizabeth K. et al., eds. *The Woman Question*. 3 vols. Chicago and London: University of Chicago Press, 1983.

Henley, William Ernest. "In Hospital: Rhymes and Rhythms." In *A Book of Verses*, 1–48. 1888. Reprint, London: David Nutt, 1897.

Herstein, Sheila R. "The *English Woman's Journal* and the Langham Place Circle: A Feminist Forum and Its Women Editors." In *Innovators and Preachers: The Role of the Editor in Victorian England*, edited by Joel H. Wiener, 61–76. Westport, CT, and London: Greenwood, 1985.

Hervey, Nick. "Gull, Sir William Withey." In *Oxford Dictionary of National Biography*. Oxford University Press, 2004; online ed., https://doi-org.uml.idm.oclc.org/10.1093/ref:odnb/11730.

Hilton, Mary, and Pam Hirsch, eds. *Practical Visionaries: Women, Education and Social Progress 1790–1930*. Harlow, Essex: Pearson; New York: Longman, 2000.

Holcombe, Lee. *Victorian Ladies at Work: Middle-Class Working Women in England and Wales 1850–1914*. Hamden, CT: Archon, 1973.

Howsam, Leslie. "'Sound-Minded Women': Eliza Orme and the Study and Practice of Law in Late-Victorian England." *Atlantis* 15, no. 1 (1989): 44–55.

Jordan, Ellen. *The Women's Movement and Women's Employment in Nineteenth Century Britain*. New York and London: Routledge, 1999.

Judd, Catherine. *Bedside Seductions: Nursing and the Victorian Imagination, 1830–1880*. New York: St Martin's, 1998.

Keep, Christopher. "The Cultural Work of the Type-Writer Girl." *Victorian Studies* 40, no. 3 (1997): 401–26.

Kittler, Friedrich A. *Discourse Networks 1800/1900*. Translated by Michael Metteer with Chris Cullens. Stanford: Stanford University Press, 1990.

Knight, Adrienne. "The Great Nursing Dispute of Guy's Hospital 1878–1880." *Journal of the Royal College of Physicians of London* 31, no. 2 (1997): 208–14.

Kranidis, Rita S. *The Victorian Spinster and Colonial Emigration: Contested Subjects*. New York: St Martin's Press, 1999.

Ledger, Sally. *The New Woman: Fiction and Feminism at the Fin de Siècle*. Manchester: Manchester University Press; New York: St Martin's, 1997.

Leighton, Dorothy. *Disillusion: A Story with a Preface*. 3 vols. London: Henry, 1894.

Levitan, Kathrin. *A Cultural History of the British Census: Envisioning the Multitude in the Nineteenth Century*. New York: Palgrave Macmillan, 2011.

Liggins, Emma. *George Gissing, the Working Woman, and Urban Culture*. Aldershot, HPH, and Burlington, VT: Ashgate, 2006.

– *Odd Women? Spinsters, Lesbians and Widows in British Women's Fiction, 1850s–1930s*. Manchester: Manchester University Press, 2016. ProQuest Ebook Central, https://ebookcentral.proquest.com/lib/umanitoba/detail.action?docID=4705464.

Longley, Margaret Vater. "Writing Machines." In *Proceedings of the First Annual International Congress of Shorthand Writers*. Chicago: Brown and Holland, 1881: 14–16.

Lonsdale, Margaret. *Sister Dora: A Biography*. Leipzig: Tauchnitz, 1880. https://archive.org/details/sisterdoraabiogoolonsgoog.

Lowe, Graham S. *Women in the Administrative Revolution: The Feminization of Clerical Work*. Toronto and Buffalo: University of Toronto Press, 1987.

Lucas, John. "Harkness, Margaret." In *Oxford Dictionary of National Biography*. Oxford University Press, 2004; online ed., https://doi-org.uml.idm.oclc.org/10.1093/ref:odnb/56894.

Lysaght, Elisabeth J. *A Long Madness*. 3 vols. London: Charing Cross: 1877.

Maggs, Christopher J. *The Origins of General Nursing*. London: Croom Helm, 1983.

Malton, Sara A. "Illicit Inscriptions: Reframing Forgery in Elizabeth Gaskell's *Ruth*." *Victorian Literature and Culture* 33, no. 1 (2005): 187–202.

Manton, Jo. *Sister Dora: The Life of Dorothy Pattison*. London: Quartet, 1977.

Marsh, Richard. *The House of Mystery*. London: White, 1898. British Library, Historical Print Edition.

Meade, L.T. [Elizabeth Thomasina Meade Toulmin Smith]. *A Girl in Ten Thousand*. New York: Burt, c. 1900. https://babel.hathitrust.org/cgi/pt?id=uc1.aa0014831903. Originally serialized in the *Young Woman*, 1894–95.

Mitton, Geraldine. *A Bachelor Girl in London*. London: Hutchinson, 1898. British Library, Historical Print Edition.

Moore, Judith. *A Zeal for Responsibility: The Struggle for Professional Nursing in Victorian England, 1868–1883*. Athens, GA, and London: University of Georgia Press, 1988.

Moore, Norman. "Moxon, Walter." Revised by Michael Bevan. In *Oxford Dictionary of National Biography*. Oxford University Press, 2004; online ed., https://doi-org.uml.idm.oclc.org/10.1093/ref:odnb/19467.

– "Sturges, Octavius." Revised by Michael Bevan. In *Oxford Dictionary of National Biography*. Oxford University Press, 2004; online ed., https://doi-org.uml.idm.oclc.org/10.1093/ref:odnb/26749.

Morten, Honnor, and H.F. Gethen. "The Story of a Nurse." In *Tales of the Children's Ward*, 28–64. London: Sampson Low, Marston, 1894.

Mullin, Katherine. *Working Girls: Fiction, Sexuality, and Modernity.* Oxford: Oxford University Press, 2016. doi:10.1093/acprof: oso/9780198724841.001.0001.

Mumm, Susan. *Stolen Daughters, Virgin Mothers: Anglican Sisterhoods in Victorian Britain.* London and New York: Leicester University Press, 1999.

Nightingale, Florence. *Notes on Nursing.* London and New York: Appleton, 1860.

Nord, Deborah Epstein. *Walking the Victorian Streets: Women, Representation, and the City.* Ithaca and London: Cornell University Press, 1995.

Payn, James. *Thicker Than Water.* London: Longman, Green, 1885.

Perkin, Harold. *The Rise of Professional Society: England since 1880.* London and New York: Routledge, 1989.

Peterson, Jeanne M. *The Medical Profession in Mid-Victorian London.* Berkeley and London: University of California Press, 1978.

Poovey, Mary. *Uneven Developments: The Ideological Work of Gender in Mid-Victorian England.* Chicago: University of Chicago Press, 1988.

Price, Leah. "Grant Allen's Impersonal Secretaries: Rereading *The Type-Writer Girl*." In *Grant Allen: Literature and Cultural Politics at the Fin de Siècle*, edited by William Greenslade and Terence Rodgers, 129–41. Aldershot, HPH, and Burlington, VT: Ashgate, 2005.

Price, Leah, and Pamela Thurschwell, eds. *Literary Secretaries/Secretarial Culture.* Aldershot, HPH, and Burlington, VT: Ashgate, 2005.

Prochaska, F.K. (Frank). "Burdett, Sir Henry Charles." In *Oxford Dictionary of National Biography.* Oxford University Press, 2004; online ed., https://doi-org.uml.idm.oclc.org/10.1093/ref:odnb/38827.

– *Women and Philanthropy in Nineteenth-Century England.* Oxford: Clarendon, 1980.

Pykett, Lyn. *The "Improper" Feminine: The Women's Sensation Novel and the New Woman Writing.* London and New York: Routledge, 1992.

Rappaport, Erica D. *Shopping for Pleasure: Women in the Making of London's West End.* Princeton, NJ: Princeton University Press, 2000.

Reader, W.J. *Professional Men: The Rise of the Professional Classes in Nineteenth-Century England.* London: Weidenfeld and Nicolson, 1966.

Reynolds, K.D. "Norton [née Sheridan], Caroline Elizabeth Sarah." In *Oxford Dictionary of National Biography.* Oxford University Press, 2004; online ed., https://doi-org.uml.idm.oclc.org/10.1093/ref:odnb/20339.

Ritchie, Anne Thackeray. *Old Kensington*. London: Smith, Elder, 1873. https://babel.hathitrust.org/cgi/pt?id=inu.32000006997615;view=1up; seq=1. First published serially in *Cornhill Magazine* (April 1872–April 1873).

Rivers, Bronwyn. *Women at Work in the Victorian Novel: The Question of Middle Class Women's Employment*. Lampeter, Wales: Edwin Mellen, 2005.

Silverstone, Rosalie. "Office Work for Women: An Historical Overview." *Business History* 18, no. 1 (1976): 98–110.

Smith, Johanna M. "Textual Encounters in *Eliza Cook's Journal*: Class, Gender and Sexuality." In *Encounters in the Victorian Press: Editors, Authors, Readers*, edited by Laurel Brake and Julie F. Codell, 50–65. Houndmills and New York: Palgrave Macmillan, 2005.

Steinbach, Susie L. *Women in England, 1760–1914: A Social History*. New York: Palgrave Macmillan, 2004.

Summers, Anne. "The Mysterious Demise of Sarah Gamp: The Domiciliary Nurse and Her Detractors, c. 1830–1860." *Victorian Studies* 32, no. 3 (1989): 365–86.

Sutherland, Gillian. "Education." In *Social Agencies and Institutions*, edited by F.M.L. Thompson, 119–69. Vol. 3 of *The Cambridge Social History of Britain, 1750–1950*. Cambridge: Cambridge University Press, 1990.

– *In Search of the New Woman: Middle-Class Women and Work in Britain 1870–1914*. Cambridge: Cambridge University Press, 2015.

Swenson Kristine. *Medical Women and Victorian Fiction*. Columbia: University of Missouri Press, 2005. PDF e-book.

Thurschwell, Pamela. *Literature, Technology and Magical Thinking, 1880–1920*. Cambridge: Cambridge University Press, 2001.

Tosh, John. *A Man's Place: Masculinity and the Middle-Class Home in Victorian England*. New Haven, CT, and London: Yale University Press, 1999.

Tropp, Asher. *The School Teachers: The Growth of the Teaching Profession in England and Wales from 1800 to the Present Day*. London: Heinemann, 1957.

Van-Helten, Jean Jacques, and Keith Williams. "'The Crying Need of South Africa': The Emigration of Single British Women to the Transvaal, 1901–10." *Journal of Southern African Studies* 10, no. 1 (1983): 17–38. http://www.jstor.org/stable/2636814.

Vicinus, Martha. *Independent Women: Work and Community for Single Women, 1850–1920*. Chicago: University of Chicago Press, 1985.

Waddington, Keir. "The Nursing Dispute at Guy's Hospital, 1879–1880." *Social History of Medicine* 8, no. 2 (1995): 211–30.

Wagner, Tamara S. "Victorian Failed Emigration and the Superfluity Debates: Elizabeth Murray's *Ella Norman*." *Journal of Victorian Culture* 20, no. 1 (2015): 101–20. https://doi-org.uml.idm.oclc.org/10.1 080/13555502.2014.990729.

Walker, Lynne. "The Entry of Women into the Architectural Profession in Britain." *Woman's Art Journal* 7, no. 1 (1986): 13–18.

Walkowitz, Judith . *City of Dreadful Delight: Narratives of Sexual Danger in Late-Victorian London*. Chicago: Chicago University Press, 1992.

Wardle, David. *English Popular Education 1780–1975*. 2nd edition of *English Popular Education 1780–1970*. Cambridge: Cambridge University Press, 1976.

Watson, John, ed. *What to Do with Our Boys and Girls*. London: Ward, Lock, Bowden, 1892.

Webster, Rachel. "'I Think I Must Be an Improper Woman without Knowing It': Fallenness and Unitarianism in Elizabeth Gaskell's *Ruth*." *Victorian Network* 4, no. 2 (2012): 10–28.

Wiener, Joel H., ed. *Innovators and Preachers: The Role of the Editor in Victorian England*. Westport, CT, and London: Greenwood, 1985.

Williams, Raymond. *Marxism and Literature*. Oxford and New York: Oxford University Press, 1977.

Young, Arlene. "'Entirely a Woman's Question'? Class, Gender, and the Victorian Nurse." *Journal of Victorian Culture* 13, no. 1 (2008): 18–41.

– "Ladies and Professionalism: The Evolution of the Idea of Work in the *Queen*, 1861–1900." *Victorian Periodicals Review* 40, no. 3 (2007): 189–215.

– "The Rise of the Victorian Working Lady: The New-Style Nurse and the Typewriter, 1840–1900." BRANCH: *Britain, Representation, and Nineteenth-Century History, 1775–1925* (2015). http://www.branchcollective.org/?ps_articles=arlene-young-the-rise-of-the-victorian-working-lady-the-new-style-nurse-and-the-typewriter-1840-1900.

Zellers, John A. *The Typewriter: A Short History, on Its 75th Anniversary, 1873–1948*. New York: Newcomen Society, 1948.

Zimmeck, Meta. "Jobs for the Girls: The Expansion of Clerical Work for Women, 1850–1914. In *Unequal Opportunities: Women's Employment in England 1800–1918,* edited by Angela V. John, 153–77. Oxford: Blackwell, 1986.

Index

Vera, "Under the Red Cross: A Narrative of Hospital-Life with the Prussians in France," 79–83, 85, 86

Vicinus, Martha, 173n22

Walkowitz, Judith, 36

Warwick, Countess of (Daisy Greville), 193n87

Watson, Lily: "A Modern Mistake," 87

Webster, Rachel, 185n2

Western Mail: "Our Daughters," 163, 167; suicide, 122; typewriters, 120–2, 193n87

Westminster Review, 16, 110; male nurses, 43; nursing, 38

Whyte-Melville, George, 179n73; "The Strong-Minded Woman," 35–7, 39, 53, 59. *See also* Strong-Minded Woman

Wicks, William: "Found by a Letter," 136–7; 139

Williams, Rachel, 35

Williams, Raymond, 4

Wilson, H. Mary: "In Warwick Ward," 87–8; "On Monmouth Ward," 87–8

Woman's Herald, 4, 16, 60; nursing, 117–18; typewriters, 121. See also *Work and Leisure*

Woman Question, 13, 15, 18, 22, 27

women's press, 5, 9, 14, 16–19, 22, 25–28; employment advice, 158–61; nursing, 31–4, 75–7, 117; nursing crisis 39, 55–6; office work, 104–5, 107–8; professionalism 27–34; typewriting, 112–21. *See also* mainstream media; *individual media publications*

Work and Leisure, 5, 16, 26; nursing, 55, 75–7, 184n65; typewriting, 115, 120. See also *Woman's Herald*

Young Woman, 16, 97–100, 119

Zellers, John, 114–15